Vital Resonances

To mum, dad and Jenny

Vital Resonances

Encountering Film with Varda, Haneke and Nancy

Francesca Minnie Hardy

EDINBURGH
University Press

Edinburgh University Press is one of the leading university presses in the UK. We publish academic books and journals in our selected subject areas across the humanities and social sciences, combining cutting-edge scholarship with high editorial and production values to produce academic works of lasting importance. For more information visit our website: edinburghuniversitypress.com

© Francesca Minnie Hardy, 2021, 2023

Edinburgh University Press Ltd
The Tun – Holyrood Road
12 (2f) Jackson's Entry
Edinburgh EH8 8PJ

First published in hardback by Edinburgh University Press 2021

Typeset in 11/13 Monotype Ehrhardt by

Manila Typesetting Company

A CIP record for this book is available from the British Library

ISBN 978 1 4744 3695 3 (hardback)
ISBN 978 1 4744 3696 0 (paperback)
ISBN 978 1 4744 3697 7 (webready PDF)
ISBN 978 1 4744 3698 4 (epub)

The right of Francesca Minnie Hardy to be identified as author of this work has been asserted in accordance with the Copyright, Designs and Patents Act 1988 and the Copyright and Related Rights Regulations 2003 (SI No. 2498).

Contents

List of Figures   vi

Acknowledgements   vii

Film, Resonance and the Senses   1

Seeing with Oneself: Regarding Jean-Luc Nancy on Film   20

La Pointe Courte: Avoid Contact with the Eyes and Skin, May Cause Irritation   58

Time of the Wolf: Denatured Disaster Movie, Underwhelming Apocalypse, or the New Normal?   80

Teenage Dreams in *The Seventh Continent*   88

Le Bonheur: Happiness Made and Remade   112

The Singular Plural of Seeing in *Cleo from 5 to 7*   119

Caché: If These Walls Could Talk   142

Bad Resonance in *The Piano Teacher*   151

Documenteur: A Resonant Picture   172

Bloody Resonance   177

Bibliography   192

Index   205

Figures

1	*The Gleaners & I* (2000), a film by Agnès Varda	14
2	*The White Ribbon* (Michael Haneke, 2009)	15
3	*La Pointe Courte* (1954), a film by Agnès Varda	59
4	*The Time of the Wolf* (Michael Haneke, 2003)	85
5	*The Seventh Continent* (Michael Haneke, 1989)	98
6	*Le Bonheur* (1965), a film by Agnès Varda	115
7	*Cleo from 5 to 7* (1961), a film by Agnès Varda	130
8	*Caché* (Michael Haneke, 2005)	148
9	*The Piano Teacher* (Michael Haneke, 2001)	164
10	*Documenteur* (1981), a film by Agnès Varda	175
11	*Happy End* (Michael Haneke, 2017)	184
12	*Varda by Agnès* (2019), a film by Agnès Varda	189

Acknowledgements

This book took far too long to write. Indeed, it's taken so long that my thanks really are a work of excavation. Emma Wilson's unwavering support during my time as a postgraduate student, when this book began, remains peerless. At Edinburgh University Press, Gillian Leslie and Richard Strachan's kindness and patience enabled this book to happen. In all this time there have been many colleagues and friends at the universities of Aberdeen, Cambridge, Greenwich, Middlesex and Nottingham Trent who have generously supported fledgling ideas and false starts. I would particularly like to thank Katherine Groo, Paul Flaig, Jenny Chamarette, Laura McMahon, Matilda Mroz, Patrick Phillips, Gregory Sporton, Nicky Bowring, Rebecca Butler, Cüneyt Çakirlar, Anna Dawson, Martin O'Shaughnessy, Dave Woods and Anna Backman Rogers. Justin Clark deserves a special thanks for the many hours he spent listening to me during the book's development and I'd like to say a particular thank you to Rory Waterman who spent years living with me and the book. A final, and long overdue, thanks to mum, dad and Jenny.

Film, Resonance and the Senses

> The disillusioned writer and the insensitive critic are alike in discounting the very thing for which one goes to the cinema: the extraordinary resonances which a director can provoke by his use of actors, decor, movement, colour, shape, of all that can be seen and heard.[1]

Resonance is a (seemingly) passive yet pervasive concept in film studies. In theory (and practice) it constitutes a quasi-instinctual, linguistic beat that unwittingly rhythms your reading and writing. You might come to notice its frequency more frequently now. It litters pages but is rarely commented upon except for the occasional Romantic denigration.[2] Resonance, then, we might believe, is critically risky. Its prevalence, however, is remarkable and codes its nominal, adjectival and verbal forms as profoundly malleable, that is, as plastic as the titular fly of Yoko Ono's 1970 film, which 'not only denotes [its] eponymous insect, but an imperative to take wing [. . .] turn[ing] the noun designated by the title back into a verb, inviting us to soar'.[3] Like Ono's short, and Ara Osterweil's account of it, resonance's risks, as we will come to see, dovetail embodiment and ethereality, fleshiness and flight, and thus they may be worth it, and worth investigating, given what they permit us to do. Indeed, in the briefest of initial surveys of resonance, and its relationship to cinema, we can see how it conjoins diametrically opposed theories of spectatorship, each admittedly offering nightmare visions in its own way. Forged in loss of the object, of motor skills, of consciousness, the presumed vacancy of Christian Metz's spectator-fish reveals itself to be not so much 'a place of absence' as one of resonance.[4] Trapped in the auditorium-cum-aquarium, wherein 'viewing in the cinema leads to no good',[5] in this hollow spectator-fish, Metz suggests 'the purity of [the film's] disembodied utterance will resonate more clearly'.[6] Attempting, as she describes it, to make good on this cinematic viewing experience, and others, Vivian Sobchack gives film a body that 'exists as the visible visual relation between an embodied eye and a sensible world'.[7] She continues:

> The *radical* and *primary* perceptual correlation that is visible as the film is a correlation not *mediated* by instruments, but *enabled* by them. As an accomplishment of perception and its expression, the film is enabled by its mechanisms much as our bodies provide us with the sensing and sensible means to accomplish our perceptual and expressive intentions in an intended and expressed object. Thus, in a sense quite different than relating cinematic technology to our own human bodies, the mechanisms and technological instrumentation of the cinema can be understood as the film's body, functioning as its sensing and sensible being at and in the world.[8]

Sobchack playfully summarises her thinking by ventriloquising *Blade Runner* (Ridley Scott, 1982) replicant Roy Baty who 'says [to his creator] with an irony that resonates through the viewing audience [. . .], "If you could only see what I've seen with your eyes"';[9] it is '[t]he reversibility of cinematic perception and expression' that bestows such a set of eyes, that allows such irony to resonate.[10] Despite their radical differences, then, both Metz and Sobchack give an account of cinematic spectatorship which understands film as resonant: a channelling, perhaps a distortion, of worldly experience, be it ideology or sensibility, emitted via waves of light and sound.[11] Cinema thus becomes something of a wave phenomenon, that is, matter in movement. Arguably, then, in this fleeting overview, resonance 'resonates'; however, aside from vaguely acting as a conduit for images, memories and emotions, as well as implying an originary, inescapable togetherness, exactly what resonance is, what to resonate means, is neglected.

Vital Resonances addresses this neglect and I was first struck by the relationship between resonance and cinema after reading Roland Barthes's 'Leaving the Movie Theater' for the first time, although at the time I didn't know that this was what I had been struck by – I was still searching for the word: resonance. Here Barthes, a self-confessed fan of black-and-white film, with something of an ambivalent attitude to film sound, gives a kaleidoscopic, *jouissant* account of the cinematic viewing experience.[12] Lingering somewhere between psychoanalytic and phenomenological film theory, thanks to his two bodies – one 'narcissistic', the other 'perverse'[13] – which admit him two ways of going to the cinema, he describes film as a 'festival of affects'.[14] Already the critical air is pregnant with possibility and uncertainty – affect is, after all, polygonal – a charge reflected in the darkness that preoccupies Barthes's idle body and mind.[15] For saying nothing of the images on-screen, and very little about leaving the cinema, it soon becomes apparent that Barthes's intervention is very much about being physically and psychically in the auditorium, rather than (simply) lost to film's (al)lure. Shrouded in 'the very substance of reverie', this dark 'is also the "color" of a diffused eroticism; by its human condensation, by its absence of worldliness [. . .], by the relaxation of postures', spectatorship here becomes an assemblage of lassitude.[16] Repression and respiration chase after each other – breath and warmth commingle with dreams – innocence, immanence and transcendence jostle for primacy, whilst the musculature hinges these physical and psychical states together: legs, lungs, lower lumbar lounge alongside the image-repertoire, a collocation Barthes refutes elsewhere: 'The reader who cannot write projects his image-repertoire (the narcissistic zone of the psyche) very far from his muscular, carnal body, the body of *jouissance*.'[17] Embodiment neighbours ethereality, fleshiness neighbours flight once again. The 'film' finally emerges:

> In that opaque cube, one light: the film, the screen? Yes, of course. But also (especially?), visible and unperceived, that dancing cone which pierces the darkness like a laser beam. This beam is minted, according to the rotation of its particles, into changing figures; we turn our face toward the *currency* of a gleaming vibration whose imperious jet brushes our skull, glancing off someone's hair, someone's face.[18]

The movie theatre here is cast as a vibratory field. Beams, jets, particles rebound. The film dances and pierces the colour of the viewing space, it brushes up against the bodies in the room, ricocheting off their features. Barthes, then, figures film as inherently resonant, that is, as matter in movement and through this assemblage he invests the film with a floating (im)materiality that renders us in-visible – phenomena Davina Quinlivan and Osterweil pursue in their respective work on breathiness and eroticism in cinema. Necessary to the 'breathing visuality' Quinlivan posits, for instance, is an interstitial appreciation of both visibility and materiality: the seam between the seen and unseen, between physicality and incorporeality, fruitfully tiptoed through a style that 'invites a sensual appreciation of the filmic foregrounding of breathing'.[19] It is, after all, 'by way of techniques of the visible – especially modalities of camera work and editing [. . .] – that the cinema realizes its most immaterial function of putting us in touch with the invisible'.[20] Osterweil's in-visibility echoes this liminality: 'Pitched into darkness, we become "in-visible" – not in the superhero sense of being imperceptible, but in the sense that we become so intertwined with the film [. . .] that we can no longer distinguish between [. . .] its "flesh" and our own.'[21] Cradled within its dancing cone, which emanates from the screen, Barthes's idle body could thus be described as being caught up within such pulmonary and epidermal configurations. Breath to breath and flesh to flesh, he attunes to an ecstatic cinematic viewing experience which conceives cinema as a wave phenomenon. Diffuse, erotic, excessive, ethereal, (im)material, in-visible, intimate, resonance here is the colour of cinema.

In his celebrated *Metaphors on Vision*, Stan Brakhage echoes a similar preoccupation with innocence, materiality and colour mentioned by Barthes:

> Imagine an eye unruled by manmade laws of perspective, an eye unprejudiced by compositional logic, an eye which does not respond to the name of everything but which must know each object encountered in life through an adventure of perception. How many colours are there in a field of grass to the crawling baby unaware of 'Green'? How many rainbows can light create for the untutored eye? [...] Imagine a world alive with incomprehensible objects and shimmering with an endless variety of movement and innumerable gradations of color. Imagine a world before the 'beginning was the word'.[22]

We are, of course, beginning with a word – resonance – a word that sees green, a word that unwittingly embarks upon the adventure in perception that Brakhage desires, that is, a way of seeing centred on a pristine worldliness that is driven by encounters. If resonance is the colour of cinema, then, this green is the colour of resonance, colours resonance, for, arguably, it is this very state that film critics revert to when they evoke it. Take, for instance, the following observation from Matilda Mroz:

> In *Cinema and Modernism*, David Trotter asks the following question: 'does cinema . . . deal in *meanings* at all'? He continues, 'Deborah Thomas remarks of a detail of décor in a scene in Capra's *It's a Wonderful Life* (1945) that although the detail does not "mean" or "symbolise" anything, it *resonates*'.[23]

Resonance here signifies an absence of stable, easy signification – a linguistic, but not necessarily rhetorical, failure – whilst pointing up its enigmatic critical power and its affinity for a world alive with incomprehensible objects and shimmering with an endless variety of movement and innumerable gradations of colour. In this way, resonance is a quintessential postmodern concept, this -ism's various -nesses – flatness, depthlessness, pastness and so on – sketching out imprecision, such fuzzy logic a symptom of its degrading, cannibalistic appetite.[24] Resonance is not so indiscriminately hungry, yet such is its potency that it is called upon when language, and even meaning itself, fails. Indeed, (such) failure is at the heart of resonance; a disinvestment from straightforward linguistic codes animates it – it does not mean, it does not symbolise, it resonates. Such is its power that Anne Rutherford indexes it as 'murky'.[25] Discussing Theo

Angelopoulos's *Ulysses' Gaze* (1995), she notes how 'These corporeal, material intensities which cycle between filmmaker, film and audience could perhaps best be described in murky, indistinct terms like sympathetic vibration, as redolent as they are with indefinables like intuition, feeling, resonance, or intensity.'[26] If the role of theory is to clarify the cinematic viewing experience, then, the murk of resonance is clearly antithetical to these aims.

The murk of resonance motors Elena del Río's concluding discussion of Carlos Reygadas's *Battle in Heaven* (2005):

> That the film is thus building a resonance between Marcos and Christ seems irrefutable. The resonance 'resonates' precisely because it is both congruent and absolutely incongruous. It triggers the proximity between two subjects utterly dispossessed and marked by suffering, yet it also triggers an infinite distance between them: if Christ's dispossession awaits the promise of a future glory and power, Marcos' dispossession turns its back on any such promise of transcendence, and instead remains 'vertiginously within itself', exclusively dependent on its immanent affects and intensities.[27]

Here resonance is substantive and verbal, definite and indefinite. It is congruence and conflict, consonance and dissonance. It is proximity and distance, mimicry and contagion. It offers a glimpse of transcendence, but it is stubbornly, vertiginously immanent. Resonance 'resonates', it serves as a conduit, and del Río's tautology is performative yet telling: her use of scare quotes, a staple of resonance's textual renderings, literally highlights the murky place that it occupies within the vernacular of film studies. Such bracketing off marks up its uncertain linguistic contours, while gesturing towards its promises of contingency and an excessive (emptying out of) meaningfulness. In stark opposition to, and moreover despite, its acoustic origins, and Michel Chion's call for precision, '"Why say 'a sound', when we can say 'crackling' or 'rumbling' or 'tremolo'? Using more exact words allows us to confront and compare perceptions and to make progress in pinpointing and defining them"', resonance's own rumblings refuse such exactitude.[28]

Sobchack is less suspicious of resonance; however, she too catalogues it amongst another bunch of indefinables, and likewise highlights the challenge it poses to critical film language. 'What have we, as contemporary media theorists, to do with such tactile, kinetic, redolent, resonant, and sometimes even taste-full descriptions of the film experience?', she writes of a medley of effervescent responses to films as diverse as *The Piano* (Jane Campion, 1993), *Speed* (Jan de Bont, 1994) and *Toy Story* (John Lasseter, 1995).[29] Resonance here becomes part of a multisensory address; it is a sonorous counterpart to touch, taste, smell and movement, a part of the 'rebounding' encounter with film Sobchack posits: 'Watching *The Piano* [. . .] my skin's desire to touch streams toward the screen to rebound back on itself and then forward to the screen again and again.'[30] For film studies, then, resonance is 'troublesome', to forge something of a methodological kinship with Rosalind Galt's work on the pretty where prettiness troubles through its links to ornament's feminine surpluses and superficiality's suspicious depthlessness.[31] According to Galt, 'the pretty exerts a demand that images be read precisely at the point of their aesthetic exclusion, a practice that might reveal different shapes for the global cinematic body',[32] and significantly, it is resonance that animates Galt's closing aspirations for her pretty project which envisage 'a future for the pretty image as an aesthetic field uniquely able to voice a cinematic ethics of worldliness through the resonance of the decorative image'.[33] It is the image of a textile, exploding heart in Claire Denis's *L'Intrus* (2004) – constructed from multicoloured streamers blowing in the wind – that inspires this future, its voice, which exceeds the streamers' gentle rustle in the wind, coordinating a subtle although emphatic multisensory encounter between spectator and screen. Perhaps rebounding in the way Sobchack describes above, in essence, their psychedelic burst prompts the whole image to vibrate as it bathes us in the colours, textures, sounds and rhythms of the streamers which in turn become colour, texture, sound, rhythm, thanks to cinema's capacity 'to reveal the world as experience and flux' in what Tiago de Luca determines realism of the senses:[34] 'the sheer expressiveness of reality, which, escaping intentionality, asserts itself as purely sensible presence'.[35] What matters here is matter, as Sobchack claims, what matters is 'the "mattering" of all matter', and resonance facilitates this very mattering through its inherent affinity for matter in movement.[36] Film, moreover, facilitates this mattering of all matter because by design, and however it moves, it is nothing more than matter in movement. Filmstock whirs in the projector frame to frame; transitory configurations of light, colour, sound and movement flash up on the screen, swiftly replaced by others. From shot to shot, scene to scene, sequel to sequel, film creates meaning materially – that is, as matter in movement.

Film Studies' Bodily Turn

Resonant, worldly matter momentarily takes us outside of film studies and towards Jane Bennett's *Vibrant Matter: A Political Ecology of Things* and her 'horizontal' understanding of materiality: 'It draws human attention sideways, away from an ontologically ranked Great Chain of Being and toward a greater appreciation of the complex entanglements of humans and nonhumans.'[37] Here Bennett calls for 'a countercultural kind of perceiving' where we, the *mes*, see, hear, smell, taste, feel the swarms, confederacies, confederations, conjunctions, clusters, alloys and assemblages of humans and non-humans, 'life' and matter, and their coextensive evanescence, affects, agency and power, that constitute the world, as well as our selves, and which are understood without recourse to the limiting categories of context, constraint, tool or soul.[38] This is a world brimming with not-quite-subjects – actants – and of an embodied yet radically displaced self that is itself filled with '"foreign" materialities'.[39] But a world that is not alienating and where in fact the encounter is vital and where all agency is distributive.[40] A mute world, which demands a sensitive ear, where the *its* outnumber the *mes*. And in keeping with the resonant bestiary that has emerged across these pages – flies, fish, silkworms[41] – it is also a world of history-making and culture-enabling worms as well as a world full of philosophy: Massumi's affect, Spinoza's conatus and Deleuze and Guattari's operators, assemblages and virtualities. Thus, in Brakhage-like fashion, Bennett endorses an adventurous, never completely self-possessed way of apprehending the world, that enriches an account of the worldliness of resonance and of resonance as matter in movement:

> In a vital materialism, an anthropomorphic element in perception can uncover a whole world of resonances and resemblances – sounds and sights that echo and bounce far more than would be possible were the universe to have a hierarchical structure. We at first may see only a world in our own image, but what appears next is a swarm of 'talented' and vibrant materialities (including the seeing self). [. . .] A touch of anthropomorphism, then, can catalyze a sensibility that finds a world filled not with ontologically distinct categories of beings (subjects and objects) but with variously composed materialities that form confederations.[42]

Initially invested with seemingly straightforward acoustic contours, resonance risks being reducible to the obverse of its visual counterpart: resemblances. The worlds resonance and resemblance uncover are understood as auxiliary. Resonance further risks being freighted with a certain critical conservatism through recourse to anthropomorphism, which in turn threatens an unsustainable, antimaterialist anthropocentrism. Soon enough, though, resonance precipitates as a catalyst for a way of being in and with the world that is attuned to the vibrant matter of which it is composed, albeit one that residually remains bound to a human framework. Its noise, its clamour, goes out into the world as a sort of transcendent, yet immanent, address, enchaining life and matter, brains and buildings, thereby disclosing a world of *its* and revealing that *we* are not alone. We *are* vital materiality, we are surrounded by it, although we do not always see it that way.⁴³ Indeed, the 'animal-vegetable-mineral-sonority cluster' that I therefore am is hard to keep sight of.⁴⁴ Fundamentally, then, resonance displaces the seeing self as the centre and apex of this world and acquires a worldliness that is isomorphic with 'the inflection of matter as vibrant, vital, energetic, lively, quivering, vibratory, evanescent, and effluescent'.⁴⁵ Resonance and materiality intimately correspond.

In spite of this displacement, however, Bennett's argument is 'motivated' by a peculiar self-interest.⁴⁶ Strange in its generosity, this self-interest pursues an encounter with matter that rejects the 'habit of parsing the world into dull matter (it, things) and vibrant life (us, beings)'.⁴⁷ Resonance undoubtedly refuses such parsing out. It does not quarantine matter and life and – technically speaking, at the very least – neither does, nor can, cinema: it cannot help but capture 'the sheer *senses* [the world] emanates'.⁴⁸ As we have already seen through the work of de Luca, del Río, Osterweil, Quinlivan, Rutherford and Sobchack, film studies has by no means been indifferent to the bankruptcy that Bennett sees in the way of ordering the world that upholds the life–matter binary. Indeed, it is the bankruptcy seen in theories of spectatorship such as Metz's spectator-fish which has been a central inspiration for film studies' recent bodily turn. This turn lends a careful ear to a vital materiality and as Sobchack's pioneering intervention states: 'This is a vision that knows what it is to touch things in the world, that understands materiality', an understanding that pivots on spatiality and intention, texture and solidity.⁴⁹ Resonance, moreover, is foundational to this turn, although it doesn't appear to have noticed. In fact, in keeping with the soft touch of much of its critical literature – the feel of velvet, the (frustrated) tactility of a sari, the skin of a lover's body – the reader is unlikely to be aware of this. Whilst, then, resonance has consistently been a footnote to film studies' bodily turn, *Vital Resonances* finally places it at the forefront of our encounter with film.

Tacitly, then, resonance is already a powerful critical and rhetorical tool invoked at crucial moments of theoretical insight, which for Martine Beugnet, signifies a 'run against the long-held belief that valuable experience and knowledge must necessarily come as a process of "enlightenment" that distances us from the unreliable input of sensual perception'.⁵⁰ In essence, she continues, 'we have to unlearn before we can learn to see and feel again'.⁵¹ Taking stock of this unlearning, Jenny Chamarette considers what such practices have taught us:

> What is also at stake are affective, precognitive, proprioceptive encounters with the screen image, that take on such significance in the film theory of Vivian Sobchack, Laura U. Marks and Jennifer M. Barker, among others. Instances such as haptic

visuality might be considered more productively not as the insistence of some semi-empirical examples where the eye 'touches', but as a contact of the abstract and the concrete in thinking embodied ontological relationships to and with the specific visuality of cinema. Haptic visuality is a strategy not only to apprehend the image but also to apprehend what it is to be present to the image, to share its actual and virtual spatialities and temporalities, beyond representation.[52]

Such unlearning and apprehension started in earnest with Sobchack's *The Address of the Eye: A Phenomenology of Film Experience* – a titular address that, like resonance, operates both nominally and verbally, as a self-address as well as an address to elsewhere: 'It is a visual address always housed in a situated body experienced as "mine" and yet always also able to extend itself to where that body is not.'[53] According to Sobchack, resonance galvanises the unlearning that the bodily turn teaches, centred on the synaesthetic configuration of the senses that it celebrates, whereby this address is '[r]esonant with the body's other senses (particularly those of touch and sound)'.[54] She later posits how

> I am able to see texture. My sense of sight is pervaded by my sense of touch. Smell is cooperative with taste and taste with sight. [. . .] My sense of sight, then, is a modality of perception that is commutable to my other senses, and vice-versa. My sight is never only sight – it sees what my ear can hear, my hand can touch, my nose can smell, and my tongue can taste. My entire bodily existence is implicated in my vision.[55]

In seeing texture, Sobchack shows how '[s]eeing is both *synaesthetic* and *synoptic*', both commutable and comprehensive, upon which its understanding of materiality is predicated.[56] Yet despite this understanding, the murk of resonance starts to emerge: 'The film's vision [. . .] perceives and expresses the "sense" of fabrics like velvet or the roughness of tree bark or the yielding softness of human flesh.'[57] What the film perceives and expresses is only the 'sense' of rough*ness* or soft*ness*. Once more these scare quotes perform inexactitude, which Sobchack repeats in later critical moments when attempting to find the right word:

> Thus, although generally I appear to be a polite visual 'listener' who seldom visibly and audibly interrupts or argues with my invited guest's narrative unless I am encouraged to do so by the form of her discourse, I am nonetheless actively engaged in an invisible and inaudible comparison of the guest's experience and performance with my own. [. . .] And in fact I may 'see' what my guest sees.[58]

With less hostile echoes of replicant Roy Baty, Sobchack's use of scare quotes depicts the murk of resonance. They both point up and attempt to contain its enigmatic critical power, which here structures the commutability and synopsis between the body's senses; vision, touch and hearing operate in resonance, which in turn realises such 'listening', which in turn realises and permits us to partake in the film's knowing vision. Equally, this murk points up cinema's material undulations: as a polite visual 'listener' I do more than look. Rather, I am cradled within the floating (im)materiality that the film is. Resonance, both rhetorical and experiential, thus clarifies. It makes any description of the cinematic viewing experience legible, if not explicit.

Published a year later, Steven Shaviro's *The Cinematic Body* inflects resonance with a living-dead quality via the zombie. Somehow animate and animating, according to Shaviro, cinematic 'zombies do not [. . .] stand for a threat to social order from without. Rather', he continues, 'they *resonate* with, and refigure, the very processes that produce and enforce social order. That is to say, they do not mirror or represent social forces; they are directly animated and possessed [. . .] by such forces.'[59] In spite of the infection that ravages their bodies and minds, effectively collapsing the two to produce a de-Cartesian horde, the zombies' rotting flesh channels social order and actively constitutes it. Their groans may outstrip linguistic codes, but their shuffling feet and stiff, staccato limbs perpetuate the status quo. Their bodies, as both abstractions and sensual, cinematic images, are thus resonant, a process which extends to the spectator who is 'drawn into proximity with them. The participatory contact that they promise and exemplify is in a deep sense what we most strongly desire.'[60] Resonance here is mimesis and contagion, and the horde, of which we become a part, thus forms a sort of a resonant assemblage, delivering an undead distributive agency – the zombie perhaps the perfect embodiment of a vibrant materiality that does not discriminate between life and matter.[61] Significantly, resonance once again structures.

Laura U. Marks continues this trope in her highly influential account of haptic visuality, where 'the eyes themselves function like organs of touch'.[62] Here resonance is perhaps at its most fundamental across the bodily turn, for it is the very hinge of her thesis – to combat the silence of 'the verbal and visual archives' – and, moreover, of its principal paradigm.[63] Resonance, then, dovetails the material and the social, as above, via Marks's proposal of 'an order of the *sensible*'[64] – essentially a repository for extradiscursive audio-visual 'noise', which we likely register as 'a gap between the seeable and the sayable', and which we likely see or hear as sub-dialogue sounds, for example, grunts, zombie groans, or orphaned images, glitches and objects.[65] This order houses the stuff that cannot be readily recuperated by dominant cinematic and symbolic regimes, which ceaselessly endeavour to suppress these slippages. Marks, however, lets these slippages stand: 'What does not register in the orders of the seeable and the sayable may *resonate* in the order of the sensible.'[66] Resonance, then, is the order of the sensible; it organises what escapes the distance senses, or what they distrust – arguably, this is the 'film' as Barthes saw it – and, following Sobchack, haptic visuality is resonance thanks to its synaesthetic sensory configuration. Touch, vision, movement, or rather, skin, eyes, muscle, and of course image, form another resonant assemblage:

> Haptic looking tends to move over the surface of its object rather than plunge into illusionistic depth, not to distinguish form so much as to discern texture. It is more inclined to move than to focus, more inclined to graze than to gaze.[67]

Looking in this way, then, is an inclination, an invitation and a reconfiguration of the typical power dynamic at the heart of cinematic spectatorship – dialogic, rather than monologic.[68] Yet through such reciprocity, as Marks details, '[w]hen vision is like touch, the object's touch back may be like a caress',[69] there is a coincident counterargument to be made: that the bodily turn is fundamentally unresonant owing to the closed experiential circuits it establishes, that is, encounters with film that 'are not', according to Mroz, 'extended into time'.[70] Although writing with specific reference to Sobchack's rebounding mentioned above, Mroz's thinking can be productively applied to any of the key bodily turn paradigms which upon closer inspection materialise as disappointingly, almost inflexibly, paradigmatic. Supposedly impressionistic encounters, hinging on contingency, and revelling in somatic confidence and knowledge, these encounters are overwhelmingly staged between individual *mes* and individual films, even film stills warns Mroz. These encounters are thus restrictively dyadic. Sobchack's rebounding and Marks's haptic visuality narrowly take place between skin and screen, whilst a triptych of attempts to restage the maternal figure and relation inspire Marks's thesis.[71] These problematically paradigmatic dyads reach their apotheosis in Jennifer M. Barker's account of the cinematic musculature.

Ostensibly bulking up Sobchack's filmic body, Barker embeds her muscular thinking in discussions of empathy, that is, affective and physical reactions that cycle between artwork and viewer:

> When the film swivels suddenly with a whip pan [. . .] we feel those movements in our muscles because our bodies have made similar movements [. . .]. When the film 'ducks' or 'swerves' or 'races' or 'stalks' its subjects or 'crashes' into something, we can relate, having performed many of these basic gestures ourselves, in our own way.[72]

Resonantly, Barker draws on Eugène Minkowski's 'reverberation' in order to flesh out her empathetic thinking, which itself reads like an account of resonance:

> If, having fixed the original form in our mind's eye, we ask ourselves how that form comes alive and fills itself with life, we discover a new dynamic and vital category, a new property of the universe: reverberation (*retenir*). It is as though a well-spring existed in a sealed vase and its waves, repeatedly echoing against the sides of this vase, filled it with their sonority. Or again, it is as though the sound of a hunting horn, reverberating everywhere through its echo, made the tiniest leaf, the tiniest wisp of moss shudder in a common movement and transformed the whole forest, filling it to its limits, into a vibrating, sonorous world.[73]

The vase, the forest become vibratory fields, full of matter in movement, and to understand reverberation as exclusively acoustic, Minkowski stresses, 'would be the intentional mutilating of it'; rather, it is a mutual, material tingling.[74] It is this sense of reciprocity that Barker seeks to uphold. Reciprocity, however, soon gives way to response: 'the film's gesture [. . .] demands a reply of some kind from the attentive spectator's body. It evokes a corresponding, but not predetermined, gesture from our bodies.'[75] Despite Barker's efforts to maintain contingency, what ultimately emerges is foreclosure:

> the film is to our bodies like car is to driver: we live through it vicariously, allowing it to shape our own bodily image. It becomes our proxy, our vehicle for movement and action, as well as the thing that provides us a safe haven from which to experience real danger.[76]

Barker's mention of a 'safe haven' compounds this principle, intimating that instead of stimulating the actual muscles, the spectatorial body hides behind the body of the film whereby her muscly disposition is nothing more than a charlatan, an empty gesture. We are thus driven into very familiar critical terrain for the film serves as nothing more than our 'screen surrogate': 'a main controlling figure with whom the spectator can identify'.[77] We hitch a ride and thereby share in its 'active power' and control in 'forwarding the story, making things happen'.[78] In effect, we are back in the tank with the other spectator-fish, but this time around it is the film's embodied utterance that resonates more clearly. Any real danger, as well as the dangers of resonance's murk, are safely bracketed off.

Resonance and the bodily turn thus share a linguistic and experiential bracketing off and *Vital Resonances* seeks to reattune to the synoptic quality of perception which has been consistently overlooked in the wake of Sobchack's seminal intervention. It does so through a series of close encounters with the work of two of the most ostensibly disparate European filmmakers: Agnès Varda and Michael Haneke. Varda's margins – women, the precariat, the elderly – and Haneke's bourgeois milieus – Paris, Vienna, second homes – appear oppositional. Yet Varda's recent collaborations with the Fondation Cartier pour l'Art Contemporain (2006–) and Miu Miu (2015) indicate an inadvertent rapprochement *de luxe* between the two filmmakers, whilst Haneke's recent turn towards ageing, and euthanasia, in *Amour* (2012) and *Happy End* (2017) suggests a corresponding inscription of self within their respective film worlds: the former an unusually personal family portrait for the usually inscrutable *auteur*.[79] *Vital Resonances*, however, brings together Varda's and Haneke's bodies of work through more humble means: the cabbage.

A Walk amongst the Cabbages

'Green'. Then trees to the left of the frame, leaves to the right, and finally rows and rows of Renaissance-perspective-defying cabbages. Cabbages as far as the eye can see. Cabbages on the very surface plane of the image (Figure 1). A field. A voice intones that 'The harvest of the cabbage is over' and a quick pan to the right reveals this declaration to belong to a man – a judge? – explaining how those cabbages that remain can now be gleaned. Then red. Red tomatoes, to match the leather binding of the penal code, which is then read aloud: 'Article R- 26.10. Here – gleaning is allowed from sunrise to sunset. First requirement. The second requirement is that gleaning occurs after the harvest is over.' Fully attired in his robes and planted in the field of cabbages, the judge describes how little change there has been to the legislation concerning gleaning over the centuries. Since at least the sixteenth century the poor, wretched and deprived have had the right to glean the remains of the harvest. What of those who want for nothing but glean anyway, asks a voice off-screen. Reassuringly, one may glean for pleasure. 'Now if you don't mind', continues the judge jovially, 'I'll take a walk in the cabbages.' Enrobed, and with code in hand, the sight of the judge trundling through the leftover cabbages produces a pleasing yet dissonant image: the black robe, white cravat and red penal code map the rule of Law amongst the greens and browns of the pastoral. Legislature mixes with legumes, as it has unchanged for over 500 years. Varda then gleans of her own accord. This a mental, rhizomatic gleaning, which has always been free of governance, that records a medley of vegetation by exploiting a range of cinematic techniques: cabbages in close-up,

Figure 1 *The Gleaners & I* (2000), a film by Agnès Varda © 2000 ciné-tamaris.

a slow-motion magnolia in extreme close-up, saturated sunflowers, grainy landscapes shot through a car window.

Black, white and greys. The shades of yesteryear. A black smock and white collar. The shades of the Pastor. The shades of patriarchal law. A psalm is read aloud. Then a back comes into view. A scythe irrepressibly, but gently, swings at the shoulder. Footsteps jostle with musical airs to echo the judge's trundling. The camera stops at a gate. Then, rows and rows of Renaissance-perspective-respecting cabbages (Figure 2). The scythe swings upwards and soil and spliced cabbages shoot outwards from the blade. Exertion sounds out and the scene plays out like Foley in reverse. The wind picks up and a series of vignettes surveys the professional, domestic and sexual servitude the characters find themselves edged towards or trapped in – Schoolmaster, Baroness, Steward, Governess – until we find ourselves back at the cabbage patch. Heavy footsteps. The camera tracks the village children as they approach it, stopping as they inspect the damage. The children peel away and the camera pans. Servitude is momentarily restored until a remarkable shot sunders it: an image of butchered cabbages. Entirely devoid of depth, it is impossible

Figure 2 *The White Ribbon* (Michael Haneke, 2009). Reproduced with kind permission of the director.

to fix the scale of this image. At first, we wonder: what is it? Has it been observed through a telescope, camera lens or microscope? Is it a close-up, or a long shot? In essence, its presence obliterates (film) language. Haptic, it obliges us to be present. Dissonant, we struggle to explain it. Resonant, it is an (a)signifying intensity.[80] A close-up of the Baroness seeks to do some of the affective work here, her face subtly etched by disgust and quiet devastation. Later in the film her incomprehension will crystallise into an understanding of the rot at the heart of the village prompting her departure. For now, though, she simply walks away, whilst the Baron and Steward take a walk amongst the cabbages.

In and between Varda's *The Gleaners & I* (2000) and Haneke's *The White Ribbon* (2009), cinema is manifestly matter in movement. It is terrestrial and vegetal, texture and solidity. It is colour. It is sound, crunch, slice, voice, rustling, and movement, proxemics, props and people. In and between the two films, moreover, and their respective walks amongst the cabbages, resonance precipitates. Indeed, the cabbage becomes resonance itself. Its murk muddies through excessive, deferred, materially constituted meanings – infinite cabbages in long shot, cabbage corpses in extreme close-up – but it also clarifies violence, precarity, pragmatism and pleasure. It is verbal. It coordinates plant and village life. It is substantive. It embodies the processes that manage social (dis)order. The cabbage resonates. Resonance resonates. But how to keep sight of these resonances? For this we turn to French thinker Jean-Luc Nancy.

Notes

1. V. F. Perkins quoted in John Gibbs, *Mise-en-scène: Film Style and Interpretation* (London: Wallflower, 2002), p. 59.
2. See, for instance, Sarah Cooper, *The Soul of Film Theory* (Basingstoke: Palgrave Macmillan, 2013), p. 65.
3. Ara Osterweil, *Flesh Cinema: The Corporeal Turn in American Avant-Garde Film* (Manchester: Manchester University Press, 2014), p. 208.
4. Christian Metz, *The Imaginary Signifier: Psychoanalysis and the Cinema*, trans. by Celia Britton, Annwyl Williams, Ben Brewster and Alfred Guzzetti (Basingstoke: Macmillan Press, 1982), p. 97.
5. Vivian Sobchack, *The Address of the Eye: A Phenomenology of Film Experience* (Princeton: Princeton University Press, 1992), p. 18.
6. Metz (1982), p. 97.
7. Sobchack (1992), p. 203.
8. Ibid. pp. 204–5.
9. Ibid. p. 309.
10. Ibid. p. 15.
11. See also Laura U. Marks, *The Skin of the Film: Intercultural Cinema, Embodiment, and the Senses* (Durham, NC: Duke University Press, 2000), pp. 152–3.
12. See Roland Barthes, *Camera Lucida: Reflections on Photography* (London: Vintage, 2000).
13. Roland Barthes, 'Leaving the Movie Theater', in *The Rustle of Language*, trans. by Richard Howard (Berkeley: University of California Press, 1989), p. 349.
14. Ibid. p. 346.
15. See Brian Massumi, *Parables for the Virtual: Movement, Affect, Sensation* (Durham, NC: Duke University Press, 2002).
16. Barthes (1989), p. 346.
17. Roland Barthes, *The Grain of the Voice: Interviews, 1962–1980*, trans. by Linda Coverdale (Evanston: Northwestern University Press, 2009), p. 241.
18. Barthes (1989), p. 347.
19. Davina Quinlivan, *The Place of Breath in Cinema* (Edinburgh: Edinburgh University Press, 2012), p. 134.
20. Elena del Río, *The Grace of Destruction: A Vital Ethology of Extreme Cinemas* (New York: Bloomsbury, 2016), pp. 13–14.
21. Osterweil (2014), p. 5.
22. Stan Brakhage, 'From *Metaphors on Vision*', in *The Avant-Garde Film: A Reader of Theory and Criticism*, ed. by P. Adams Sitney (New York: Anthology Film Archives, 1987), pp. 120–8 (p. 120).
23. Matilda Mroz, *Temporality and Film Analysis* (Edinburgh: Edinburgh University Press, 2012), pp. 4–5.

24. See Fredric Jameson, *Postmodernism, or, the Cultural Logic of Late Capitalism* (London: Verso, 1991).
25. Anne Rutherford, *What Makes a Film Tick? Cinematic Affect, Materiality and Mimetic Innervation* (Berlin: Peter Lang, 2011), p. 175. Despite this murk, Rutherford frequently draws on resonance across her discussion of embodied spectatorship; an indefinable she defines as 'a kind of "co-presence" of affect and signification, a relationship that does not privilege one over the other' (p. 130).
26. Ibid. p. 175.
27. Del Río (2016), p 115.
28. Michel Chion quoted in Lucy Fife Donaldson, *Texture in Film* (Basingstoke: Palgrave Macmillan, 2014), p. 140. Donaldson's study of texture resonates with my own on resonance, especially in its sympathy towards a more synoptic appraisal of film spectatorship and style: 'One specific framework I've proposed is to consider the intermeshing of vertical (the materiality of decor, props, dialogue, characters and their interaction, performance and physical action, pitch, amplitude and register) and horizontal (editing, music, rhythm, pattern and movement, repetition) textures' (pp. 165–6).
29. Vivian Sobchack, *Carnal Thoughts: Embodiment and Moving Image Culture* (Berkeley: University of California Press, 2004), p. 54.
30. Ibid. p. 78.
31. Rosalind Galt, *Pretty: Film and the Decorative Image* (New York: Columbia University Press, 2011), p. 98 and p. 53.
32. Ibid. p. 37.
33. Ibid. p. 304.
34. Tiago de Luca, *Realism of the Senses in World Cinema: The Experience of Physical Reality* (London: I. B. Tauris, 2013), p. 3. De Luca 'start[s] from the premise that spectatorship is embodied' thereby 'set[ting him] free to concentrate on sensory modes of production and address as expressed through current realist cinema' (p. 2). See also Luis R. Antunes, *The Multisensory Film Experience: A Cognitive Model of Experiential Film Aesthetics* (Bristol: Intellect, 2016), which departs from a similar multisensory position: '[N]ot only *can* our brains perceive an audiovisual medium in a multisensory way, but they *must* do so because there is no other way for our perception to occur. Our natural, not exceptional or synesthetic, way of perceiving is multisensory' (p. 3).
35. De Luca (2013), p. 80.
36. Sobchack (2004), p. 302.
37. Jane Bennett, *Vibrant Matter: A Political Ecology of Things* (Durham, NC: Duke University Press, 2010), p. 112.
38. Ibid. p. xiv.
39. Ibid. p. 36.
40. Ibid. p. 6.

41. Barthes (1989), p. 346.
42. Bennett (2010), p. 99.
43. Ibid. p. 14.
44. Ibid. p. 23.
45. Ibid. p. 112.
46. Ibid. p. ix.
47. Ibid. p. vii.
48. De Luca (2013), p. 11.
49. Sobchack (1992), p. 133.
50. Martine Beugnet, *Cinema and Sensation: French Film and the Art of Transgression* (Edinburgh: Edinburgh University Press, 2007), p. 6.
51. Ibid.
52. Jenny Chamarette, *Phenomenology and the Future of Film: Rethinking Subjectivity beyond French Cinema* (Basingstoke: Palgrave Macmillan, 2012), p. 234.
53. Sobchack (1992), p. 261.
54. Ibid. p. 25.
55. Ibid. p. 77–8.
56. Ibid. p. 133.
57. Ibid.
58. Ibid. p. 272.
59. Steven Shaviro, *The Cinematic Body* (Minneapolis: University of Minnesota Press, 1993), p. 87.
60. Ibid. pp. 96–7.
61. Ibid. p. 52.
62. Marks (2000), p. 162.
63. Ibid. p. 76.
64. Ibid. p. 31.
65. Ibid. p. 36.
66. Ibid. p. 111. My emphasis.
67. Ibid. p. 162.
68. Ibid. p. 150.
69. Ibid. p. 184.
70. Mroz (2012), p. 30. Resonance is also a key pillar of Mroz's thinking (pp. 4–5).
71. Marks (2000), p. xi.
72. Jennifer M. Barker, *The Tactile Eye: Touch and the Cinematic Experience* (Berkeley: University of California Press, 2009), p. 75.
73. Eugène Minkowski quoted in Barker (2009), p. 78.
74. Eugène Minkowski, *Vers une cosmologie: Fragments philosophiques* (Paris: Fernand Aubier, 1936), p. 101. My translation.
75. Barker (2009), p. 80.
76. Ibid. p. 110.
77. Laura Mulvey, 'Visual Pleasure and Narrative Cinema', *Screen*, 16 (1975), 6–18 (p. 12).
78. Ibid.

79. See Peter Conrad, 'Michael Haneke: There's No Easy Way to Say This . . .', *The Observer*, 4 November 2012 <http://www.guardian.co.uk/film/2012/nov/04/michael-haneke-amour-director-interview> (last accessed 29 June 2020).
80. Massumi (2002), p. 41.

Seeing with Oneself:
Regarding Jean-Luc Nancy on Film

Listening: This is at the same time a title, an address, and a dedication.[1]

Jean-Luc Nancy might be regarded as the most cinematic philosopher – both in writing and on screen – for the diminutive professor has to date 'appeared' in eight films that explore his singular-plural being as transplant patient, friend, teacher, husband, actor, thinker.[2] At times these audio-visual encounters embody an extension of Nancy's textual musings, such as Marc Grün's *Le Corps du philosophe* (2003) and Phillip Warnell's *Outlandish: Strange Foreign Bodies* (2009). At others their philosophical remit is more collaborative, for instance, Claire Denis's ambiguously titled *Vers Nancy* (2002) and David Barison and Daniel Ross's *The Ister* (2004). In other instances, he is more obliquely 'adopted' by filmmakers, as is the case in Denis's *L'Intrus* (2004) and Nicolas Klotz's *La Blessure* (2004), and Nancy even has one bona fide acting role under his belt, playing printer Jean-Luc Cinan, less ambiguously moving towards Nancy here, in Rabah Ameur-Zaïmeche's *Les Chants de Mandrin* (2012).[3] With an honourable mention for Warnell's *Ming of Harlem* (2014), to which he contributed a poem, Nancy has enjoyed a steady on-screen presence throughout the noughties, a steadiness mirrored by his textual musings. This attention includes *The Evidence of Film*, a book-length study on the cinema of Iranian director Abbas Kiarostami, a collection of articles published in cultural reviews *Vacarme* and *Remue* and a quartet of pieces in the journal *Trafic*.[4] Alternatively, these interventions take in Plato's discrediting of images, the Hegelian dialectic, the Kantian schema and ecotechnics, placing a vast panorama of Western thought into dialogue with cinema.[5] Indeed, in an article surveying recent film theory in France, Sarah Cooper catalogues Nancy as one of the leading figures responsible for the 'abiding interest in film' that the philosophical intelligentsia of *l'Hexagone* continues to demonstrate.[6]

We might, then, justly describe Nancy's approach to cinema as esoteric, not least because his critical encounters with film, and responses to them, frequently take in a select set of players.[7] Select too is Nancy's cinematic taxonomy. He sees two cinemas, which each forge a different relationship with the world. The principles of the first classification observe typical representational means that 'take advantage of all the possibilities of film at once and in an intense way: image, sound (music, special effects), words'.[8] In the second, championed by Nancy and his respondents, film resists these same possibilities:[9]

> Cinema – its screen, its sensitive membrane – stretches and hangs between a world in which representation was in charge of the signs of truth, of the heralding of a new meaning, or of the warrant of a presence to come, and another world that opens onto its own presence through a voiding where thoughtful evidence *realizes* itself.[10]

To realise/*Réaliser* here is as pregnant as the world that cinema creates, 'translating [. . .] as producing or making a film', and, accordingly, it is the very act of filmmaking, cinema itself, that unleashes the evidentiary possibility that the world *is*:[11] 'if one day I happen to *look* at my street on which I walk up and down ten times a day, I construct for an instant a new *evidence* of my street'.[12] This mobile, mundane meandering, moreover, keenly complements what else emerges from the pages of Nancy's reflections on film: an account of the philosopher as a cinemagoer.

Echoing Barthes's account of spectatorship in 'Leaving the Movie Theater', Nancy in *The Evidence of Film* intermittently mentions the cuboid dimensions of the *salle*, described as an 'opaque cube'[13] and 'looking box',[14] respectively, which is entered by a dynamic 'beam of light'.[15] Whilst in 'Cinéfile et cinémonde', and again aping Barthes,[16] he notes how cinema 'saturates daily life' thanks to the arthouse cinemas and multiplexes that limn cities and out-of-town retail parks, new releases and reruns that adorn their screens, sweeping marketing campaigns that emblazon public transport, television shows dedicated to the film industry and how it has even given birth to a whole substratum of language: the movies, pictures, flicks.[17] 'Cinema', he says, 'is everywhere'.[18] It flashes up within the currency of the everyday:

> When we look at a landscape from a train, plane or car, or when we suddenly fix an object, a detail on a face or an insect [. . .] when we encounter a remarkable, strange, surprising or disconcerting situation, but also whilst drinking a coffee or climbing down stairs.[19]

Each of these scenarios, Nancy suggests, elicits a proclamation of 'that's cinema' and despite his putatively arcane engagement with cinema, there is likewise a fundamental ordinariness to his reflections on film.[20] Nancy undoubtedly goes to the movies. Indeed, in his figure of the *cinéfile*, who hovers ambiguously between the casual and the furtive onlooker that *filer* implies, Nancy embeds the act of going to the cinema into the very fabric of (his) spectatorship.

Tellingly, Amy Sherlock's recent analysis of Francesca Woodman's photography via Nancy reveals an inherent (pseudo-)spectatorship engrained within the very makeup of his thought through the recurrent mention of exposure. Determining it 'a linchpin uniting the registers of the aesthetic and the ontological' and noting how it resonates 'with the technical register of photography generally', her careful thinking distils how '*exposure* simultaneously invokes the scene of viewing or exhibition space [. . .] and the community of viewers'.[21] In this way, Sherlock folds an additional social dimension into the inextricable tangle of sensible, technical and affective dimensions that make up Nancy's understanding of the artwork.[22]

In a decidedly Nancean vernacular, we might consider that his cinema-going and the body of work it inspires, whether cinematic or written, *compear*; a complex term that dismantles the myth of a common being predicated on fictional foundations.[23] It does so by observing the relentlessly expository logic that drives Nancean thought through a set of insistently corporeal contours:

> Compearance is of a more originary order than that of the bond. It does not set itself up, it does not establish itself, it does not emerge among already given subjects (objects). It consists in the appearance of the *between* as such: you *and* I (between us) – a formula in which the *and* does not imply juxtaposition, but exposition.[24]

Nancy's responses to cinema constitute such exposition(s), for it is in, and only in, such an encounter that this work materialises, and in turn, this work compears with the work of others, as Laura McMahon explains in her own intervention on Nancy, cinema and touch: 'What is privileged here is a form of relationality, of *being-with*, of co-exposure, as viewer and image come into contact, shape and give rise to one another.'[25]

Writing, of course, requires reading, and compearance necessitates a peculiarly uncorked, yet parenthetical and matricial, perusal which Nancy's conception of 'literature' encapsulates:

> Literature does not come to an end at the very place where it comes to an end: on its border, right on the dividing line – a line sometimes straight (the edge, the border of the book), sometimes incredibly twisted and broken (the writing, reading). It does not come to an end at the place where the work passes from an author to a reader,

and from this reader to another reader or to another author. It does not come to an end at the place where the work passes on to another work by the same author or at the place where it passes into other works of other authors. [. . .] It is unended and unending.[26]

Graphically echoing the murk of resonance, this motile, knotty, literature shapes Nancy's writing. Kristen Lené Hole, for example, whose own work on Nancy, film and ethics compears with the interruptive quality of Nancean 'literature', and its 'continually reopening the world to a meaning that it *is* but that it cannot master', understands Nancy's philosophy 'as a fugue, with variations on the same themes echoing and "chasing" each other throughout his voluminous oeuvre'.[27] Resonance is such a fugue with mention of it nestled in Nancy's meditations on music in *The Sense of the World* where he tackles the seam between sensibility and signification inherent to sonority, and how this seam is central to sense, and the very condition of meaning, as well as the superlative makeup of the sonorous register:[28] 'This register is like the line of contact between the most interior', that is, the internal stirrings of the body, 'and the most exterior [. . .]: sound is, as it were, the least incorporated of matter'.[29] Nancy continues:

> After having been heard, it still remains somewhere out there, and not merely like color and line vis-à-vis. Rather, it resonates elsewhere, at a distance, in an exteriority that is spaced out in all the other directions and that the ear *hears* along with the sound, as the opening of the world. Sound has no hidden surface.[30]

However, Nancy soon claims that 'resonance *itself* is lost,[31] although a later flight in his work implies otherwise, as we shall see in far greater detail below.[32]

This fugue suggests something of a Deleuzian crystalline structure, part actual, part virtual. By means of such writing readers of Nancy's work are ceaselessly caught up with literature's lines, twists and breaks, and each time that Nancy trails off, each time that he interrupts himself, what you, I, we allow to be said remains secret, yet shared, forcing us to obey his master's voice, whose body is hidden from view, and thereby obliging us to take up an acousmatic position.[33] Always blind to him, as Nancean readers, we are cautiously rendered pseudo-disciples of his 'teachings' and all of this secrecy leads inexorably to, or perhaps from, listening. From the 'secret intimacy of sin and forgiveness' of confession, to outposts 'where one could listen in secret', from eavesdropping to espionage, from telephony's 'affair of confidences or stolen secrets' to a question:

> What secret is at stake when one truly listens [. . .] when one tries to capture or surprise the sonority rather than the message? What secret is yielded [. . .] when we listen to a voice, an instrument, or a sound just for itself?[34]

These are our stakes here when defining resonance and we realise them thanks to a series of case studies taken from across Varda's and Haneke's oeuvres which invite us to listen to a medley of yielding materials: wood in *La Pointe Courte* (1954) and *Time of the Wolf* (2003), water in *The Seventh Continent* (1989) and *Le Bonheur* (1965), textiles in *Cleo from 5 to 7* (1961) and *Caché* (2005), and letters in *The Piano Teacher* (2001) and *Documenteur* (1981).

Our listening to Nancy lies somewhere between sonority's capture and message, and throughout the following pages we will establish how the Nancean vernacular is itself resonant: co-articulated through its co-exposure with the reader, that is, through the encounter. In essence, we are the lines, twists and breaks of 'literature', making Nancy's thought a peerless critical and conceptual match for *Vital Resonances*.[35] Equally, Varda and Haneke share an appreciation of the encounter. Speaking in 1962, for example, Varda proclaimed:

> According to their possibilities, people meet for an instant, a minute, or a lifetime. They have one encounter or ten in their existence, or they don't have any. But everyone, one way or another, needs it. Those who know it are already less unhappy than those who don't. . . . This need is essential.[36]

According to Varda, then, encounters fuel our very being, and Haneke asserts a similar position in relation to cinema-going:

> A hundred people in front of a screen [. . .] see not one film, they see a hundred different films. I provide a construct and nothing more – its interpretation and its integration into a value and belief system is always the work of the recipient.[37]

Haneke evokes an almost matricial structure of cinematic reception. A screen, a film, is purely generative, nothing more, and both Varda and Haneke inadvertently demonstrate a profoundly Nancean understanding of otherness in their respective appraisals of the cinematic encounter – we *are*, film *is* relationally constituted – happy accidents, and resonances, that promise a fruitful encounter between the three.[38]

Nancy might realise such encounters with the stone. Hard and modest, the stone, and its inherent minerality, recurs across his work where it does not dissolve in thought,[39] but rather takes on Heidegger, and his stony worldlessness, and articulates what it is to be a body in the world and to build a world contra the 'stupid', 'self-enclosed', 'stone-like identity' (metaphorically) postulated in Denis's *Vers Nancy*.[40] According to Nancy, Heidegger forgets the stone's weight, surfaces and, that most quintessential of stony properties, rolling: 'the *contact* of the stone with the other surface, and through it with the world as the network of all surfaces'.⁴¹ The stone, then, is just as much a part of the world as the unfortunate walker, or philosopher, who stubs a toe on it.⁴² Indeed, such injury, or encounter, which we might be tempted to attribute to its stupid, self-enclosed, stone-like identity testifies to its very being-in-the-world, to its very worldliness. Stone and toe collide, establishing brute difference, contact without fusion, tact through indelicacy, yet this stony contact 'does not', as Nancy elaborates, '"handle" things (*betasten*) [. . .]. But it does *touch* – or it *touches on* – with a passive transitivity. It is touched, same difference.'⁴³ The stone, then, might be indifferent to the stream and the fly, yet the current and the six hairy legs attest to the impossibility of any supposed stony identity. Through this 'brute [chiasmic] entelechy', there is a sort of blind compearance at work that divorces touch from instrumentalisation, identification and appropriation, with which Heidegger's schema burdens it, and gives rise to a world that '*a priori* consist[s] in being-among, being-between, and being-against', that is, shared.⁴⁴ Stone and toe tiptoe this being:

> Without that – without this impalpable reticulation of contiguities and tangential contacts, without the play (interstice, interval, and escape) of a geared down *being-toward*, where *toward* has less the connotation of a mere opposition to *in* than the connotation of sense disengaged and delivered from the *in* – there would be no world. 'In itself', the thing is 'toward' the *other things* that are close, proximate, and also very distant because there are several of them.⁴⁵

It is quite literally along the edges of the stone 'in itself', then, that the Heideggerian poverty is exposed as short-changing the stone: '*Corpus*: all bodies, each outside the others, make up the inorganic body of sense' which makes up the world.⁴⁶ Overall, though, says Marie-Eve Morin, the stone puzzles, its goal 'to turn our attention radically away from our own experience, our own living bodies, toward what Nancy calls the sense of the world'.⁴⁷ Yet as Morin recognises, and as we shall see in greater detail below, we can never escape its minerality, it exists within us, and thus its invitation to turn toward the sense of the world cannot be declined: encounter is vital.⁴⁸ Indeed, in a resonant fugue,

> not even the silent attestation of the being-placed-there of stones remains truly beyond music: still, already, there is the rustling of the world, the grating, crackling, 'background' noise, the noise without noise, or rather, even simply, the mineral stupor that is still the surprise of the world.⁴⁹

The stone, then, is but another resonant vehicle of the Nancean lexicon; it informs his thinking and our encounters with it, as well as our encounter with the sense of the world.

Resonance, then, as we shall come to see, is (at) the very heart of Nancy. Our listening to Nancy, moreover, discloses that there is an altogether stranger, more intimate anatomy associated with his work on cinema, an anatomy of orifices that encompasses the heart, mouth, lungs and ears, perhaps even more so than the eyes, as well as the biggest organ of all, the skin and its pores. This altogether stranger, more intimate anatomy includes the fluids that are intimately related to them, from breath to blood to body odour to 'gossamer words',[50] that I will elucidate here in order to show how Nancy's encounter with film truly does come from the heart and how it in turn is affected by all that passes through it. Or, to put it another way, if resonance is (at) the very heart of Nancy, then his heart resonantly beats beneath his writings on the image via a writing and reading process akin to his exscription, for if meaning is only inscribed through its passing through what Morin calls a 'material point', 'the flesh of a lip, the point of a pen or of a stylus', then Nancy's heart is the point of such material inscription. After all, 'it seems to' Jacques Derrida that '[a]ll that Nancy will later say about the "exscribed" essentially springs from' what he says about 'the possibility of *rejection* in general, the rejection of the body at birth as well as the rejection of one of its essential parts – a transplanted heart, for example – by the body itself'.[51] 'And since', he continues, 'it is also a matter of *self*-rejection, this source does remain essentially autobiographical.'[52] In a number of ways, as we shall see, resonance begins with these natal and cardiac rejections and the following account is thus obsessively materialist and improperly biographical, and I irrefutably take my lead from Nancy (and Derrida!).

Regarding the Impossible Image of Radical Embodiment

If there is a fundamental ordinariness to Nancy's reflections on film, born as they are from cinema-going, Nancy's turn towards aesthetics is somewhat extraordinary, and began shortly after he underwent the heart transplant detailed in 'The Intruder'. Despite Ian Balfour's suggestion, then, that this shift in critical attention occurred 'almost all of a sudden', thinking along these lines, we might say that following his transplant Nancy's thought itself underwent a major procedure: a more sustained turn towards the image in, for example, *Les Muses* (1994)/*The Muses* (1997), *The Evidence of Film* (2001), *Au fond des images* (2003)/*The Ground of the Image* (2005), *Nous sommes: la peau des images* (2003)/*Being Nude: The Skin of Images* (2014).[53] Any interrelation, moreover, between Nancy's heart transplant and cinema may seem a stretch, but such are its filmic resonances that this experience has produced no fewer than three cinematic adoptions – begging the question: is there something fundamentally filmic at the heart of Nancy's *greffe*?[54] The heart, then, Nancy's heart, is the first part of the altogether stranger, more intimate anatomy which pilots this chapter's improper biography.

Temporarily adopting the (occasional) pastoral register of the Nancean filmic vernacular, we might determine this turn, and Nancy's interest in cinema in particular, a scion. For in *The Evidence of Film*, his most sustained treatment of film to date, Nancy defines the 'verily cinematic' as 'the budding and opening of a look in the middle of ordinary turbulence'.[55] A heart transplant perhaps surpasses the parameters of ordinary turbulence. But then again, what turbulence could be more ordinary than a heart beating in its thoracic niche? The aftercare routine that Grün's *Le Corps du philosophe* introduces us to, a nurse's visit, a hospital trip, a doctor's appointment, instils a very ordinary timbre into the extraordinary world of the graftee. Nancy of course explores such a narrative in his earlier tract 'The Intruder' wherein he listens in on the arrhythmia of his faulty heart, a sensation that surges forth with a quotidian flash of cinema: 'when climbing stairs' he 'feel[s] each release of an "extrasystole" like the falling of a pebble to the bottom of a well'.[56] A verily cinematic image that repeats: *l'escalier, c'est du cinéma*. '[T]he dark red muscular mass' of his fleshy heart unites the mineral and the liquid and whereas before there had always been silence, the unequivocal white noise of being, a 'potent, silent evidence that was holding things together so uneventfully', where formerly he 'had never identified [him]self as this body, even less as this heart', Nancy is moved to conceive this self as an image.[57]

Nancy foreshadows this coincidence between image-hood and selfhood (and minerality) in *The Muses* where, taking up an imaginative residence in the grotto of the first image-maker(s), being and the image are shown to be irreducibly caught up with each other: 'Thus, the painting that begins in the grottos (but also the grottos that painting invents) is first of all the monstration of the commencement of being, before being the beginning of painting.'[58] Nancy's grotto residence thus intimates an originary imagistic quality to being, and in 'The Intruder' Nancy negotiates such a conflation and attempts to picture his heart/body through a series of in-text questions when 'suddenly concerned with and *watching*' (t)his heart, (t)his body, he asks: 'How do you become a representation to yourself? And a montage of functions?'[59] Montage sets a verily cinematic tone and

Nancy had already attempted such assembly in *Corpus* where the body is consistently, yet confusedly, catalogued.[60]

> Corpus: a body is a collection of pieces, bits, members, zones, states, functions. Heads, hands and cartilage, burnings, smoothnesses, spurts, sleep, digestion, goosebumps, excitation, breathing, digesting, reproducing, mending, saliva, synovia, twists, cramps, and beauty spots. It's a collection of collections, a *corpus corporum*, whose unity remains a question for itself.[61]

Nancy's reflections here roam the body like a movie camera where in the final edit embodiment is effectively enumerated and *corps* comes to constitute *corpus*.[62] Significantly, as *corpus corporum*, questions remain, just as Nancy maintains later in 'The Intruder' when he ponders '[w]hat does it mean to replace a heart? Representing the thing is beyond me.'[63] This from the thinker for whom '[a] body is an image offered to other bodies, a whole corpus of images stretched from body to body.'[64] Through the necessity for a replacement pump, as Philip Adamek summarises, '[n]othing is represented other than, perhaps, the disruption of representation.'[65] Hollower still is Nancy's description of the transplant of his wasted heart which 'imposes an image of passing through nothingness, a flight into space emptied of any propriety or intimacy, or else, conversely, an image of that space intruding upon the inside of me: feeds, clamps, sutures, and tubes'.[66] In effect, it imposes the image of an orifice. The originary intimacy and irreducibility between image- and selfhood are thus outstripped by a 'vivid' alienation.[67]

Constitutive of this orificial ontology, we might imagine Nancy beside himself, gawping down at his chest which he archaically describes as 'gaping' (*béant*).[68] *Bouche bée*, '[w]riting and thinking like this, mouth agape',[69] Nancy's gaping mouth matches the former silence of his body and it likewise opens onto the struggle to represent because it presents a 'third' term beyond the 'conceptual opposition' that opening/closing signifies.[70] This gaping is Nancy's permanent post-operative state. He is 'closed open' – the gap(e) between graphically inscribing, and exscribing, how this 'gaping cannot be sealed back'.[71] This gaping seals Nancy's chest cavity as orifice. Indeed, 'The Intruder' alongside *Corpus*, *Ego Sum* and *The Inoperative Community* embody Nancy's 'opus-corpus',[72] each of them plumbing its 'orificial depths'.[73] Apnoea, gasps, exhalations connote breath and suggest the lungs in 'The Intruder', whilst *Corpus* is full of holes. In the 'list of gleanings' and 'ongoing stammer of bits and pieces'[74] Nancy proffers how '[t]he head [. . .] consists only of holes [. . .]. Pupils, nostrils, mouth, ears are all holes, carved flights out of the body';[75] orifice here encapsulates extrusion, expropriation *par excellence*.[76]

Nancy ties this pocked 'countryside' to the visual regime:[77]

> It's no surprise that our thoughts [. . .] and images are swallowed up in holes, instead of lingering within reach of their sides: caverns, crying mouths, hearts pierced through, *interfices et urinam*, skulls with staring eyeholes, castrating vaginas, not openings, but evacuations, enucleations, collapses.[78]

Here the orificial ontology that Nancy acutely experiences within his own chest extends to art history and we detect further holes in his account of cinema and evidence. Evidence, after all, realises itself through a voiding – of the representational possibilities of cinema – and it 'always comprises a blind spot within its very obviousness',[79] 'keep[ing] a secret or an essential reserve'.[80] Blindness risks reigning here, as he notes earlier in *Corpus*: 'But slits, holes, and zones do not present things to be seen, do not reveal anything: vision does not penetrate'.[81] Vision, Nancy continues,

> glides along swerves and follows along departures. It is a touching that does not absorb but moves along lines and recesses, inscribing and exscribing the body. A mobile, unstable caress, seeing the image in slow motion, fast-forwarded, or frozen, seeing as well with *touches* from other senses, smells, tastes, timbres, or even, with sounds, from the senses of words (the 'sure' that yields 'pleasure').[82]

Kinetic, tactile, durational, olfactory, acoustic, this vision is festooned with touches from other senses; as proponents of the bodily turn might put it, an embodied look accrues. As Jessica Barnfield summarises, 'Nancy configures the revelation of the visual through the sensual'[83] and in its sensuous *sure*ty it recalls *expeausition*, a Nancean 'neologism',[84] homophonous with exposition.[85] Anne O'Byrne evocatively plies this Nancean formula of folding, to paraphrase Derrida, by noting how it 'fold[s] *peau*, French for skin, into a word that otherwise suggests the work of vision. We are *expeaused* skin to skin and flesh to flesh.'[86] Likewise, it hints at one of Nancy's favourite expressions, *à fleur de*,[87] a locution which encompasses the epidermal, a sense of being right up at the surface of something, and the orificial, a sense of being 'at the edge of' something.[88] Skin, reading, pores, poring, a curious corporeal and ocular porousness precipitates through which vision becomes a gliding caress, an orificial look that (anxiously) circles caverns, crying mouths, hearts pierced through, skulls with staring eyeholes, castrating vaginas without the solace of banks that we might scale to sanctuary. It is a look engendered by the altogether stranger, more intimate anatomy associated with Nancy's work on the image and which his gaping chest cavity seals: a body lost and gained to its host, a body inscribed and exscribed by a look that presents not an image of *the* body but a body in bits.

An Epic of the Mouth

Pupils, nostrils, nipples aside, the most obvious orifice is the mouth and despite *béance*, Nancy's gaping chest is not a silent space; neither is it a place for viscera, but rather for voice(s). Following the (wasted) heart, then, Nancy's chest cavity becomes enmeshed with the second major orifice of his engagement with cinema: the mouth. According to Nancy – but who is this 'I' after all? as he asks in 'The Intruder' – the mouth possesses a primary role in his oeuvre, a 'motif' that he says has never left him.[89] Yet, as he admits, since *Ego Sum* he has remained largely silent on it, 'as if [. . .] waiting [. . .] for a special occasion, the sudden discovery of the opportunity for an epic of the mouth'.[90] Cinema is perhaps this opportunity and his filmic adopters, Denis and Klotz, grant his thinking such special occasions. *Beau Travail* (1999), Nancy writes, 'must be understood like a shout before a right mess: "Oh, good job!"'[91] Shed of sarcasm, this shout cries out 'in [the film's] final images', where Denis Lavant's Galoup is animated by 'the vital intensity of a precise and feverish dance in a dimly-lit basement club to a song of which the title (another secret title to decipher) is rhythm of the night'.[92] His body, enveloped by the music, dancing within a body of light, comes to form the lynchpin of the material, musical medley that hyperbolises and rarefies the cinematic apparatus here: camera, light, movement, darkness, stillness, bodies. Its nice work, by no means a shambles but a resurrection, confects looking, scents it, festoons it, with a joyous multisensory address. Klotz's adoption, *La Blessure* (2004), occasions a second epic. Remarkably distinct in terms of affect, Nancy describes the film as a 'dirge';[93] a slow lament 'that the title nominates as its design, namely the wound which endures as scar'.[94] The *expeausition* of its low, lasting rumble poignantly extends our look in time.

Like Denis and Klotz, as noted above, *Corpus*, *Ego Sum*, 'The Intruder' and *The Inoperative Community* give us mouths. Hearts in mouths, ventriloquising mouths in and alongside bellies, dry mouths, mouths in eyes, mouths in mouths. They orchestrate an opera of orifices despite Nancy's own self-avowed reticence on the theme.[95] *Ego Sum* features a lengthy meditation on the mouth:

> The mouth: through which breath flows, and with breath sound, and within sound the immaterial sense finely woven in the phonemes, in their resonances, their harmonies, and their background noise. The mouth: through which food is absorbed, the digestion of which metabolizes energies in the delicate arrangement of muscular, nervous, and hormonal capacities giving rise to gestures, actions, passions, and the words that accompany, follow, or precede them. The mouth: through which emerges one of the major openings of the body, a body that exists only by being exposed from

top to bottom and all the way through to influxes, affluxes, and refluxes of its near and far extremities, as well as of its entrails, always caught up, again and again, in the pushes and repulsions of the agitated masses among which it is thrown. The mouth: this jetty that says 'I', sometimes shouting it and at other times stifling it.[96]

What materialises here is a fairly classic mouth. It eats, it soughs, and above all it speaks. This is a vocal mouth and despite *béance*, voices litter 'The Intruder'. According to Adamek, a voice 'giv[ing] an account of its own disarray'[97] scores Nancy's pages, complicating the autobiographical credentials of the text. Whilst for Peggy Kamuf it is 'the other's speech', its 'intrusion', that suddenly opens 'a void' in Nancy's chest 'in a precise, punctual speech act: "il faudra une transplantation" [You will need a transplant . . .]'.[98] This confluence between the voice and the void suggests that speech here operates like the surgeon's scalpel to make an orifice of Nancy. Despite for Nancy, then, 'the truth of the subject [lying in] its exteriority and its excessiveness: its infinite exposition',[99] the elision of vacancy and vocality implies that there is something happening on the inside too – a word foreign to the Nancean vernacular, its intrusion rhetorically opening it up to new spaces for reflection – to which we shall return in earnest in this book's conclusion.

Indeed, such is Nancy's disdain for our innards that he unflatteringly describes them as 'a sack crammed with rumblings and musty odors' with the '[m]uscles, tendons, nerves and bones, humors, glands, and organs' bagged up therein thought of as merely 'functionalist formalisms'.[100] Within Nancy's gaping chest cavity, though, these rumblings become imbricated with vocality, with the orifice of the mouth, and in doing so forge a curious point of contact across Nancy's oeuvre and his philosophical dialogue 'Distinct Oscillation':

- The speaking voice has its own form, its sonorous image. See for yourself: when I say 'sonorous', do you not have an image? Do you not discern a round 'o'-'o'-'o' . . .?
- Oh, oh! I see what you're saying: I see the voices that I hear! I see them so well, in fact, that the spoken text calls up, as though from out of itself, the face of its voice, the movement of its lips, the passing glimpse of the inside of the mouth, of the tongue and the teeth, and of the whole articulatory cinema, not to mention of the overall expression of the face.[101]

With the voice, then, comes a whole articulatory cinema: face, lips, mouth, tongue, teeth are all seen in it and speech becomes an invitation for spectation: *la voix, c'est du cinéma*. In this way, as Nancy writes elsewhere, this articulatory cinema sounds out the body's extension (and its interiority):

> Of course the body also declares in language: there is mouth there, tongue, muscles, vibrations, frequencies, or else hands, keyboards, graph traces, and all the messages are long chains of material scratches and grafts. But it's precisely a question of what, in language, no longer involves the message, just its exscription.[102]

Skimming anatomy and sonority, sense and resonance, the mouth is the site of their intertwining. They compear.

Whilst we might mistake the mouth for a place of stability, as a place that masters meaning fluently and which with each utterance creates meaning anew, by design the mouth gapes. Who is this 'I' that shouts and stifles after all? *Bouche bée*, it demands to be heard, but it does not make sense. The mouth, in the Nancean tongue, then, is a turbulent site. As Sara Guyer summarises: 'Nancy demonstrates that the mouth is the occasion of a constitutive disruption of subjectivity, that is, the emergence of the so-called subject in and as this disruption' – perhaps akin to how the doctor's speech opens up the cavity in Nancy's chest, which in turn unsettles his heretofore silent sense of subjecthood.[103] In this manner, Guyer details, 'Nancy recasts Cartesian subjectivity according to a convulsive chasm – which is also a chiasm',[104] for as Nancy stipulates: 'The mouth is the opening of the *Ego*, *Ego* is the opening of the mouth.'[105]

Convulsive, chasmic, chiasmic, cinematic, the Nancean gob bears grinning parallels with Galoup's dancing, or rather Galoup's dancing chiasmically bears uncanny parallels with the Nancean gob: convulsive, chasmic, chiasmic, cinematic. Here, there, wherever, and whenever, he might be, he is all explosive, exorbitant *ego* – a subject in formation, a singular site that beats. He *is* his frenzied, careful movements. Like a fricative expulsion of satisfaction and wonder which *'resounds previous to the voice, inside the throat [. . .] just a column of air pushed from the chest in the sonorous cavity, the cave of the mouth that does not speak'*[106] – he gapes between body and soul; to lean on another Nancean neologism that we shall encounter below, he is âmmmmm: a body beaten by its sense of body – and it is in this way that cinema might be considered Nancy's epic of the mouth.[107] Beating beneath his writings on film, it inaudibly mutters *à fleur d'image*, that is, in the whole articulatory cinema of camera, light, movement, darkness, stillness, bodies. It mouths, it resonates and here it segues us into the 'two forms of mouthwork' that the convulsive, chasmic, chiasmic, cinematic,

Nancean mush involves:[108] orality and buccality. One refined and rarefied, the other less so:

> Os, oris, oral mouth is the face itself taken metonymically for this mouth that it surrounds, carries, and makes visible, this mouth that is the passageway for all kinds of substances, first of all of this aerial substance of a discourse. *Bucca*, on the other hand, is the puffed-up cheeks, the movement, the contraction/distension of breathing, eating, spitting, or speaking. Buccality is more primitive than orality. Nothing is yet taking place there, and above all, that has always-already spoken there yet. But an unstable and mobile opening forms at the instant of speaking. At this instant, nothing can be discerned; *ego* does not want to say anything, *ego* only opens this cavity.[109]

Orality, then, is a discourse-filled mouth. The philosopher's mouth. My mouth. Your mouth. Buccality is a mouth filled with murmurs and groans,[110] the animal, the inchoate, in the human, which the philosopher's mouth, my mouth, your mouth all possess: 'a friction, the pinch or grate of something produced in the throat, a borborygmus, a crackle, a stridency where a weighty, murmuring matter breathes'.[111] Both mouths are, however, capable of producing crap. For, as Nancy describes, 'words' – the preserve of the oral mouth – are 'the body's effluvia, emanations, weightless folds in the air escaping the lungs and warmed by the body'.[112] These are 'gossamer words, evaporating into the sky'.[113] In this way, then, the sonorous image of the speaking voice is waste: 'o'-'o'-'o', oozing. Like images, the self is excreted too: 'From excrement to the outgrowth of nails, hairs, or every kind of wart or purulent malignity, it has to put outside, and separate from itself, the residue or excess of its assimilatory processes, the excess of its own life.'[114] Trash talking and talking shit take on a whole new meaning.

Exposed to his own insides, then, Nancy's constitution as an artistic 'subject' could be said to have emerged from the beats that his heart skipped. Indeed, his entire aesthetic philosophy could be understood as a waste product of his wasted heart, an extreme case of self(hood) (in) expropriation, and its coincident orifices, which is intimately and irreducibly caught up with image-hood. Like the explosive, exorbitant *ego* of Galoup, Nancy *is* his arrhythmic heart – reflected in the staccato cataloguing of (his) *corpus*. Nancy's entire aesthetic oeuvre is perhaps not so much an epic of the mouth, then, but an orificial epic, and it is thus that his heart mouths and resonates beneath his writings on the image. Not least because it precipitates the look that buds and opens in the middle of ordinary turbulence, a look that starts to emerge as Nancy's own body becomes more conspicuous, a look that is in fact ordinary turbulence, to which cinema can give shape, sense and form, especially when it tunes in to the peculiar resonance of regard that prevails amongst Nancy's writings on the image: care, respect, distance, tact where to regard sees the spectator 'test oneself with regard to a meaning one is not mastering'.[115] To paraphrase Nancy, then, in the end, looking is nothing other than this, and it is in this way that we regard the impossible image of radical embodiment, for the challenge to representation that the strained silence of his body poses tacitly informs Nancy's relationship to film and spectatorship.

Despite himself, then, and in the wake of his heart transplant, an orificial aesthetic ontology leaks out of Nancy's gaping chest cavity, and, in this struggle to represent, a series of impossible images well up inside him – android, zombie, intruder – significantly, not through imagination (imagination fails, after all), but from his very corporeality, from the body's murky silence.[116] The contingency, moreover, between a profoundly lived experience and the birth of Nancy's aesthetic turn reiterates just how his reflections on film are themselves born from actual encounters with the material culture of cinema-going. They compear. This murky silence, though, is no silence at all because there is always the sound of blood, breath, borborygm, that is, the sounds of the intimate, orificial anatomy at the heart of Nancy's thinking on the image and hearing the heart brings us to the ears.

A Fancy, Pretty Line of Thought

To regard/*Regarder* thus places a very particular demand upon any visitor to Nancy's thought: to test oneself with regard to a meaning one is not mastering. Indeed, how we listen in on certain, always critical words is fundamental to the very fabric of Nancy's work, where each case of 'tuning in' offers a new perspective on what was once familiar.[117] Any visit to his philosophy, then, is such a test. *Sens*, for instance, the critical cornerstone for much of Nancy's thinking on being, is shot through with a linguistic and conceptual multiplicity and can be triply rendered in English across his output as the (five) senses, meaning and direction,[118] 'rendering meaning dynamic and relational rather than fixed or closed, possessable or masterable'.[119]

Nancean *sens*, then, that elemental 'stuff' of being,[120] is thus, as Stephen Barker posits, laminate and polyvalent, thereby enjoying an almost isomorphic resonance with what it falteringly denotes:[121] 'prior to or in excess of any relation between signifier and signified, and [. . .] in excess also of any fixed linguistic signification'.[122] Equally, and to point up further the (isomorphic) inherency of such audition to Nancy's thought, *entendre* can be translated as both to hear and to understand, and listening (*écouter*) itself is critically, conceptually and philosophically engaged with in an eponymously titled tome.[123] Early in this text, Nancy figures this verbal distinction in emphatically guttural terms: 'the slight, keen indecision that grates, rings out, or shouts between "listening" and "understanding"'; terms that excoriate the buccal in the oral and, moreover, in the aural.[124] Further precisions situate these differences as contextual, rather than rasping. This, then, is an audition that involves a linguistic and phenomenological cleaving. It is an aurality that distinguishes hearing as understanding which 'is already each time to understand at least the rough outline of a situation' from listening as a 'straining toward a possible meaning [. . .] that is not immediately accessible'.[125] *Écouter*, as Brian Kane determines, 'holds open the threshold between sense and signification'.[126] What cleaves hearing from listening, then, is the disposition of the latter towards corporeal and significatory ambiguity and materiality. Such listening, which, as we shall see below, Nancy structures as resonance, is emphatically attuned to the mechanics of *sens*: motile, sensory, pregnant. It is here that Nancy issues a discreet, yet unintended, call for how to approach his philosophy. When doing so we have '[t]o be all ears',[127] which succeed the (gaping) heart and mouth as our primary organising principle, and not according to some righteous do-goodery – after all, *sens* does not exceed signification 'because it consists in a signification so elevated, sublime, ultimate, or rarefied that no signifier could ever manage to present it'[128] – but rather these ears are 'immersed entirely in listening, formed by listening or in listening, listening with all [their] being'.[129] Indeed, Nancy's thinking has always been immersed in listening. Certainly, there is an anxious, edgy listening to 'his' body throughout 'The Intruder' and it is by means of such writing that Nancy insists that we listen hard(er) to his words whereby any encounter with his work operates as an exercise in our exposure to *sens*.

Thinking about listening returns us to the middle of ordinary turbulence. Although turbulence is a largely liquid or aerial phenomenon, Nancy loans it more terrestrial contours, whilst 'tun[ing] in to' what Jane Bennett describes as its 'strange logic'.[130] Turbulence's strange logic hosts matter in movement – its collisions, congealing, disintegration – which deftly dovetails with what I term the arabesque logic of Nancy's thought, and which in turn dovetails with his approach to the image. Simply put, the arabesque is a fancy, pretty line. It is a florid line that whorls and flows, and its whorls and flows take in the world, splaying and stringing out its materiality and vitality, plucking its raw materials from the earthly world of things found in nature – leaves, vines, flowers, seed pods – and reimagining them in manifold ways to establish new configurations of worldly sense.[131]

Its endless ramifying ricochets the non-hierarchical worldly sense it strings out, its material, technical disposal of being arguably doing the work of philosophy. Nancy's philosophy does, of course, do (some of) this work, and we find such juggling of the materiality of the world at the very heart of his thinking on being singular-plural: 'Being singular plural: these three apposite words, which do not have any determined syntax [. . .] mark an absolute equivalence.'[132] Unfettered and amorphous, a broad account of being singular-plural likewise suggests that it hinges on a comparable structuring principle to, even reads like a description of, the arabesque:

> The ontology of being-with is an ontology of bodies, of everybody, whether they be inanimate, animate, sentient, speaking, thinking, having weight and so on. Above all else, 'body' really means what is outside, insofar as it is outside, next to, against, nearby, with a(n) (other) body, from body to body, in the dis-position. Not only does a body go from one 'self' to an 'other,' it is *as itself* from the very first; it goes from itself to itself; whether made of stone, wood, plastic, or flesh, a body is the sharing of and the departure from self, the departure toward self, the nearby-to-self without which the 'self' would not even be 'on its own'.[133]

Non-hierarchically and non-anthropocentrically cataloguing all bodies, syntactically speaking the decentred disposition of bodies accommodated by Nancy's being singular-plural echoes the staccato rhythm of the arabesque's ornament: its compound surface growing in similar ways to Nancy's compound mode of being. Fundamentally, these other bodies partake in a vital part of our own vital being, for without these other bodies there would be no man, no us, no we: 'We would not be "humans" if there were not "dogs" and "stones".'[134] 'For Nancy', Christopher Watkin summarises, 'togetherness is otherness'[135] and whilst Nancy does not straightforwardly extend this sense of togetherness to his writings on the image, just as Nancy's being singular-plural tussles with the arabesque line, the line plays a pivotal part in Nancy's understanding of the image and of art writ large: 'The "essence" of art is not in a temple but in a trace, in the singular unicity of a naked trace on a naked canvas.'[136] The line thus enjoys an integral structural role: 'Making an image', he writes, 'means producing a relief, a protrusion, a trait, a presence.'[137] This trait, or line, though, is not just about image-making. Indeed, within Nancy's thought it becomes the arbiter of imagery, for in 'The Image – The Distinct' he posits that:

> The image, clear and distinct, is something obvious and evident. It is the obviousness of the distinct, its very distinction. There is an *image* only when there is this obviousness: otherwise, there is decoration or illustration, that is, the support of a signification.[138]

This line, then, hierarchises. It sets out what, according to Nancy's taxonomy, an image is or can be. As Rosalind Galt puts it, Nancy 'separate[s] it from the quotidian world of meanings and things', that is, from ordinary turbulence.[139] Ontologically speaking, though, the everyday motors Nancy's thinking, 'explor[ing] the sense of the world, in particular its circulations, relations, singularities, inoperable implications and certainly the polymorphy and polyphony of the banalities of common life'.[140] Such exploration very much reads like the stringing out of the arabesque, and Nancy conducts this exploration in a somewhat stuttering manner which in turn arabesques. This arabesque is the issue of tautology: a fault in style, its repetitions tachycardic, aping the paroxysm of the wasted heart at the heart of Nancy's thinking on the image and which here addresses one of his key correspondences: *sens/monde*.

In *The Sense of the World* Nancy describes how '*world* is not merely the correlative of *sense*, it is structured as *sense*, and reciprocally, *sense* is structured as *world*. Clearly, "the sense of the world" is a tautological expression.'[141] Sense and world, he continues, are coextensive:[142]

> The word *world* has no other unity of sense other than this one: a world [. . .] is always a differential articulation of singularities that make sense in articulating themselves, along the edges of their articulation (where *articulation* should be taken [*doit se prendre*] at once in the mechanical sense of a joint and its play, in the sense of a spoken offering, and in the sense of the distribution into distinct 'articles'). A world joins, plays, speaks, and shares: this is its sense, which is not different from the sense of 'making sense'.[143]

Thinking about audition, as we are here, we might permit ourselves a momentary sensory lapse, mistaking *se prendre* for *entendre* to turn up the hum of worldly presentation, for this coextensivity of *sens* and *monde* quivers and at their very articulation one hears the murmur of sonority. It is, after all, sound and its resonance that 'the ear *hears* [. . .] as the opening of the world'.[144] Indeed, the coextensivity of *sens* and *monde* pivots on a noisy, lively charge where the quivering of these relations, circulations, intersections among singularities reticulates all vital beings and being's reticulation quivers with the relations, circulations, intersections among singularities, where 'reality is a kaleidoscope of multiplicity whirling deliriously, composing the very limit conditions of experience and resisting appropriation by a meaning-bestowing mind'.[145] Nancy's ontology here truly is aquiver and this noisy, lively charge is the parsing hinge of being singular-plural, Nancy's 'non-essentialized ontology of being-with',[146] where relation is primordial.[147]

Zsuzsa Baross observes as much in an oblique account of being singular-plural which centres a machinic, fissural resonance as its structuring principle:

> Resonance is a vibration, a current, a wave of tension, an intense pleasure or as it may be the case, repulsion, traverses simultaneously but differently bodies at a distance, agitating their composite parts or particles differently. Yet the third term is not the wave, the current, the rhythm, or the tension that agitates. It is resonance itself. The wave, the agitation, the tension do not come to bodies from the outside. It is in their resonance – something they have differently in common – that they encounter one another, consummate as it were their nuptial *in* resonance.[148]

Resonance here functions as a third term in the Nancean vernacular, like gaping, and, as a decidedly bodily contact it recalls the 'messy' togetherness that is otherness of Nancy's radical ontology, whereby resonance resonates by means of our bodies' incommensurability:[149] something they have differently in common. According to Baross, then, and without making direct mention of Nancy's distinct work on resonance, resonance is the measure of our incommensurability, of the messy togetherness that is otherness. Inadvertently peeling resonance away from sonority, following Baross, and of course Nancy, *we* resonate.

In *Listening*, Nancy more emphatically pronounces this noisy, lively, parsing hinge:

> Communication is not transmission, but a sharing that becomes subject: sharing as subject of all 'subjects'. An unfolding, a dance, a resonance. Sound in general is first of all communication in this sense. At first it communicates nothing – except itself. At its weakest and least articulated degree, one would call it noise. [. . .] In a body that opens up and closes at the same time, that arranges itself and exposes itself with others, the noise of its sharing (with itself, with others) resounds.[150]

Illustrating what Sarah Hickmott describes as 'the essential sonority of the being-with',[151] Adrienne Janus playfully conceives this noisy choreography as one body 'sounding out' another whereby we (all) are 'listening subjects' and as listening subjects we *are*.[152] We resonate. This subject, whilst graphically hinting at the murk of resonance explored in the first chapter, echoes Nancy's closed open post-operative state, and stages the old orificial adage '[t]he ears have no eyelids' after all, acutely reminding us that 'animal bodies, in general – the human body, in particular – are not constructed to interrupt at their leisure the sonorous arrival'.[153] We are bodies full of holes, a corpus of holes, a porousness through which the patent sensuousness of the world flows. The arabesque surreptitiously bursts into the midst of this noisy choreography for, as we saw above, in its ornamental, decorative, sinewy form, it is an unfolding. It is also a dance, and this accrual of materiality and corporeality dovetails with resonance. The arabesque, then, brings us wholeheartedly to resonance.

Revealing the Richness of Resonance

Resonance is at the very heart of Nancy's philosophy and, although a slim volume amongst his oeuvre, *Listening* is a rich and revealing one. More revealing perhaps is that *The Nancy Dictionary* defines resonance as exclusively, and dismissively, auditory: an 'ontology of sound – which is nothing more than a structure of infinite referrals and deferrals'.[154] Revealing because whilst it acknowledges the murmur of sonority that subtends the coextensivity of *sens* and *monde*, it essentially prunes Nancy's rhetoric by failing to attend to the material, motile murmur of *sens/monde* that coincides with its sonority. Resonance undoubtedly involves the ear. Yet this audition untethers resonance from sonority and foregrounds how it deals with matter in movement. The stakes of this listening both engender and entail the critical context for this dual objective through its cleaving of hearing and listening. For this listening does not limit itself to the workings of the ear and instead celebrates the carnality of sound: its capacity to brush up against our epidermal superficies and flow through our inner recesses. Fundamentally, it points up the emphatically material nature of sound, reminding us that acoustic vibrations are material vibrations that move in space and time.[155] The arabesque logic of Nancean thought effectively redresses his earlier claims for sound as the least incorporated matter. Meaning-making via Nancean listening is not, then, 'an acoustic phenomenon (or not merely [. . .] one) but [. . .] a resonant meaning, a meaning whose sense is supposed to be found in resonance, and only in resonance'.[156] Otherwise put, meaning is not, indeed cannot be made in a vacuum. Such sense is thus irrefutably corporeal, singular-plural, relational and protean. We, after all, resonate, yet resonance does not respect the relentlessly expository logic that drives Nancean thought, although it does maintain its insistently corporeal contours. Indeed, resonance conjoins the most interior and the most exterior and through resonance the sense of the world flows through us. Nancy's discussion of timbre reflects this altogether stranger, more intimate (auditory) anatomy.

Atypically, timbre is not an ambiguous term within the Nancean vernacular although it is proximal to his work's prevailing lexical resonances. Avowedly singular-plural in its centring of irreducibility, '[t]imbre is above all the unity of a diversity that its unity does not reabsorb', which 'opens, rather, immediately onto the metaphor of other perceptible registers: color

(*Klangfarbe*, "color of sound" [. . .]), touch (texture, roundness, coarseness), taste (bitter, sweet), even evocations of smells. In other words, timbre resounds with and in the totality of perceptible registers'.[157] Timbre thus recalls the budding and opening of the material, motile look in the middle of ordinary turbulence, a look which skirts and skims and is scented with touches of other sensory registers and which is consonant with Nancy's convulsive, chasmic, chiasmic emergence as an artistic subject. Timbre thereby prepares us for the materiality and corporeality of resonance, stakes that Nancy explicitly introduces when drawing parallels between the drum and the body:

> Timbre can be represented as the resonance of a stretched skin [. . .] and as the expansion of this resonance in the hollowed column of a drum. Isn't the space of the listening body, in turn, just such a hollow column over which skin is stretched, but also from which the opening of a mouth can resume and revise resonance? A blow from outside, clamor from within, this sonorous, sonorized body undertakes a simultaneous listening to a 'self' and to a 'world' that are both in resonance.[158]

Murky at best – a 'self' and a 'world' in resonance – there are hints of the convulsive, chasmic, chiasmic Nancean gob here, the hum of the mmmmm in âmmmmm choreographing this murky self and world. Indeed, Nancy catalogues the entire intimate, orificial anatomy of his listening and thinking on aesthetics: through blows and clamours, through conspicuous convulsions, skin, ear and mouth are all cast at the heart of resonance.

Despite mention of blows and clamouring, however, Hickmott remarks how this sonorous, sonorised body is suspiciously silent with Nancy less concerned about 'the "beat" itself' than the rhythm,[159] that is, 'the gap *between* the beats that allows the temporal-spatial matrix to unfold'.[160] If, though, the murmur of sonority subtends the coextensivity of *sens* and *monde*, its hum silences silence, even if Nancy is deaf to it. This rhythm, moreover, returns us to the arabesque, for eschewing 'simple succession', this matrix

> is present in waves on a swell, not in a point on a line; it is a time that opens up, that is hollowed out, that is enlarged or ramified, that envelops or separates, that becomes or is turned into a loop, that stretches out or contracts, and so on.[161]

Like the arabesque, then, through the articulated lines of resonance's dispersive temporal-spatial matrix we attune to the swelling, ramifying, looping of worldly sense, that is, to the quivering sense of the world strung out. Nancy reorients us further to this strung-out worldly sense when ramifying voice, which we must no longer hear, or understand, as an exclusively human, or verbal, form of communication, but rather as emblematic of the linguistic and phenomenological cleaving that is a specifically Nancean listening:

> we have to understand what sounds from a human throat without being language, which emerges from an animal gullet or from any kind of instrument, even from the wind in the branches: the rustling toward which we strain or lend an ear.[162]

Rustling is a modest sound. Yet like the stone it turns us towards the sense of the world, and its inherent noisy charge, and through a sort of sideways listening – what Bennett might call a countercultural perception[163] and what Nancy does call a straying – we reach the apotheosis of Nancy's resonant listening by reaching the weakest strain of sound: noise. Such listening proffers more materiality, more movement, more autonomous subjects, an unfolding which abandons old hierarchies and reorients our encounter with the quivering sense of the world. In the midst of this mundane symphony the soul emerges,

> that skin stretched over its own sonorous cavity, this belly that listens to itself and strays away in itself while listening to the world and while straying in all directions, that is not a 'figure' for the rhythmic timbre, but it is its very pace, it is my body beaten by its sense of body, what we used to call soul.[164]

Galoup's ghost reappears and thanks to this intimate, orificial anatomy, self and world resonate, the distant resonates in the close, and the close resonates in the distant, the self resonates in the other, the oral in the buccal, the animal in the human, the visual in the acoustic.

Fundamentally, then, the tautology, coextensivity, motility and sonority of *sens* and *monde* that make up resonance's dispersive temporal-spatial matrix pivot on a resonant vitality, itself tautologically meaningful. That is, not just sonorous, but sensuous, corporeal, fleshy and worldly, and which realises the arabesque logic of Nancy's sense of the world. Resonance thus coordinates our co-exposure to and co-articulation of the sensible, intelligible world. It is the touch we make with it, it is how it touches us, how we make sense of and grasp it. It attunes us to the shared corporeal, material contours of life; it is the very kernel of our encounter with others that we are, yet it does not subsume our own rhythms. For Nancy, then, bodies are in resonance, reciprocally producing, informing, shaping the other, and filtered through Nancean thought resonance emerges as a materialistically minded modality of perception.

Resonance thus emerges as a verb and what Nancy considers 'the work's *doing*': 'its manner of doing and making, what it does to sense or how it *makes sense*'.[165] Nancy's work's doing is resonance and his philosophy precipitates as the ultimate 'resonance chamber' wherein the dark red muscular mass of his wasted heart, and the gaping cavity of his chest, opened up as much by the penetrating voice of the surgeon as by the scalpel, and the cavity of the ego as mouth, find themselves caught up with the dark red muscular and fibrous cavity of the womb.[166] From hearts in mouths, then, to hearts in wombs, we, as does Nancy's thought, risk an essentialising, mythic impulse:[167]

> The womb[*matrice*]-like constitution of resonance, and the resonant constitution of the womb: What is the belly of a pregnant woman, if not the space or the antrum where a new instrument comes to resound, a new *organon*, which comes to fold in on itself, then to move, receiving from outside only sounds, which, when the day comes, it will begin to echo through its cry? But, more generally, more womblike, it is always in the belly that we [. . .] end up listening, or start listening. The ear opens onto the sonorous cave that we then become.[168]

The arabesque logic of Nancy's philosophy somewhat exacerbates this set of terms because he also risks this register when he states that 'the image is always material', a consideration which quickly becomes engrained in a compromising material history:[169]

> But *matter* is first *mother* (*materies* comes from *mater*, which is the heart of the tree, the hardwood), and the mother is that from which, and in which, there is distinction: in her intimacy another intimacy is separated and another force is formed, another same is detached from the same in order to be itself.[170]

Several things are (re)born here. In the first instance, the Nancean gob tongues this cry. It is chasmic and chiasmic and it is through these qualities that this cry embodies the very structure of resonance and the sonority of being-with. Its clamour goes out into the world, a world of noise, which is noisy before the cry's arrival into it, and which its clamour echoes. This cry effectively re-establishes a certain anthropocentrism which Nancy's earlier comments on animal gullets, instruments and wind effectively horizontalise when reorienting our encounter with the sensuousness of the world. If resonance is his work's doing, then, this cry undoes some of this work, an undoing which dovetails a more pressing issue; the image here materialises as 'woman', for if the image is always material, then equally it is always engrained in this arcane, yet not so secret, maternal material history. Once again being seen, whether on-screen, in text, on canvas, puts women at risk. This conception, moreover, appears to ignore the decentring of identity that motors singular-plural being, in its rejection of the open-ended, unfettered, amorphous syntax that (un)structures Nancy's radical ontology by means of its apparent attempt to fold the unfathomable vastness of being into one essentialised single, rather than a singular-plural, body: life giver. If matter comes from mother, then, and mother comes from wood, it would appear that the philosopher cannot see the wood for the trees because despite the promise of distinction, of separation, of detachment that underwrites Nancy's understanding of matter, '"Matter" is [. . .] first the very difference through which *something* is possible, as *thing* and as *some*',[171] the maternal-feminine blithely underwrites all matter: 'The mother is the consistency proper to difference.'[172]

Coincident with this retrograde treatment of women's bodies, however, is the cavernous quality of the body which wrests the abovementioned mucous, mythic cavities away from any sense of essentialism, for these mucous cavities are also configured as caves. '"Silence" [. . .] an arrangement of resonance' gives us 'all [the body's] resounding cave'.[173] Enwombed, '[t]he ear opens onto the sonorous cave that we then become'.[174] The cave is of course the canvas of the first image-maker through whose muscular gesture being and the image are irreducibly caught up, and Nancy's aesthetic turn itself cascades from a comparable muscular gesture – *scalpel* – whilst his thesis on resonance understands the subject as an echo.[175] Caves are surely the paradigmatic site of echoes wherein, across Nancy's work, self, image, subjectivity, body, world are resonantly constituted. The cave therefore offers a means to resolve the tensions prompted by the mucous, mythic cavities of the mouth, the womb, the heart, and instead embraces what we have differently in common with the radically distinct corpora that populate the world, with human and non-human life, with animate dogs and inanimate rocks, and of which resonance is the very measure: our shared minerality: 'But I would no longer be a "human" if I did not have this exteriority "in me", in the form of the quasi-minerality of bone.'[176] Despite our differences from dogs and rocks, then, without which we would cease to be distinctly human, without the mineral content of our bones, which draws us closer to dogs and rocks, for they too possess mineral-rich skeletons, we would cease to be singularly human. Similar to the resonant matrix of the womb, then, our shared minerality is a measure of aliveness, of vitality, but one that eschews essence whereby rather than the fecundity of the womb functioning as the embodied and literal giver of life, a mineral technicity instead articulates and reticulates our compound mode of being. Indeed, this mineral technicity is another, profoundly Nancean tautology: the ear hears sound, and its resonance, as the opening of the world, whilst the ear opens onto the sonorous cave that we become, a cave which (already) resounds in 'silence' and which echoes the mineral stupor of the world. This mineral technicity thus underwrites Nancy's *sens/monde* correspondence and in a further marker of resonance as his work's doing, the cave crystallises as an exemplary site of image capturing in his most-sustained discussion of cinema to date, and it is to cinema that we now turn, and which eventually returns us to Nancy's 'differential' conception of matter.[177]

From *Corpus Corporum* to *Corpus Imāginum*

How, though, does Nancy give us a cinema of resonance? He does so, in part at least, through an account of film that stresses the autonomy of objects which foreground waveforms: 'The antenna searches the sky, searches for the air waves carrying these images that make people talk, bet, vibrate [. . .], these images that are woven into social relations as much, if not more, than dreams.'[178] This autonomy of objects experientially overlaps with the intimate, orificial anatomy that Nancy's engagement with aesthetics takes in: heart, mouth, ears, skin, lungs and, of course, eyes. Cars, cranes, caves, even the camera, materialise as signal boxes capable of picking up, or to use Nancy's preferred term, of capturing, images. Characters, for instance, drive for miles in order to secure mobile phone reception. Cranes too operate as antennae whereby filming, and in turn looking, become (akin to) thinking:

> one [. . .] begins to swivel, sole slow element moving [. . .]. This brings to mind some questions on the means to obtain this image: did anyone communicate with the crane by telephone or was it a matter of waiting for a propitious moment? Yet these distanced thoughts do not leave the film: they are part of the look that the filmmaker rouses and drives with the arm of the crane. They set this gaze in motion toward the film itself and inside of it.[179]

There is a moving poetry to this industrial site/sight. The eye-mind wanders and wonders, which discloses an echoey, resonant quality to vision – a regard, if we recall, that is a test in relation to a meaning one is not mastering. Looking effectively becomes encaved, bouncing off the internal walls of the film. On occasion, however, these waves touch upon a discomfiting sense of usurpation.

Cinema, indeed the look itself, is regarded as elemental and 'ubiquitous': 'it can take in everything, from one far end of the earth to the other [. . .] and it can show its pictures everywhere'.[180] Relentlessly terrestrial, thus turbulent, and apparently contagious, therefore airborne(?), in this somewhat alarming understanding of film, cinema comes to form its own resonant matrix: it swells, it ramifies, it envelops. A proto cave – a tear, a crack, a fissure – condenses a great deal of these possibilities:

> In *Life and Nothing More* the torn picture is not just split by a crack: it is, in itself, both a crack or a fissure and a continuous tie between the past (shown by the man

in the picture with his old-fashioned pipe) and the present (shown by the character's, the filmmaker's gaze). The image opens one look onto the other: the picture's and the onlooker's. This opening provides a space, a distance both necessary and respectful, and at the same time it works as a relation. The film is not a representation, it is an attraction for a look, it is a traction all along its movement, while it also defines a side of the space – the side of the box where the projection of the film, the interception and presentation of the image occur [. . .]. Kiarostami's screens bear much less resemblance to a theatre displaying scenes from a fable or a demonstration than to a hollowed-out passage where the pictures slip through, a passe-partout in framing, or a device allowing still pictures to pass through a slide projector.[181]

Rhetorically faithful to the mineral technicity elucidated above, this unholy holey image schematises what Nancy calls the *cinémonde*: 'a world, our world, of which the experience is schematised – in the Kantian sense, that's to say made possible in its configuration – by the cinema'.[182] Cinema here schematises a world, our world, which in turn schematises continuity, or contiguity, of past and present, as well as the future looks of the spectators to come. Beyond our world it bears witness to Nancy's world, that is, his orificial ontology, his thinking, our ideas and Kiarostami's images swallowed up in, or passed through, holes – *interfices et urinam* – the 'hollowed-out passage where the pictures slip through' recalling the passage through nothingness that Nancy sees when told that he must have a transplant, pushing the cinematic logic of his heart even further. Equally, Nancy's mention of attraction and traction here recalls the force(s), wave(form)s and pressure that he senses in cinema, in particular, and in images, in general, and the ethical, material regard that they engender, which he juxtaposes with the material culture of cinema-going, and which in turn precipitate as a pool of resonances that are intercepted. Subject to subject, then, with nary a threat of an objectifying, mastering gaze between film and spectator, just as resonance is the measure of our corporeal incommensurability, something we have differently in common, of the messy togetherness that is otherness, it is likewise the measure of these looks that regard each other. On this account, capturing images is resonance and Nancy inadvertently confirms as much when he embeds the very structure of resonance, its straying, into his thinking on cinematic reception. He writes:

> as long as there is *cinémonde*, there is this existential which configures us in relation to its manner of refashioning the world or life, of giving back the real to itself in a conjoining form of imitative capture and enigmatic estrangement, in close proximity and scintillating distance.[183]

Capturing images, then, sets the world aquiver, a world, like resonance, that we partake in as both superlatively near and far away.

Alongside this ubiquity, Nancy expressly details how 'motion pictures comprise an *internal multiplicity*, or even several: pictures, images as such, music, words, and finally movement'.[184] Nancy's multiplicity comes up short here. It does, however, recall his enumerative cataloguing of the body as a collection of collections, a *corpus corporum*, and, once more following Nancy, we might incorporate the image in a similar fashion, that is, as *corpus imāginum*: evidence, fissure, gape, hole, intimate, line, material, obviousness, orificial, pleasure, skin, world. We perhaps do not recognise the image per se here. Worse still, this may seem a twee rhetorical move, aping his master's voice for a cheap pseudo-intellectual ploy. But it is Nancy himself who unwittingly endorses such cataloguing. In fact, it constitutes the very fabric of what we might call his aesthetic syntax, for the image's 'intimate materiality'[185] is freighted with multiplicity where 'the image is not only visual: it is also musical, poetic, even tactile, olfactory or gustatory, kinesthetic, and so on'.[186] *The* image is flush with a material multiplicity, a materiality predicated on difference, a materiality that is differential, and, like the cave, a materiality that can navigate us out of mythologising cul-de-sacs whatever strain of cinema it observes.[187] Janus productively summarises Nancy here, who, she says,

> is not describing the plurality of the arts so much as indicating the plurality of the image as a kind of *resonance form* – that is, a differential, imaginary form that allows us to describe as a singularity that which is actually a dynamic plurality of shared multiple elements that 'resonate' or move between one form, state, or sense and another.[188]

Graphically marking up the murk of resonance, emphatically bracketing off the ambiguity at its rhetorical heart, in the Nancean vernacular, the image is but a placeholder for a *corpus corporum*, that is, for a *corpus imāginum*: differential, gape, gustatory, hole, imaginary, intimate, kinaesthetic, material, multiple, musical, obviousness, orificial, pleasure, plural, poetic, resonance, singular, skin, tactile, visual, world. In Nancean tones, moreover, the image attunes us to the very particular demand that Nancy places upon his reader: to test oneself with regard to a meaning one is not mastering, to remain alert to the sense of the world, of words, and of the self, as resonance. Nancy's engagement with cinema furnishes us with an especially resonant example of the resonant listening integral to his thought because just how we should tune in to the verb to film/*filmer* emerges as a cornerstone of this work. Like *sens* and the auditory, then, to film/*filmer*, in Nancean terms, is shot through with a linguistic and conceptual multiplicity and each time that we hear it we must recalibrate its frequency. We must, then, catalogue to film/*filmer* as *corpus imāginum*.

Cinema's *corpus imāginum* offers up an entire corpus of parts: multi-zonal like the 'acephalic and aphallic [. . .] modulation of skin'.[189] Writing in *Corpus*, Nancy catalogues skin as: 'variously folded, refolded, unfolded, multiplied, invaginated, exogastrulated, orificed, evasive, invaded, stretched, relaxed, excited, distressed, tied, untied'.[190] Skin here is multiply material like the image, and it is the recuperation of the epidermis into the Nancean encounter with film, as a sort of throwback to its diaphanous etymology, that fleshes out the corpus of to film/*filmer* further. In the first instance this occurs through Nancy's response to Denis's *Trouble Every Day* (2001) where he charts how:

> Tenderly, attentively, with difficulty and at length it makes an image of the skin: it doesn't just show skin, but slips it into the plane of the image, it tends to confuse the screen with the skin, it films skin where filming would mean *following, filtering, freezing*.[191]

This is no simple skin-show.[192] Filming here is far from simply recording a picture or reproducing the world; skin becomes 'akin to light itself',[193] its 'material support'.[194] To film/*filmer* becomes fleshy, transparent, thereby reloading the phenomenological, ontological and sensual folds and contours of *expeausition*. More than this, though, this tender, attentive, difficult and 'durational' filming affirms to film/*filmer*'s resonances by multiplying the qualities integral to its manner of making sense.[195] Following, filtering, freezing correspond with scrutiny, porosity, rigidity, each of them materially and experientially distinct. These distinctions attest to the image's material multiplicity, to its resonance, to an understanding of the image as a placeholder for a *corpus corporum*, that is, for a *corpus imāginum*, for here to film/*filmer* is equally movement, rarefaction and stasis. To film/*Filmer* is following, filtering, freezing, scrutiny, porosity, rigidity.

In Klotz's *La Blessure*, it is skin again that schematises the *cinémonde*. Here, though, the tear in the skin is far more discreet: a laceration upon a leg instead of the licentious devouring of lissome teenagers and labia. Yet its impact on Nancy's thinking, and on his viewing and listening, is no less profound and here it is the porosity of skin, its reversible touching, its irritability and excitability, its absorption of the outside and inscription of 'marks from within – wrinkles, spots, warts, peelings – and marks from the outside, which are sometimes the same, or else cracks, scars, burns, slashes' that seeps into Nancy's response to the film.[196] It is not, however, the mortification of flesh that sets its *cinémonde* aquiver:

> It's a film that needs to be heard (*entendre*) [. . .]. It needs to be heard (*entendre*) right up against its slow and insistent images, right up against its light and its colours.

> It's not characters who speak in the image, it's the image that speaks, it's the black skin, striped fabrics, the winding road that sound out.[197]

Reminiscent of the whole articulatory cinema of the mouth, the image that speaks becomes an invitation for spectation: *la voix, c'est du cinéma*. What's more, it furthers our claim for cinema being considered Nancy's epic of the mouth. Here again it beats beneath his writing and thinking on film, it inaudibly tongues right up against its imagery. Indeed, this spectation pivots on an understanding of *the* image as multiply material, as a corpus of vibratory parts. Nancy thus invites the spectator to tune in to the slow, insistent, material vibrations of the image, right up against the corpus of its many parts, that is, right up against its light, its colours, the skin of its protagonists, its mise-en-scène, body parts, even sensations and sentiments. The otology the cinematic image engenders here centres on resonance. Nancy, however, appears deaf to the rhetorical resonances with which his thought is aquiver, for he instructs the spectator to hear (*entendre*) rather than to listen (*écouter*). Otherwise put, to risk the (al)lure of the already each time of understanding, however rough the outline.[198] As Nancy's own description of the spectatorial encounter with *La Blessure* makes irrefutably clear, though, the spectator submits to a profoundly Nancean listening here for its speech fractures into a medley of different material frequencies. Its timbre reorients our encounter with the quivering sense of the world and we thus listen to, that is, right up against, the corpus of its many parts; we listen right up against and at their very articulation. We *are* this listening. It *is* the touch that we make with it. As such, *La Blessure* exceeds 'a song, unwound and filmed' and burgeons forth as a fully material élan.[199] To film/*Filmer* is thus to make the *sens*uousness of the world resonate, to move all its bits about, 'the world [that is] there in all parts and offers itself to the senses – its colours, odours, savours, sounds, presences, withdrawals'.[200] Accordingly, then, film precipitates as the ultimate resonance form, that is, as matter in movement through its many component parts – cinematography, editing, mise-en-scène, colours, textures and sounds – that resonate with and between each other in order to create meaning materially. If resonance, then, is film's doing, then Nancy is the thinker for film.

The orality of *La Blessure*, however, should not be silenced, for these words are wounding, thereby recalling the scalpellic voice of the surgeon that makes an incision in Nancy's chest. Furthermore, at the bottom of these (wounding) whispers in the dark is a moist breathiness which opens onto the final material and anatomical registers of Nancy's engagement with film: ether and the lungs. 'Light, air and breath' encompass this ether,[201] all of which 'belong to the element of film as its media, through which it passes'.²⁰² There is an undoubted resonant quality to this luminous, breathy element which extends cinema's vibratory field well beyond the traction of the screen, and whilst Nancy initially declines the principle that film's 'support [. . .] does not extend in all directions, like air through which sound travels',²⁰³ he later testifies: 'As long as it is projected it vibrates.'²⁰⁴ His own response to *La Blessure* confirms as much, the different sensory registers of the film's material élan floating towards the spectator in the air. For like the acoustic, material vibrations of sound through air, the multiply material vibrations of the cinematic image 'travel[. . .] through space'.²⁰⁵ Speaking of the images caught by one of the many antennae that make up Kiarostami's cinema, Nancy describes how such imagery is 'like ether in a frame', but as his own spectatorship detailed above clearly demonstrates, it cannot be contained therein.²⁰⁶

This final push towards the ether chimes with Nancy's onset experience with director Rabah Ameur-Zaïmeche. A self-professed onset 'neophyte',²⁰⁷ Nancy nonetheless offers an intriguing account of the relationship between editing and meaning and, moreover, of the 'status' of the so-called '"finished" film'.²⁰⁸ Nancy here problematises this status, even the very possibility of ever finishing a film, by conceiving editing not as an exercise in binding meaning and holding it fast, but rather as an exercise in creative yielding. '[T]he finished film', according to Nancy, 'is never the only imaginable film', with '[e]ach film [. . .] rich with others'.²⁰⁹ This abundance emerges from the fact that in proposing one particular point of view via its final edit, the film 'distances' its material from a multiplicity of other possible or latent films, each just as imaginable as the 'actual'.²¹⁰ As such, the finished film is merely a placeholder for a multiplicity of others that ectoplasmically halo it as a floating aura.²¹¹ In this way 'a work is nothing other than a trigger for interpretations, that is to say, for openings and explorations of meaning – to show that which does not signify but which signals towards a sense that is always renewed'.²¹² Cinema here is *sens* and redolent of Nancy's account of Kiarostami's cinema, which is full of signal boxes, director, camera, screen, film are all such devices through which the sense of the world resonates, whereby to float/*flotter* shimmers with virtuality, that is, with circuits of imagination and memory and with the ambiguity and materiality of resonance. To float/*Flotter* as to film/*filmer* is, then, evocative and Nancy reads the logic of evocation as akin to resonance's dispersive temporal-spatial matrix: 'It does not establish [presence] any more than it supposes it already established. It anticipates its arrival and remembers its departure, itself remaining suspended and straining between the two: time and sonority, sonority as time and as meaning.'²¹³

To film/*Filmer* is once more to make the sense of the world resonate, and across Nancy's writings on cinema a corpus of to film/*filmer* resonates. Across the following chapters we will be adding to this corpus and further exploring resonance's doing through the resonant encounters with the sense of the world that Varda's and Haneke's cinema realise. If we resonate, then what does it mean when we say, 'it resonates'?

Notes

1. Jean-Luc Nancy, *Listening*, trans. by Charlotte Mandell (New York: Fordham University Press, 2007), p. v.
2. See Laura McMahon, *Cinema and Contact: The Withdrawal of Touch in Nancy, Bresson, Duras and Denis* (Oxford: Legenda, 2012), p. 17.
3. Douglas Morrey, 'Listening and Touching, Looking and Thinking: The Dialogue in Philosophy and Film between Jean-Luc Nancy and Claire Denis', in *European Film Theory*, ed. by Temenuga Trifonova (London: Routledge, 2009), pp. 122–33 (p. 122).
4. See Jean-Luc Nancy, 'L'Areligion', *Vacarme* (2001a) <http://www.vacarme.org/article81.html> (last accessed 2 January 2020), 'La blessure, la cicatrice', *Remue* (2005a) <http://remue.net/spip.php?article742> (last accessed 5 September 2014), '*L'Intrus* selon Claire Denis', *Remue* (2005c) <http://remue. net/spip.php?article679> (last accessed 5 September 2014), 'Rien sur le cinéma', *Trafic*, 100 (2016b), 194–9, 'En Tournage Avec R.A.-Z.', *Trafic* (2011a), 79–86, 'Cinéfile et cinémonde', *Trafic*, 50 (2004), 183–90 and 'Icône de l'acharnement', *Trafic*, 39 (2001b), 58–64.
5. See Jean-Luc Nancy, *The Evidence of Film* (Brussels: Yves Gevaert, 2001c) and Nancy (2004).
6. Sarah Cooper, 'Film Theory in France', *French Studies*, 66 (2012), 376–82 (p. 379).
7. Filmmakers Claire Denis and Abbas Kiarostami are veritable stalwarts of this critical terrain, as demonstrated by the work of Ian James, 'The Evidence of the Image', *L'Esprit Créateur*, 47 (2007), 68–79, Kristin Lené Hole, *Towards a Feminist Cinematic Ethics: Claire Denis, Emmanuel Levinas and Jean-Luc Nancy* (Edinburgh: Edinburgh University Press, 2016) and Laura McMahon (2012), and special editions of *Film-Philosophy* (2008), *Journal of Visual Culture* (2010) and *The Senses & Society* (2013). Michael Haneke might also feature amongst these stalwarts thanks to the work of Eugenie Brinkema and Lisa Coulthard.
8. Ian Balfour, 'Nancy on Film: Regarding Kiarostami, Re-thinking Representation (with a Coda on Claire Denis)', *Journal of Visual Culture* (2010), 29–43 (p. 36).
9. Ibid.
10. Nancy (2001c), p. 56.

11. Philip Armstrong, 'From Appearance to Exposure', *Journal of Visual Culture* (2010), 11–27 (p. 23).
12. Nancy (2001c), p. 68.
13. Barthes (1989), p. 347.
14. Nancy (2001c), p. 14.
15. Barthes (1989), p. 347 and Nancy (2001c), p. 50.
16. Barthes (1989), p. 346.
17. Nancy (2004), p. 187. My translation.
18. Ibid.
19. Ibid. p. 188.
20. Ibid.
21. Amy Sherlock, 'Multiple Expeausures: Identity and Alterity in the "Self-Portraits" of Francesca Woodman', *Paragraph*, 36 (2013), 376–91 (p. 378).
22. See Ian James, *The Fragmentary Demand: An Introduction to the Philosophy of Jean-Luc Nancy* (Stanford: Stanford University Press, 2006), p. 228.
23. Jean-Luc Nancy, *The Inoperative Community*, trans. by Peter Connor, Lisa Garbus, Michael Holland and Simona Sawhney (Minneapolis: University of Minnesota Press, 1991), pp. 133–4.
24. Ibid. p. 29.
25. McMahon (2012), pp. 18–19.
26. Nancy (1991), p. 65.
27. Hole (2016), p. 46. Similarly, Marie-Eve Morin describes Nancy's thought as 'circular'. See Marie-Eve Morin, *Jean-Luc Nancy* (Cambridge: Polity Press, 2012), p. 2.
28. Jean-Luc Nancy, *The Sense of the World*, trans. by Jeffrey S. Librett (Minneapolis: University of Minnesota Press, 1997b), p. 84.
29. Ibid. p. 85.
30. Ibid.
31. Ibid.
32. Ibid. p. 86.
33. Nancy (2007), pp. 3–5.
34. Ibid. p. 5.
35. See Hole (2016) and Hagi Kenaan, 'What Makes an Image Singular Plural? Questions to Jean-Luc Nancy', *Journal of Visual Culture*, 9 (2010), 63–76 (p. 67).
36. Agnès Varda quoted in Geneviève Sellier, *Masculine Singular: French New Wave Cinema*, trans. by Kristin Ross (Durham, NC: Duke University Press, 2008), p. 219.
37. Michael Haneke quoted in Dennis Eugene Russell, *The Portrayal of Social Catastrophe in the German-Language Films of Austrian Filmmaker Michael Haneke (1942–): An Examination of The Seventh Continent (1989), Benny's Video (1992), 71 Fragments of a Chronology of Chance (1994), and Funny Games (1997)* (Lewiston: The Edwin Mellen Press, 2010), p. 11.
38. Hole (2016), p. 73.

39. See Marie-Eve Morin, 'Matter/Materiality', in *The Nancy Dictionary*, ed. by Peter Gratton and Marie-Eve Morin (Edinburgh: Edinburgh University Press, 2015), pp. 156–8 (p. 158) and Nancy (1997b), p. 58.
40. Hole (2016), p. 50. See also *Vers Nancy* (Claire Denis, 2002).
41. Nancy (1997b), p. 61.
42. See Mary Jacobus, *Romantic Things: A Tree, a Rock, a Cloud* (Chicago: University of Chicago Press, 2012) for more on philosophers' stubbed toes.
43. Nancy (1997b), p. 61.
44. Ibid. p. 59.
45. Ibid. p. 61.
46. Ibid. pp. 62–3.
47. Marie-Eve Morin, '*Corps propre* or *corpus corporum*: Unity and Dislocation in the Theories of Embodiment of Merleau-Ponty and Jean-Luc Nancy', *Chiasmi International*, 18 (2016), 333–51 (p. 346).
48. According to Nancy (1997b), our inescapable minerality is also overlooked by Heidegger: 'Concerning the head on which he would like to place a patriarchal hand, Heidegger forgets, first of all, that it has *also* the consistency and, in part, the mineral nature of a stone' (p. 61).
49. Ibid. p. 87.
50. Jean-Luc Nancy, 'Fifty-eight Indices on the Body', in *Corpus*, trans. by Richard A. Rand (New York: Fordham University Press, 2008a), pp. 150–60 (p. 151).
51. Jacques Derrida, *On Touching – Jean-Luc Nancy*, trans. by Christine Irizarry (Stanford: Stanford University Press, 2005), p. 58.
52. Ibid.
53. Balfour (2010), p. 29.
54. These adoptions, as previously mentioned, are: *L'Intrus* (Claire Denis, 2004), *La Blessure* (Nicolas Klotz, 2004) and *Outlandish: Strange Foreign Bodies* (Phillip Warnell, 2009).
55. Nancy (2001c), p. 22.
56. Jean-Luc Nancy, 'The Intruder', in *Corpus*, trans. by Richard A. Rand (New York: Fordham University Press, 2008a), pp. 161–70 (p. 163).
57. Ibid.
58. Jean-Luc Nancy, *The Muses*, trans. by Peggy Kamuf (Stanford: Stanford University Press, 1997a), p. 70.
59. Nancy (2008a), p. 163.
60. Morin (2016), p. 344.
61. Nancy (2008a), p. 155.
62. See McMahon (2012), p. 16.
63. Nancy (2008a), p. 165.
64. Ibid. p. 121.
65. Philip M. Adamek, 'The Intimacy of Jean-Luc Nancy's *L'Intrus*', *CR: The New Centennial Review*, 2 (2002), 189–201 (p. 193).
66. Nancy (2008a), p. 166.

67. Ibid. p. 168.
68. See ibid. and Jean-Luc Nancy, *L'Intrus* (Paris: Galilée, 2000a).
69. Nancy (2008a), p. 49.
70. Peggy Kamuf, 'Béance', *CR: The New Centennial Review*, 2 (2002), 37–56 (p. 41).
71. Nancy (2008a), pp. 167–8.
72. Ibid. p. 49.
73. Sara Guyer, 'Buccality', in *Derrida, Deleuze, Psychoanalysis*, ed. by Gabriele Schwab and Erin Ferris (New York: Columbia University Press, 2007), pp. 77–104 (p. 88).
74. Nancy (2008a), p. 53.
75. Ibid. p. 153.
76. See ibid. p. 170.
77. Ibid. p. 55.
78. Ibid. p. 75.
79. Nancy (2001c), p. 12.
80. Ibid. p. 42.
81. Nancy (2008a), p. 45.
82. Ibid. pp. 45–7.
83. Jessica Barnfield, 'Being Is an Octopus: Exploring Octopuses, Organs and Outsides in Jean Painlevé's *Les amours de la pieuvre* and Philip Warnell's *Outlandish*', *HARTS & Minds: The Journal of the Humanities and Arts*, 7 (2016) <https://www.harts-minds.co.uk/haptics-the-senses> (last accessed 27 June 2020).
84. McMahon (2012), p. 33.
85. Sherlock (2013), p. 382.
86. Anne O'Byrne, *Natality and Finitude* (Bloomington: Indiana University Press, 2010), p. 138. See also Derrida (2005), p. 14.
87. Adrienne Janus, 'Soundings: The Secret of Water and the Resonance of the Image', *Sense & Society*, 8 (2013), 72–84 (p. 74).
88. Ibid. p. 83.
89. Jean-Luc Nancy, *Ego Sum: Corpus, Anima, Fabula*, trans. by Marie-Eve Morin (New York: Fordham University Press, 2016a), p. x.
90. Ibid.
91. Nancy (2001a). My translation.
92. Ibid.
93. Nancy (2005a). My translation.
94. Ibid.
95. See Derrida (2005), pp. 24–5.
96. Nancy (2016a), p. xi.
97. Adamek (2002), p. 190.
98. Kamuf (2002), p. 39.
99. Nancy (2008a), p. 170.
100. Ibid. p. 159.

101. Jean-Luc Nancy, *The Ground of the Image*, trans. by Jeff Fort (New York: Fordham University Press, 2005b), pp. 64–5.
102. Nancy (2008a), p. 113.
103. Guyer (2007), p. 88.
104. Ibid.
105. Nancy (2016a), p. 112.
106. Nancy (2007), p. 25.
107. Ibid.
108. Guyer (2007), p. 84.
109. Nancy (2016a), p. 111.
110. See John Paul Ricco, 'Drool: Liquid Fore-speech of the Fore-scene', *World Picture*, 10 (2015) <http://www.worldpicturejournal.com/WP_10/Ricco_10.html> (last accessed 3 July 2020).
111. Nancy (2007) pp. 27–8.
112. Nancy (2008a), p. 151.
113. Ibid.
114. Ibid. p. 157.
115. Nancy (2001c), p. 38. See James (2007) and Morrey (2009), p. 129.
116. Nancy (2008a), p. 170.
117. Hole (2016), pp. 61–2.
118. See Michael Syrotinski, 'Introduction', *Sense & Society*, 8 (2013), 5–49 (p. 5), Adrienne Janus, 'Listening: Jean-Luc Nancy and the "Anti-Ocular" Turn in Continental Philosophy and Critical Theory', *Comparative Literature*, 63 (2011), 182–202 (p. 183), James (2006), p. 106, McMahon (2012), p. 32, Stephen Barker, 'De-monstration and the *Sens* of Art', in *Jean-Luc Nancy and Plural Thinking: Expositions of World, Ontology, Politics, and Sense*, ed. by Peter Gratton and Marie-Eve Morin (New York: State University of New York Press, 2012), pp. 175–90 (p. 175) and Charlotte Mandell, 'Translator's Note to *Listening*', in Jean-Luc Nancy, *Listening*, trans. by Charlotte Mandell (New York: Fordham University Press, 2007), pp. xi–xii.
119. Hole (2016), p. 43.
120. James (2006), p. 94.
121. Barker (2012), p. 177.
122. James (2006), p. 94.
123. Mandell (2007), p. xi.
124. Nancy (2007), p. 2.
125. Ibid. p. 6.
126. Brian Kane, 'Jean-Luc Nancy and the Listening Subject', *Contemporary Music Review*, 31 (2012), 439–47 (p. 439).
127. Nancy (2007), p. 4.
128. Nancy (1997b), p. 10.
129. Nancy (2007), p. 4.
130. Bennett (2010), p. xi.

131. See Galt (2011) and Laura U. Marks, *Enfoldment and Infinity: An Islamic Genealogy of New Media Art* (Cambridge, MA: The MIT Press, 2010) for a more in-depth discussion of arabesque forms and their meanings.
132. Jean-Luc Nancy, *Being Singular Plural*, trans. by Robert D. Richardson and Anne E. O'Byrne (Stanford: Stanford University Press, 2000c), p. 28.
133. Ibid. p. 84.
134. Ibid. p. 18.
135. Christopher Watkin, 'A Different Alterity: Jean-Luc Nancy's "Singular Plural"', *Paragraph*, 30 (2007), 50–64 (p. 61).
136. Nancy (1997b), p. 141.
137. Nancy (2005b), p. 66.
138. Ibid. p. 12.
139. Rosalind Galt, 'The Obviousness of Cinema', *World Picture Journal* (2008) <http://www.worldpicturejournal.com/WP_2/Galt.html> (last accessed 9 May 2013).
140. B. C. Hutchens, *Jean-Luc Nancy and the Future of Philosophy* (Chesham: Acumen, 2005), p. 3.
141. Nancy (1997b), p. 8.
142. Hutchens (2005), p. 6.
143. Nancy (1997b), p. 78.
144. Ibid. p. 85.
145. Hutchens (2005), p. 8.
146. Watkin (2007), p. 58.
147. Ibid. p. 53.
148. Zsuzsa Baross, *Encounters: Gérard Titus-Carmel, Jean-Luc Nancy, Claire Denis* (Eastbourne: Sussex University Press, 2015), p. 11.
149. Hole (2016), p. 59.
150. Nancy (2007), p. 44.
151. Sarah Hickmott, '(En)Corps Sonore: Jean-Luc Nancy's "Sonotropism"', *French Studies*, 69 (2015), 479–93 (p. 489).
152. Janus (2011), p. 189.
153. Nancy (2007), p. 14. Translation modified.
154. Brian Kane, 'Resonance', in *The Nancy Dictionary*, ed. by Peter Gratton and Marie-Eve Morin (Edinburgh: Edinburgh University Press, 2015), pp. 143–4. See also Kane (2012).
155. Nancy (2007), pp. 14–15.
156. Ibid. p. 7.
157. Ibid. pp. 41–2.
158. Ibid. p. 42–3.
159. Hickmott (2015), p. 490.
160. Ibid. p. 493.
161. Nancy (2007), p. 13.
162. Ibid. p. 22.

163. See Bennett (2010), p. 14.
164. Ibid. p. 43.
165. Nancy (2005b), p. 74.
166. Nancy (2007), p. 45.
167. Janus (2011) attempts to rehabilitate this dynamic by embedding it within an 'otocentric feminist genealogy' (p. 187) via Luce Irigaray's work on the resonant body (*corps sonore*), yet, as Hickmott (2015) counters, '[t]he recurrent slippage between the morphological and the metaphorical maternal' in *Listening* frustrates such efforts, as well as Nancy's own 'anti-foundationalist thinking' (p. 488).
168. Nancy (2007), p. 37.
169. Nancy (2005b), p. 12.
170. Ibid.
171. Nancy (1997b), p. 57.
172. Ibid. p. 184.
173. Nancy (2007), p. 21.
174. Ibid. p. 37.
175. See Kane (2015).
176. Nancy (2000c), p. 18.
177. Nancy (2005b), p. 4.
178. Nancy (2001c), p. 64.
179. Ibid. p. 30.
180. Ibid. p. 20.
181. Ibid. pp. 40–2.
182. Nancy (2004), p. 188.
183. Ibid. p. 190.
184. Nancy (2001c), pp. 22–4. My emphasis.
185. Galt (2008).
186. Nancy (2005b), p. 4.
187. Hole (2016) explores how the differential matter of film offers a way out 'of a mythologised representation of maternity' (p. 78) in Denis's *Nénette and Boni* (1996), in particular the use of close-ups, which detaches Nénette's swollen belly from her body and renders it 'alien' (p. 76).
188. Janus (2013), p. 76. My emphasis.
189. Nancy (2008a), p. 15.
190. Ibid.
191. Jean-Luc Nancy, 'Icon of Fury: Claire Denis's *Trouble Every Day*', trans. by Douglas Morrey, *Film-Philosophy*, 12 (2008b), 1–9 (p. 6).
192. Nancy (2008a), p. 33.
193. Nancy (2001c), p. 46.
194. Ibid. p. 52.
195. Laura McMahon, 'Dislocation of the Senses: Nancy on Klotz's *La Blessure*', *Senses & Society*, 8 (2013), 62–71 (p. 67).
196. Nancy (2008a), p. 159. See also McMahon (2013).

197. Nancy (2005a). My translation.
198. See also Nancy (2004) where he again suggests that in the cinema 'we are not there to listen, but to hear its imagery pass by' (p. 183).
199. Nancy (2005a). My translation.
200. Janus (2013), p. 73.
201. Nancy (2001c), p. 50.
202. Ibid.
203. Ibid. p. 48.
204. Ibid.
205. Ibid. p. 50.
206. Ibid.
207. Nancy (2011a), p. 79.
208. Ibid. p. 81.
209. Ibid. p. 82.
210. Ibid.
211. Ibid.
212. Ibid.
213. Nancy (2007), p. 20.

La Pointe Courte:
Avoid Contact with the Eyes and Skin, May Cause Irritation

It should be said that wood is one of Agnès Varda's key materials, a leitmotif of her films.[1]

We were shooting from seven in the morning until eight at night with a lunchbreak at midday. It was 34 degrees in the shade and anywhere we went I didn't spot a single tree.[2]

If, as Lucy Fife Donaldson asserts, '[a]ll films have texture', then *La Pointe Courte*, Agnès Varda's very first feature film, pushes this to an extreme.[3] *La Pointe Courte* is all texture. After all, its very first moments emit a resolute, yet discreet, material address that urgently discloses a complex of ligneous fibres, that is, the internal, wavy texture of wood. These treen textures thus figure as a material soundbite that reverberates throughout the film and embodies the augmented sonorous register that subtends Nancean ontology. It is therefore a very fitting place to start. To some, however, it simply displays the credits (Figure 3).

The film was produced, now somewhat infamously, through very meagre financial means, creating what Ally Acker's later feminist re-evaluation determines 'a nonpatriarchal, non-hierarchical way of working' thanks to the co-operative the director formed with her cast and crew.[4] Varda came to the cinema through a peculiar iconoclasm: 'Photography seemed to me too silent. It was a little "Shut up and be pretty". Pretty photos, pretty framing, it already reeked.'[5] Strangely, such a sense of iconoclasm was felt by a number of contemporary newspaper columnists, who, apparently rubbed up the wrong way by *La Pointe Courte*'s imagery, experienced almost physical reactions to the film, implying that an encounter with it nudges the spectator towards the more discomfiting edges of *expeausition*. Stranger still is that these reservations resemble each other,[6] with some suggesting the film may cause itching due to its 'fairly irritating intellectual dryness', although it is claimed that the 'agreeable'[7] ultimately wins out over the 'annoying'.[8] For others, *La Pointe Courte* represents a somewhat

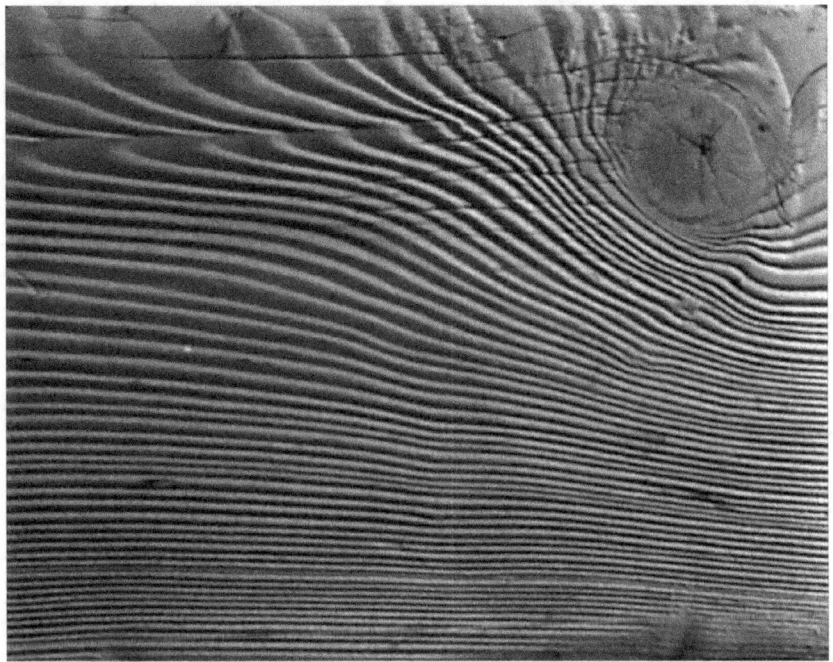

Figure 3 *La Pointe Courte* (1954), a film by Agnès Varda © 1954 ciné-tamaris.

clumsy, unthinking creature hampered by 'flaws and [. . .] blunders'[9] and a 'hive of silliness'.[10] In essence, these responses hint at a certain materiality of the film's imagery, perhaps a floating, grating (im)materiality, as if when watching it something got in the eyes, and seemingly under the skin.

What emerges here is a keen, and admittedly undesirable, texture. The film's feel is somehow offensive to (the) touch. Does this make its imagery less of an image? 'The image is desirable, or it is not an image (but rather a chromo, an ornament, a vision or representation)', writes Nancy in a further iteration of his imagistic hierarchy.[11] The most remarkable of these critical maulings is François Truffaut's 'oddly malicious' review where, as Kelley Conway details,

> he muses that Varda's resemblance to her leading man is not accidental and [. . .] facetiously expresses anxiety that he has spent too much time writing about the film's form over its content because 'it was the surest way to avoid writing the stupidities expected by the very cerebral director'.[12]

In case the reader needs reminding, when Varda's *La Pointe Courte* was seen by audiences in Paris for the first time at the Studio Parnasse in January 1956, Truffaut's directorial debut, *The 400 Blows* (1959), which bears many resemblances to its own cerebral director, was still three years away. Indeed, it is the pioneering character of Varda's oeuvre that on occasion freights its textures further by slighting her labour with the 'loose maternal association' respondents to her work cannot help but espouse: mother, grandmother, godmother, *grande dame* as reporting of her death in March 2019 subtly confirmed.[13] But we cannot blame Truffaut for that. Tellingly, even the most revered of cinephiles, André Bazin, struggled to straightforwardly desire the film's images, foregrounding the stylistic tropes that dermatologically distress:

> the author adopted a paradoxical tendency toward stylization in realism. All is simple and natural, and, at the same time, minimal [*dépouillé*] and studied [*composé*]. Perhaps I don't always agree with . . . this tendency in the images. Perhaps Agnès Varda could not forget . . . her talents as a photographer.[14]

Laudatory, yet peculiarly iconoclastic, such interpretations of the film's style as 'odd' or 'unusual' contrast with an underappreciation of the villagers' sequences,[15] considered too 'straightforward' for sustained critical attention.[16] This neglect, however, has been addressed by recent Varda criticism, which recovers the villagers' material, affective and social worlds.[17] Such criticism notes how Varda observes their daily lives, loves, labours and losses, and linguistic, domestic and political rhythms with a peculiar regard, that is, from a respectful distance, which, of course, refuses to psychologise them. Instead Varda relies on tactile, visual and aural impressions to narrate their story.[18]

Village life, though, is only half the stylistic story, for Brechtian analyses of the couple, played by Théâtre National Populaire alumnae Silvia Monfort and Philippe Noiret, are equally prevalent amongst this recent interest in Varda's maiden *long métrage*, as well as its predecessors. Having seen barely ten films before shooting her first, Varda set out to construct a film made from 'cold images'.[19] This coldness observes its subjects from a 'discreet distance'[20] and paired with the austerity of Varda's 'materialist conception of acting' it works to inhibit spectatorial identification.[21] Such an approach reduces mise-en-scène to a 'mise en place' where 'the characters express themselves concretely, by their positions on the screen, through formal relations, like a kind of puppet-performer. [. . .] Here, the relationships between images, between lines come to make up the very syntax through which I express myself.'[22] Varda here describes a sort of gestural writing and from such plasticity she sought abstraction:

> I wanted the couple to be something completely abstract. I didn't want them to be Pierre and Paul with Hélène, I wanted them to be a man and a woman who have no

name, no job. I wanted them, and it was clearly a literary idea, to be abstract and I didn't want there to be a realist dialogue.[23]

Varda's employment of music complements this literary character of their dialogue which, as Denice Orlene McMahon summarises, operates as both continuum and rupture: 'Varda uses Barbaud's atonal music [. . .] as an alienation technique in the vein of Brechtian distanciation. Importantly [however] Varda removes atonal music from its stereotypical setting, and instead uses it to convey an acute feeling of malaise.'[24] Readings of the film's material world as metaphors for the protagonists' thoughts and feelings, however, compromise these Brechtian accounts. Alison Smith, for example, perceives the 'stray objects' dotted throughout *La Pointe Courte* as 'explicitly' anchored to 'a character's gaze' which in turn shapes how the spectator sees them, for example, as a 'key' to Elle's calm understanding of the couple's predicament.[25]

Equally, there is a clash between temperatures: the coldness of Brechtian distanciation produced by (the textures of) Monfort's and Noiret's performances, Varda's literary dialogue and Pierre Barbaud's score, colliding with the pervasive heat which subsumes both narrative strands. This heat horizontalises the world: '[It's] linear like a drawing on a wall, but that's a feeling. In warmer climates [. . .w]hen you are feeling a pain, the head seems to sharpen that pain, dries it out, purifies it, makes it geometric as if it were drawn.'[26] Heat, then, imposes an obvious arabesque logic, for an image on a wall is compelled to horizontalise its world(view), as well as the materiality of the world. Such logic cleaves the abovementioned object-metaphors further from looking – their aleatory configurations instead arabesque – and it is such dissonance that distils the sentiments which drive the couple's story, uncertainty and fear over the future, tentative reconciliations, social pressures, sentiments which likewise motor that of the village although in a slightly shifted, that is, societally broader and objective register: threat to livelihood, rather than romance, although this is there too through Raphael and Anna's flourishing relationship. In fact, the film as a whole 'delight[s] in contrasts [. . .] and parallels',[27] its wavy narrative 'toing and froing' between the daily lives of the residents of the eponymous fishing village, battling a municipal ban on their livelihoods, and the visit of two Parisian outsiders contemplating an end to their marriage.[28] Material dichotomies, and (mis)understandings of the film's material world, have thus long dominated *La Pointe Courte* criticism, spanning the film's two halves and drawing up opposing territories, such as light and shadow,[29] iron and wood,[30] black and white.[31]

From Bazin's uncertainty to Truffaut's cruelty, from Brechtian distanciation and atonality to material oppositions, and even the queasy instrumentalisation of Varda's pregnancy, *La Pointe Courte* accrues texture in a medley of ways: through criticism, through industrial context, through style and through narrative.[32] So too does wood. Varda, for instance, describes how 'In *La Pointe Courte*, I presented a couple in crisis; they are not only in the process of breaking up but also of splitting off from society.'[33] The textu(r)al ramifications of the couple's splitting off neatly echo the materiality of wood, for both wood and the structure of the film can be split along the length of their grains, yet by design each clings faithfully to its other half. This chapter therefore asks readers to reattune to the film's material world, to shift from understanding to listening. Essentially, it asks readers to listen to wood.

Seeing the Wood for the Trees

Nowhere is such listening more obvious than during *La Pointe Courte*'s opening sequence. Indeed, responses to the film are readily canonising it, for the very first moments of Varda's very first feature film never fail to elicit comment. These voices add to its seemingly mundane textures: a plank of wood and a series of starched white sheets flapping in the wind. Whilst these sheets connote part of the village's daily grind, specifically women's labour, the film's timber preface recalls the palpable sense of urgency with which contemporary, and occasional collaborator, Jean-Luc Godard asserts wood to be Varda's filmic material *par excellence*. The very first image of her very first film affords us such a ligneous inference through the exposed wood grain that greets our eyes. Not all critical eyes, however, converge on this internal, textured ornament, and while these voices tend to harmonise, with *La Pointe Courte*'s expanded authorship weighing on many interpretations to produce a reading of the film's opening as plural, dialectical and economical, when *La Pointe Courte* proper begins constitutes a critical fracture.[34] Smith and Conway, for example, suggest that the film commences 'with a tracking shot down the main street of the village', deferring its start until after the credits have rolled.[35] To take this post-credit moment as the beginning of *La Pointe Courte*, however, marks the first misunderstanding of its material world, for the entire film issues from wood's internal, textured ornament.

Rebecca DeRoo's fascinating examination of the film's neo-realist credentials lends support to this thinking, for '[w]hile', as she writes, 'the opening credits announce that it is a film "by Agnès Varda and the inhabitants of La Pointe Courte"', Varda's filmmaking 'suggests that we question how much the film's workers and villagers speak for themselves, and whether we as viewers can truly see and hear them'.[36] DeRoo's critique centres on *La Pointe Courte*'s triptych of 'local airs', understood as music, breeze and atmosphere, and which, despite appearances, thwart any claim for authenticity and code the spectator as an outsider through processes of erasure, dubbing and corporeal opacity. In all iterations, these airs are literally bracketed off, graphic marks which not only hint at the murk of resonance but demand that the spectator reorient their encounter with the film. For instance, whilst these local airs are listed as part of the opening titles, the individual musicians are 'uncredited', unlike professional composer Barbaud, and the music's local meaning is not shared; and whilst the wind ostensibly animates the 'unpeopled' scene, owing to a faulty recording device, its howls are dubbed.[37] As such, the local airs that we hear are nothing more than an approximation, an imitation.

When watching *La Pointe Courte*, then, we must stay alert to the secrets of its local airs and, irrespective of a Nancean lens, the film demands a peculiar strain of listening, frequently inducing an anxious, edgy audition. When Elle first arrives in the village, for example, we hear the excruciating noise of a sander: metal butchering wood. First heard off-screen, this noise dissolves the usual narrative indicators, drowning out voices and undoing the customary audio-visual hierarchy – a frank reminder of our essential corporeal vulnerability to and fundamental precarity in relation to sound. We are not, after all, at leisure to stem its encroachments. Similarly, all voices had to be added in post-production with the actual voices of the villagers replaced by those of actors. The film is thus 'underscored by [a] rift between sound and image'[38] whereby it possesses 'no sonorous perspective',[39] unmooring the villagers, and the couple, from their bodies. Whilst this sense of precarity resonates more broadly with the film's wider thematic parallels – a love and livelihood in peril – and reminiscent of the problematic object-metaphors discussed above, indicative of an acoustic identification with Elle, following a Nancean framework, it likewise augments their materiality. For produced thus they (dis)embody materiality's differential character, which cinema's material multiplicity both embodies and hyperbolises, and which in turn hyperbolises an understanding of cinema as an epic of the mouth. This contact with wood, moreover, recalls the stakes of Nancy's resonant listening: its concern for the temporal-spatial matrix of sonority, rather than its messages, its sonorous attack, its disclosure of worldly sense that is motile, material and messy, that is, a world that is motile, material and messy. It overwhelms any threat of the already each time of understanding, for we fail to (immediately) surmise a context for these mechanised wails. Wood thus distils (the sense of) the world.

The violence and discomfiture of this later ligneous episode are absent from *La Pointe Courte*'s earliest encounter with wood, yet during its initial wooden whittling the fact that wood limns its local airs is not so secret. Woodwind instruments play the music that fills the air, which by their very physicality betray such inference. Indeed, the entire opening sequence is lined with wood, and as if in response to Varda's own iconoclasm it is here that we witness cinema inventing itself when an originally static shot, which is deftly evocative of rootedness, tightly frames the exposed wood grain, then smoothly pans left before seamlessly becoming a tracking shot which telescopes the village's wooden ramparts. Photography discreetly becomes cinematography, horizontalising materiality. Slowly, the camera advances until it chances upon a suited man beneath what the film's second protagonist reveals to the uncultivated spectator is a fig tree. Upon encountering this man, the camera's mechanical neck cranes a little and then relinquishes its view of him in favour of a more rustically attired figure who quickly reports the other man's presence in the village. In electing to follow this second man, the camera retraces its original steps, coiling around and taking the spectator back with it. The camera continues to pursue this winding as it traverses a household full of children, then it records piles of wood until it finally reacquaints the spectator with the local man as he creeps and clambers over rooftops in order to regain sight of the health inspector. As he peers, he completes a further coil by reversing the original perspective from which we observed the besuited man, a circular inscription reinforced by a cat curled up in a net in the following shot. The smooth formation of straight growth lines as the camera tracks and pans is therefore interrupted by its backtracking, its arabesques materially mimicking knot formation in the trunks and branches of trees. Cinematography thus etches a second knot into the film and consequently the visual image becomes grainier through a thickening up of the image through this cascade of ligneous inferences.

Thanks to such graininess, the worldliness of wood again burgeons, a burgeoning that Nancy's wider wooden witterings reflect and whereby wood precipitates as the material *par excellence* for both Varda and Nancy. Indeed, Nancy's own arboreal encounter effervesces with bodily and *sensuous* abundance:

> I see this green tree shining in the sunlight, I am in it, I pass into it, I merge with it – to the point where this confusion forestalls itself because it resounds in me as an approach to an unimaginable intimacy. [. . .] 'I' become the green of the tree and the sunlight in which 'I' find 'myself' – I sense myself, I feel myself [. . .] – here, the green, the precise green of this precise tree, the precise gleam of this moment of sunshine – comes back to itself in such a way that it becomes precisely 'this' green,

this nuance, this meaning or this aspect, which furthermore is at the same time a touch and also vaguely some part of a smell, a sound, or a taste.[40]

Haloed by light, Nancy's arboreal encounter is paradigmatic of his thinking on being and the body. Demonstrative of the arabesque logic of his philosophy, it stages the budding and opening of a look in the middle of ordinary turbulence, deepening this look's terrestrial contours, transforming any ordinariness into the extraordinary, whilst embodying the very structure, or timbre, of resonance: the self and worldly sense (un)folding through tension and rebound, deployment and redeployment, venturing and return. It is, after all, only in the return to the self that I am, this I is, myself. I am only 'I' in my exposure to others: 'I am' articulated thus – 'my "subjectivity" is itself firstly a body among others, sensing the others and sensed by those others'.[41] It is a 'space of resonance, of relay'.[42] Here, then, the self strays and in straying sight discloses the sensual, fracturing perception into many sensory wavelengths, which further affirms the corporeal contours of Nancy's arboreal encounter:

> Once more the body – and that it senses: that it is a plural unity of senses [...]. 'A body' means that the same one sees, hears, smells, tastes, experiences motion, warmth, contraction, expansion, emptiness, exasperation, vertigo, tension, scansion, disequilibrium, speed, variety, confusion, waiting, transport, vitality, abatement, retreat, nausea, etc. – without going further in the multiplication of these rough categories (as we would have to do by breaking down or 'cutting up' [*(dé)taillaint*] sight into sight of colours, of shades, of lines, of forms, of volumes, of depths, of movements, of compactness, of lights, of transparencies, of brightnesses, of grains, of invisibilities ...).[43]

Freighted with its own ligneous inference – '"cutting up" sight into colours, shades, lines' – green here supersedes the rustling of the wind et al. in staging the noisy choreography of being (a body in the world). There is even some trace of the convulsive, chasmic, chiasmic, cinematic Nancean gob tonguing below as singular sites beat against other singular sites.[44]

Fundamentally, then, the tree, Nancy's own wooden, material soundbite, engenders a critical and ontological whorl, and reminiscent of Brakhage's green, the tree soon reticulates a resonant vitality which hinges the tautology, coextensivity, motility and sonority of *sens* and *monde*:

> In broader terms: this green becomes this green 'in me' but as 'I' also become its nuance, its gleam, and some part of the sap which runs through it, some part of its exuberant growth taken from the soil, the rain and the sun, some part of its contrast with other colours, and with forms, densities and turning shapes which surround it (the trunk, other plants) so this green becomes 'this' green in itself and

for itself. [. . .] This does not only happen 'for me', subjectively, since this also happens for and through all sorts of other innumerable 'perceptions', those of animals – birds, spiders, squirrels – which at the same time have a relation to the same tree, but also for and through all the other possible exchanges between trees and plants more or less easily made in their growth, between the gleams, reflections, shadows which change values, which enhance or diminish each other.[45]

What emerges from Nancy's treen encounter, then, is the kaleidoscopic appraisal of being that his thought gives us and in pointing up its emphatically dizzying qualities it sketches out how bodies sound each other out. We resonate, after all, and resonance is the very kernel of our encounter with others that we are, yet whereby our own rhythms are not subsumed by the rhythms of those other bodies. So dizzying is this encounter that it teeters Nancy's thought onto the edges of unfamiliar critical terrain: namely, an autolytic sense of interiority. What is on the inside of Nancy's work on the body, for instance? What happens to Nancy's thinking when it stumbles upon its own insides? What happens to Nancy's philosophy when its arabesques ineluctably lead there? Safely bracketed off, though, this 'in me' graphically undermines its own assertions, whilst staking a claim for our insides, that is, for trunks, both fleshy and arboreal, to which we shall return in the book's conclusion. Here, then, this 'in me' persists *à fleur de* and Nancy's encounter with this tree distils a resonant matrix which reveals a body/self and world in resonance.

The originary resonance of such an encounter, however, is not always enough. We want (some) sensation(s) to linger longer. We 'want[. . .] to grasp and replay, to intensify the sensation itself', like a wall painting in a hot climate, like the sensation of wood.[46] It is this desire, a further tautology of Nancy's thought, that prompts an image-making gesture: '"This" green becomes a work of painting, or a photo; but it can also switch to a rhythm, or a sonority, etc.; or become a work of words.'[47] The (Nancean) image as a placeholder for a *corpus corporum*, that is, for a *corpus imāginum*, is very much in evidence here, furthering the critical and ontological whorl, and it clusters a curious Nancean aesthetic aggregate: image as flower.

A Little Piece of Material Cinema in the Palm of your Hand

Frontal, colourful, ornamental, the flower recalls the tendrils of the arabesque. Indeed, floral forms predominate in this decorative form and thus are antithetical to Nancy's hierarchical thinking on the image. Yet the flower winds its way to the very heart of one of his favourite locutions: *à fleur de*. 'The *fleur*', he writes, 'is the finest, most subtle part, the very surface, which remains before one and which one merely brushes against [. . .]: every image is *à fleur*, or is a flower.'[48] Tellingly, these floral tones resonate with edges and the epidermis, with the distal and the proximal; they demand that we tune in to their specific phenomenal resonances and open onto the altogether stranger, more intimate anatomy that Nancy's engagement with the image facilitates. Indeed, the image as a flower, or *à fleur*, condenses a great deal of Nancy's thinking on the image, whilst housing untapped critical potential:

> What [the image] transports to us, then, is its very unbinding, which no proximity can pacify and which thus remains at a distance: just at the distance of the touch, that is, barely touching the skin, *à fleur de peau* ['touchy']. It approaches across a distance, but what it brings into such close proximity is distance.[49]

According to Nancy, then, the image as a flower is intimate and itchy, yet remote, echoing something of the irritation expressed by some contemporary respondents of *La Pointe Courte*, and its touchiness cuts up touch. Here to flower/*effleurer* means to raze, to brush, to caress and across the pages of *The Evidence of Film* the flower persists as (resonant) paradigm through a relationship to touch which dovetails with colour.

Touch first appears in the text with reference to narrativity and how a protagonist attempts to touch upon a sought-after experience through impersonation and usurpation, and my thinking here usurps an existing tally of touches by Ian James who counts just one isolated mention:[50]

> Nancy indicates that '*Evidentia* came to Latin as a translation of the Greek *enargeia*, which speaks of the powerful and instantaneous whiteness of lightning', and he immediately adds, 'It touches in an instant and prevents any gripping'. Throughout this essay evidence is associated rather more with the lexicon of luminous energy, visibility, sight, lighting and gaze than it is with that of touching or caressing. Here the language of touch is evoked briefly to indicate once again that, however much the 'powerful whiteness' of evidence might impose itself upon the gaze of the spectator, it is nevertheless not something which is possessed or grasped, but something that, touched upon, remains distant.[51]

Offered up and dissipated in the same instant, this vestigial touch reloads the touchiness of the image *à fleur*, its floral bursts subsequently operating similarly to Nancean evidence. Mention above of unbinding, for example, (re)attunes us to the peculiar resonances of regard and its attending to a meaning one is not mastering. Whilst this configuration of touch here is indisputable, James's touch tally, however, is inaccurate and thus indifferent to the series of touchy mentions that punctuate *The Evidence of Film* and which involute a further critical and ontological whorl because these additional touches articulate an approach to cinema that is subtended by the materiality and motility of resonance and its arabesques of worldly sense. After all, evidence is not just about pregnancy, that is, a onetime reconfiguration of experience, but equally its enchaining.

Let us take, for instance, another of Nancy's critical florets: 'I say a "flower".'[52] Here Nancy considers how sense becomes material through exscription:

> Sense consists only in being woven or knit together. Text is textile; it is the material of sense. But sense as such has no material, no fibers or consistency, no grain or thickness. Sense 'as such' consists precisely in nothing other than weaving together an 'as such'.[53]

The flower, and 'its parcel of silky fibres', soon precipitates as principal vehicle of such weaving:[54]

> 'To image' must be heard as a transitive verb whose action, however, cannot act on an object. I can illustrate a discourse by giving a concrete example, but this remains secondary in relation to the sense [. . .]. If, by contrast, I say that I image this discourse (for example, the discourse that says, 'I say "a flower"'), this is something completely different: I present its saying with its said; therefore I say 'a flower' or rather, here, I say, 'I say a flower', and the image is there, palpable as the impalpable in this saying of the saying, this movement of the needle in the stitch that already links saying to flower, but also 'saying' to 'speaking', 'singing', 'evoking', and 'flower' to 'scent', 'petal', 'wilting', 'floret', 'flora', or 'flame' – and so many others that are absent.[55]

Nancy's definition of 'to image' here arguably stems from his heart transplant, which inspired his aesthetic turn, for its inability to act upon an object parallels his incapacity to picture the removal and replacement of his wasted heart except as orificial, ecotechnical and intrusive, as procedure, rather than picture. Instead of picturing, 'saying' and 'flower' enchain, and we are reminded of to film/*filmer* as to float/*flotter* and its synergies with evocation which mirror the temporal-spatial matrix of resonance. Here 'saying' and 'flower' are merely placeholders for a multiplicity of other doings that ectoplasmically halo them as a floating aura and which hint at the material multiplicity of the Nancean image and its status as a placeholder for a *corpus corporum*, that is, for a *corpus imāginum*.

Through the flower the whole articulatory cinema of the mouth materialises too:

> From one language to another, there is always a diminution of signification and an increase in sensation. The text images itself. If I say 'flower', *fleur*, *Blume*, *fior*, I do not say the same flower and yet I also do not say the flower itself (the flower 'as flower').[56]

More attuned to sensation over signification, this critical floret reflects resonance, which places the flower, and all its Nancean baggage, distinctly at odds with the abrupt touch of evidentiary light. The flower in the Nancean tongue thus offers an alternative to the itchy, instantaneous issue it ostensibly proffers.

The final mentions of touch, which concern the use of colour in Kiarostami's *Life, and Nothing More* (1991), (parenthetically) crystallise this alternative:

> color too emerges little by little, by discreet touches, a few flowers, a rug, the poor-quality color print on the wall, a red, yellow and blue ceramic rooster that the child finds, and these touches will be rare, isolated among the dominant spreads of ochre, brown, gray, sable, the pale blue and green.[57]

Flashing up against a wan colourscape, such touches of colour, which are equally touches of ornament derived from lowly decorative art forms, weaving, prints, ceramics, threaten an evidentiary grasping without seizing. Yet these isolated discreet touches exert a certain pressure – a textual microcosm of being's noisy choreography. Bushy buds detach from monotone backgrounds and disrupt the timbre of pallid images: 'a bunch of red flowers, explicitly chosen for their color, stands out against the blue-grey picture of the noisy street'.[58] Timbre does not, of course, only play out acoustically; it opens onto other perceptible registers, and their respective differential qualities, to engender material vibrations that exceed the simple touch of light upon skin through the refusal to reabsorb these disruptions. Colour essentially sounds out – *Klangfarbe* – and in this way these botanical buds go some way to recover the beat that Nancy's own thesis on resonance silences for they embody the intimacy of the material blow that we are not at leisure to interrupt, and accentuate the worldliness, materiality and corporeality of resonance's dispersive temporal-spatial matrix. We thereby come to listen right up against, that is, *à fleur de*, the image which materialises as *corpus imāginum*, and it is these floral bursts, cinematic and textual, and the material multiplicity they promise, that rhythm the spectatorial encounter and thus refine resonance by allowing sensation to linger longer through drawing up material, motile arabesques of sensuous material. Fundamentally, then, the flower demands that the spectator attune to the swell of the image's material resonances, and this tuning in promotes an eschewal of succession and an appeal to the omnipresent, wave-like swell of sonorous temporality, its undulations here triggered by the colourful ornament and mobile materiality of these red, floral flourishes. This filmic topiary thus tunes us in with a look that respects the *sens*uous abundance that the world *is* just as Nancy's arboreal encounter does.

Carrying all the flower's imageness, and the specificities of the Nancean image, the flower is also favoured amongst foundational bodily turn thinkers who call upon it to signal the emphatically embodied and multisensory nature of cinematic spectatorship, as well as the synaesthesia and synopsis that underpins perception writ large:

> When I smell a magnolia, I do not distinguish as separate perceptions the act of bending to meet it, its waxy pink-and-whiteness, its unmistakable yet indefinable fragrance, the cool touch of petals on my face, and the wave of associations from my memory. [. . .] Smelling the magnolia, I mingle with it sensuously; I take on some of its qualities. [. . .] This sensuous meeting with the world is not merely an act of identification, but a function of the interplay of the senses.[59]

With stark echoes of Nancy's arboreal encounter, Laura U. Marks's intimate, intoxicating meeting with the magnolia evidences (a) body and world in resonance whereby simply taking a whiff of a floral bouquet gives way to a total sensory collapse, a jumble of movement, visuality, olfaction, tactility. Vivian Sobchack's florid experience hinges on the olfactory too:

> Although the smell of the flower is lost to the spectator's perception (if not to the filmmaker's), s/he is able, for example, to perceive the flower in an otherwise perceptually inaccessible kinetic transformation – its expansive movement from bud to flower amplified into visibility. And, although the spectator's own kinaesthetic activity is drastically reduced when watching a film, the perception of movement and its kinaesthetic 'sense' or significance seems immensely amplified because of the relative quietude of the spectator's movement. It is as if the spectator's body were kinetically 'listening' to the movement of another.[60]

Although the olfactory experience that organises Marks's synoptic sensory encounter with the magnolia above is ostensibly lost here, Sobchack's anosmic encounter with the flower's perfume parallels Marks's thanks to its expansive, amplified encounter with the sense of the world that engages an expansive, amplified strain of 'listening'. This 'listening' attends to 'sense', their respective rhetorical murk pointing up both the inexactitude and plenitude typical of resonance, which the flower attunes to here, as well as a very particular, and arguably disempowering, dynamic between spectator and film with the former considered little more than an amplifier for the murky sense of cinema. Each floral encounter, however, transforms ordinary turbulence into something extraordinary, and if wood is Varda's filmic material *par excellence*, the flower could almost be thought of as the sensuous image *par excellence*, a little living piece of material cinema in the palm of your hand.

Such an understanding, however, risks redrawing the closed circuit which typifies the bodily turn's theories of spectatorship. Through resonance's dispersive temporal-spatial matrix, which consists of green, gleam and trees, as well as soil, squirrels and spiders, instead of a confused homogeneity, the timbre of *La Pointe Courte*'s timber preface staves off this risk. It does not absorb its internal multiplicity. Rather, wood, which structures the entire opening sequence, upholds the distinctions between the senses and between the different sensible, technical registers of cinema. Indeed, wood plumbs down into the material multiplicity that the image is. Wood is vision, wood is sound, wood is movement, wood is the touch that we make with the film world. It effectively literalises Nancy's arboreal encounter and performs the noisy choreography of being, its (un)yielding (im)materiality perhaps the thing that rubbed contemporary commentators up the wrong way. My screenshot really does risk coming up short, perhaps even does serve as mere illustration, perhaps even is unresonant, because far from dumb decoration the anonymous wooden expanse plucks the ornament of the everyday from the profilmic's material surrounds and diffracts the image into many cinematic and sensory wavelengths. The looped node and striated contours of the wooden block, then, do not only cleave, but also splinter and in this way, the matt, lignin fibres of its grain supersede the brilliance of light as the film's material support and instead wood comes to structure *La Pointe Courte*, permeating its visual, audio and kinaesthetic registers. Our encounter with the film thus maps this ligneous overflow, that is, wood's permeation of the film's different material registers, and far from grounding her maiden *long-métrage* into a system that favours certain perceptions over others, Varda's relationship with wood makes the image available to a whole spectrum of perceptual engagements, materially, and microcosmically, actualising the multiplicity of encounters she believes we experience and need in life. We could say, then, that spectatorship for Varda is a case of plant life, whereby viewers are capable of being *sensuously* modified by the spoils of the image. To film/*Filmer* here, then, is to whittle/*tailler*. Indeed, to film/*filmer* is shot through with the resonant internal, textured ornament of wood and in resonance our bodies texturise the line drawing of the hot, dry, shadeless place that Varda presents in *La Pointe Courte* by threading the lignin fibres of its opening moments back into the film when it has seemingly shed its ligneous grain. In essence, *La Pointe Courte*'s wooden matrix refines Nancean resonance because wood unfailingly draws up material, motile arabesques across the film's imagery, and it is in this way that we profoundly listen to wood.

Further Wooden Whittlings

Like the green of Nancy's tree, then, *La Pointe Courte* is ligneously aquiver, and in their simplest guise these woody blows materialise as (ornamental) discreet touches thanks to the many circles and straight lines that fill the film's material surrounds. The spectator resonates with the visual rhyme that these surrounds share with wood's internal patterns through her inaugural encounter with its interior ornament and its echoes. These geometrical echoes cleave the villagers' and the couple's stories, and whilst some are quite simply articulated through an overt display of grainy form (for instance, an eel wound up in a bucket, or planks of untreated wood running parallel to a rope washing line), others flash up more discreetly. Planted amongst the characters' costumes, for example, small-scale allusions to wood's internal textured ornament can be found, such as a smoking pipe, or the striped jersey and beret worn by a number of the fishing town's inhabitants. In this iteration, the film's wooden matrix is arguably at its closest to us. We do not need to stray too far, for such sensation is refined to the point of reification. It constitutes a low hum to which we easily attune.

Alongside these small-scale allusions, however, are instances which demand a more alert listening, moments that are more rarefied. Ever present are the circles and straight lines that plainly deck out the film, but, like its opening sequence, these shapes transcend its material surrounds. These examples once again treat the image as a placeholder for a *corpus corporum*, that is, a *corpus imāginum*, and the most striking use occurs shortly after Elle has arrived in la Pointe Courte to visit the birthplace of her husband for the first time. As the couple journey to their residence, their walk is interrupted by the approach of a slow-moving train and, standing perpendicular to its passage, they are obliged to endure its cumbersome and metallic presence which comes to dominate the film's visual, aural and kinetic tracks as it edges past them: a static camera recording the train's steady screech towards the edge of the screen until its cab fills the frame, whereby modernity unexpectedly explodes into view and into the midst of the marsh and the film.[61] Transporting our view to the other side of the tracks, *La Pointe Courte* refocuses on the couple's trials, quickly cutting to an obliquely angled mid-shot. The camera then winds around the pair before stopping once again to permit them the space to walk off into the distance. Contemplated alongside each other, the kinetic content of the image, expressed by the train's slow forward motion, and the kinaesthetic quality of cinematography, realised by the camera's semi-circular movement around the protagonists, work mutually and weave wood's texture back into the film in defiance of the visual track's relinquishing its lignin fibres, and of metal's apparent dominance. In keeping with the Nancean vernacular, intrusion is just another opportunity for encounter despite the fact that in this, their first chapter, the couple are effectively victims of the village's textures. Its materiality dictates their movements.

The reciprocal play of the straight lines of the train's heavy movements and of the curvilinear motion of the camera repeats, albeit in a very different form, at a number of points during the film. In other instances, it is the faces of the protagonists captured in close-up that act as the circles, whilst the series of vista shots seen throughout the film constitute the linear complement to their round faces. Two instances again coincide with the early part of Elle's visit. The first follows a brief enquiry into whether her face has changed in the five days since the couple parted and after some reassurance from Lui, and a lingering close-up of Elle's face, he presents the village to her, and the audience, by way of a steady pan to the left which opens up a narrow, dusty track. On another occasion, we first see a vista shot until a cut to another close-up of Elle's troubled face. The pace of this change shunts wood's grain back into view and according to the Nancean floral vernacular, the cut here 'prunes the look' where once more the swirled knots and smooth contours of wood's internal ornament effloresce. Nancy further cultivates this lexis by ascribing such plant life a precise structural role;[62] he pursues this pruning further by considering how the cut 'trims its borders and its point, lightens its sharpness'.[63]

Spectatorship is thus another case of plant life, and a more expressive example takes place later in the trip as the couple wanders along the shoreline. Initially filmed in long shot, as the couple near the water's edge, a cut swiftly installs the camera behind an abandoned, broken basket lying on the sand, its woven, circular form providing a highly stylised frame to the couple's movements. As they pass in front of this wicker frame, its shape obviously reminiscent of the knot in the inaugural anonymous grain of wood, the camera dives through its cylindrical body so that we do not lose sight of the couple, although we must make do with their feet. Charting their walk at ground level, a linear travelling shot remains focused on their feet until a star-like shape, which might be the base of the broken basket, appears in the foreground of the image. Its spiked circular form, which Elle picks up and tosses into the lagoon, stalls the camera's sideways movement and again recalls the knot of the film's timber preface. In completing this motion, this beach debris and camerawork stitch the now absent lignin fibres of the opening wooden plane back into the on-screen space of the beach: the warp and weft of its tapestry gathering filaments as soon as the image acquires its wicker frame; these filaments bolstered by the travelling shot's mimicry of wood's striations; the sight of the basket's missing base likewise forming the base of the purely resonant tree trunk that our look carves out through the sequence's visual and kinaesthetic material. Our spectatorship is thus alive with the hum of worldly, woody sense which further refines resonance as a materialistically minded modality of perception – two trunks, one fleshy, one arboreal, are in resonance whereby wood is seen and felt even when absent – and this episode indicates a shifted material relationship between the film's cleaved narratives.

Chapter two of the couple's story, a lengthy scene during which they once more confront the state of their marriage, embodies this shift, and refinement, when the film whittles its most lyrical lignin. Small-scale allusions to wood's internal textured ornament – the straightness of the river bank, the roundness of bicycle wheels and their shadows on the bankside – bookmark their exchange which begins with one of the most stylised shots of the film: the couple's two heads configured as one in a fleshy homage to a Giuseppe Arcimboldo portrait. His face is shown in profile laid over hers, which looks straight on. The shot's tight framing recalls *La Pointe Courte*'s inaugural wood grain and this time from painterly stillness to movement, cinema once again invents itself. In a deft allusion to Nancy's forked films theory, whereby editing constitutes an exercise in creative yielding, rather than imposing legibility, order and meaning, the couple's faces knotted together form an anterior echo of Bibi Andersson and Liv Ullmann's comparable collapse in Ingmar Bergman's *Persona* (1966).[64] The sequence then starts to break down into a shot/reverse-shot structure, and whilst the audio track maintains a sense of this conventional filmic grammar, in a reversal of the acoustic rift that underpins the filmic bodies, the visual track cleaves. She begins to talk, but we are not privy to her response and in its place, in the disjuncture of her image, we instead see a seabird flying. We return to her face, indelibly marked by roundness, and she then walks to the right of the frame to create a perambulatory striation, thereby reiterating wood's grain. To film/*Filmer* is thus shot through with the resonant internal, textured ornament of wood and such disjuncture affirms film as the most resonant and most material of all the arts for its entire material multiplicity is ligneously aquiver.[65] The couple's conversation continues, and the formal distribution of the images alludes to the threat of their separation, the wooden frame between them materially structuring this sense of divide. Indeed, this frame consistently choreographs their movements and even when they come together in a two shot the spatial divide remains, as a wooden post scores the centre of the frame, polarising them. Wood's ligneous and bifurcating opacity endures. Despite this divide, however, due to the film's lack of sonorous perspective, their voices cleave, they remain close to each other and, moreover, close to the spectator in spite of their advances towards the shoreline. The near and the far, the distant in the close and the close in the distant, thus resonate, as does Barbaud's score, which plays non-stop during their sequences, meaning that we are always, in some way, listening to wood, and once the shot/reverse-shot structure returns, where visual inserts extracted from the village's material surrounds deputise for Elle's response, this proximity remains. He speaks, with his voice and body united by the film, then she speaks, and in this disjuncture of her image we catch a glimpse of a fisherman, different in visual content, whilst faithful to the formal design of the sequence for in agitating the surface of the water he causes it to pulsate with the ornament of the wood grain. Another facial, fleshy knot appears, wood's grain enfolded into the shape of Elle's hair, its horizontal strands aping lignin fibres, and any sense of breakdown soon accelerates: a crab, a dead cat and, unsurprisingly, planks of wood intrude upon the visual track. Each interruption halts smooth cinematic growth lines to produce a tiny knot and through these intrusions the exposed grain of wood again effloresces, which continues in earnest as this chapter draws to a close: the roundness of a child's struck face, a straight razor and an eel dovetail the film's two narrative strands.

Following this chapter, the formerly clear distinctions between the film's two halves begin to dissolve. Its alternating narrative rhythm, for instance, ceases and its strands instead intertwine. The couple and the village enjoy the joust and each party begins to comment on the other. Elle asks about the fishing; the couple's hosts diagnose their incapacity for happiness. In essence, wood's texture takes over as agitated circles – squeaky wheels, tarred fishing nets, feverish heads, a kepi – and unsettling straight lines – a cart's wobbles, hanging washing, the shuffling of crabs and eels as they advance towards a bucket – punctuate the succeeding village chapter. Fundamentally, all local airs subordinate to its textures. Raphael's walk home through the village before his short stint in jail, having been caught illegally fishing in the lagoon, anticipates the bipedal beach travelling shot. A fist that strikes a table in anger succeeds its striations. Gestures both filmic and corporeal reinscribe wood's internal ornament. This (prehensile) roundness and (bipedal) linearity echo throughout the following scene where Anna's family, seated in a row, discuss her potential relationship with Raphael. Like the film, their colloquy is ligneously aquiver. The camera then cuts to a close-up of Anna's mother's face before performing a curvilinear crane. Linearity ensues until the group gathers in a circle, a knot which Lui's prone body on the beach soon irons out. Once again, the cut prunes the look. Arguably, then, as the film progresses its chapters become grainier. *La Pointe Courte* is not, then, organised according to alternating chapters but denser blocks of wood which become more porous as it unfolds, and it is during its final sequence that the two narrative worlds intimately neighbour each other, and in resonance with wood's internal textured ornament avoiding contact is frankly impossible.

The couple prepare to leave la Pointe Courte for Paris, together. The village celebrates, together. The celebration gets into full swing and woodwind music fills the air, and our ears, evoking wood's grain which here occasions a diegetic and an extra-diegetic oscillation: the villagers jostle on the dance floor, whilst the spectator jostles with the very opening moments of the film when this music was heard for the first time. *La Pointe Courte* thus becomes a knot in the grain of cinema encased within itself, enacting a final arabesque coil which returns us to the whorls and striations of wood's internal, textured ornament from the film's opening moments. The film, however, is by no means stupidly self-enclosed. Its wooden matrix is not stony à la Heidegger, but rather akin to a Nancean stone: modest, brute and worldly. Indeed, wood is the very kernel of our encounter with the film. It is the touch we make with it, it is how it touches us and how we make sense of and grasp it. It attunes us to the shared corporeal, material contours of the villagers' and the couple's lives. In fact, it testifies that these apparently separate lives are shared, yet still distinct, and its resonances continue beyond its final frames for *La Pointe Courte* does not leave us with any sense of being wrapped up: we do not know if the couple will remain together upon their return to Paris, or whether any of the kittens will be saved from drowning following a child's request in its closing moments. In a further jostle, we do know that Varda reincarnates this final frame in her career retrospective *The Beaches of Agnès* (2008) and, moreover, that cats litter her filmography. Our final impression of the film therefore splits according to Nancy's forked films theory, which of course cleaves like wood, and the playground game of plucking petals from a flower: a kitten drowns, a kitten lives, she loves him, she loves him not.

Such terminal indeterminacy continues with Haneke's *Time of the Wolf*.

Notes

1. Jean-Luc Godard quoted in Agnès Varda, *Varda par Agnès* (Paris: Cahiers du cinéma, 1994), p. 233. My translation.
2. Agnès Varda, 'Comment j'ai fait *La Pointe Courte*', *Positif* (2009), 58–9 (p. 59). My translation.
3. Donaldson (2014), p. 1.

4. Ally Acker, *Reel Women: Pioneers of the Cinema 1896 to the Present* (London: B. T. Batsford, 1991), pp. 306–7.
5. Varda (1994), p. 38. My translation.
6. Two press reviews dated 12 January 1956 use this term (*réserves*). One, authored by Martine Monod, appeared in *Les Lettres françaises*, whilst the other was published in *Le Monde* (author unknown). See Martine Monod, 'La Pointe Courte', *Les Lettres françaises*, 12 January 1956 and Anonymous, '*La Pointe Courte* et le spectacle du Studio Parnasse', *Le Monde*, 12 January 1956.
7. Claude Beylie, 'La Pointe Courte', *Télérama*, 6 March 1962, pp. 29–30 (p. 30). My translation.
8. Monod (1956). My translation.
9. Claude Mauriac, 'La Pointe Courte', *Le Figaro littéraire*, 14 January 1956. My translation.
10. Louis Chauvet, 'La Pointe Courte', *Le Figaro*, 10 January 1956. My translation.
11. Nancy (2005b), p. 6.
12. Kelley Conway, *Agnès Varda* (Urbana: University of Illinois Press, 2015), p. 25.
13. Orlene Denice McMahon, *Listening to the French New Wave: The Film Music and Composers of Postwar French Art Cinema* (Berlin: Peter Lang, 2014), p. 141. See also Hoai-Tran Bui, 'Agnès Varda, Filmmaker and "Godmother of the French New Wave", Dies at 90', *Washington Post*, 29 March 2019 <https://www.washingtonpost.com/local/obituaries/agnes-varda-godmother-of-the-french-new-wave-dies-at-90/2019/03/29/1bcf32d0-5225-11e9-88a1-ed346f0ec94f_story.html> (last accessed 16 May 2020) and Anonymous, 'Agnès Varda, la grande Dame de la Nouvelle Vague est morte', *Paris Match*, 29 March 2019 <https://www.parismatch.com/Culture/Cinema/Agnes-Varda-figure-de-la-Nouvelle-Vague-est-morte-1615647> (last accessed 16 May 2020).
14. André Bazin quoted in Rebecca J. DeRoo, *Agnès Varda between Film, Photography, and Art* (Oakland: University of California Press, 2017), p. 28.
15. DeRoo (2017), p. 28 and Richard Neupert, *A History of the French New Wave* (Madison: University of Wisconsin Press, 2007), p. 62.
16. DeRoo (2017), p. 21.
17. See Delphine Bénézet, *The Cinema of Agnès Varda: Resistance and Eclecticism* (London: Wallflower Press, 2014), Conway (2015) and DeRoo (2017).
18. Bénézet (2014), p. 57.
19. Pierre Uytterhoeven, 'Agnès Varda de 5 à 7', *Positif* (1962), 1–14 (p. 8).
20. Alison Smith, *Agnès Varda* (Manchester: Manchester University Press, 1998), p. 66.
21. Sandy Flitterman-Lewis, *To Desire Differently: Feminism and the French Cinema* (New York: Columbia University Press, 1996), p. 223.
22. Agnès Varda quoted in Uytterhoeven (1962), p. 13. My translation.

23. Raymond Bellour and Jean Michaud, 'Agnès Varda de A à Z', *Cinéma 61* (1961), 3–20 (p. 9). My translation.
24. McMahon (2014), p. 163.
25. Smith (1998), p. 27. See also Michel Tardy, 'Notes sur deux films d'Agnès Varda', *Image et Son* (1960), 10–11.
26. Agnès Varda quoted in T. Jefferson Kline (ed.), *Agnès Varda: Interviews* (Jackson: University Press of Mississippi, 2014), p. 9.
27. Ginette Vincendeau, '*La Pointe Courte*: How Agnès Varda "Invented" the New Wave', *Current: The Criterion Collection* (2008) <http://www.criterion.com/current/posts/497-la-pointe-courte-how-agnes-varda-invented-the-new-wave> (last accessed 6 July 2013).
28. Bernard Pingaud, 'Agnès Varda et la réalité', *Artsept* (1963), 124–41 (p. 130).
29. Varda (1994), p. 39.
30. François Truffaut, '*La Pointe Courte* d'Agnès Varda', in *Les Films de ma vie* (Paris: Flammarion, 1975), pp. 325–7 (p. 326), Flitterman-Lewis (1996), p. 221, Neupert (2007), p. 62 and Varda (1994), p. 39.
31. Gilles Deleuze, *Cinema 1: The Movement-Image*, trans. by Hugh Tomlinson and Barbara Habberjam (London: Continuum, 2005), p. 121.
32. Most irritating amongst these (mis)understandings is a trio of readings which lean on an essentialising material myopia that betrays the etymological imbrication of matrix and womb, much like Nancy's thinking does, and here it is Varda's pregnant body that comes to underwrite this mythologising process. Neupert (2007) is perhaps most nauseating here: 'Varda's earliest films were vital to revising French film language, and her inspiring pregnancy with her daughter Rosalie became symbolic of France giving birth to a new cinema' (p. 333). See also René Prédal, 'Genèse d'une oeuvre: Agnès Varda et *La Pointe Courte*', in *Agnès Varda: Le cinéma et au-delà*, ed. by Antony Fiant, Roxane Hamery and Éric Thouvenel (Rennes: Presses Universitaires de Rennes, 2009), pp. 101–12 and Frank Curot, 'L'Écriture de *La Pointe Courte*', in *Agnès Varda: Études cinématographiques*, ed. by Michel Estève (Paris: Lettres modernes Minard, 1991), pp. 85–99.
33. Agnès Varda quoted in Neupert (2007), p. 60.
34. DeRoo (2017), p. 19, Conway (2015), p. 13, Bénézet (2014), p. 43, McMahon (2014) and Smith (1998), p. 65.
35. Smith (1998), p. 64. See also Conway (2015), pp. 13–14.
36. DeRoo (2017), p. 22.
37. Ibid. p. 41.
38. Ágnes Pethő, 'Intermediality as Metalepsis in the "Cinécriture" of Agnès Varda', *Acta Universitatis Sapientiae Film and Media Studies*, 3 (2010), 69–94 (p. 74).
39. See Uytterhoeven (1962), p. 13. See also Aldo Tassone (ed.), *Que reste-t-il de la Nouvelle Vague?* (Paris: Stock, 2003), p. 331.
40. Jean-Luc Nancy, 'Making Sense', trans. by Emma Wilson, in *Making Sense: For an Effective Aesthetics*, ed. by Lorna Collins and Elizabeth Rush (Oxford: Peter Lang, 2011b), pp. 215–20 (pp. 215–16).

41. Ibid. p. 216.
42. Ibid. p. 215.
43. Jean-Luc Nancy quoted in Barker (2012), p. 186.
44. See Nancy (1991), pp. 30–1.
45. Nancy (2011b), p. 216.
46. Ibid. p. 217.
47. Ibid.
48. Nancy (2005b), p. 4.
49. Ibid.
50. Nancy (2001c), pp. 20–2.
51. James (2007), p. 69. I have replaced James's use of the original French here with Christine Irizarry's English translation.
52. Nancy (2005b), p. 67.
53. Ibid. p. 66.
54. Ibid. p. 67.
55. Ibid.
56. Ibid. p. 72.
57. Nancy (2001c), p. 72. My emphasis.
58. Ibid. p. 22.
59. Marks (2000), pp. 213–14. See also Laura U. Marks, 'Haptic Visuality: Touching with the Eyes', *Framework: The Finnish Art Review*, 2 (2004), 78–82.
60. Sobchack (1992), p. 186.
61. See Bénézet (2014), p. 51 and DeRoo (2017), p. 21.
62. Nancy (2001c), p. 42.
63. Ibid.
64. Conway (2015) also makes this allusion (p. 15) and Varda's first feature film includes further premonitory visions of later European art cinema through a series of shots which anticipate the final moments of Michelangelo Antonioni's *L'Eclisse* (1962).
65. Janus (2013), p. 76. My emphasis.

Time of the Wolf: Denatured Disaster Movie, Underwhelming Apocalypse, or the New Normal?

if now you turn on the TV, in every newscast you see a little bit of the end of the world. But it's always far away, affecting other people . . .[1]

Disaster movies are, by narrative design, denatured, for they excessively recount the fall of civilisation, or its aftermath. In this way, we might classify such films as obscene, pornographic even, given their recourse to a surfeit of visuality. As such, we might annex disaster films to Linda Williams's 'gross', and lowly, body genres[2] – pornography, horror, melodrama – and their attendant concerns with systematic excesses and bodily fluids: cum, blood and tears, respectively.[3] Generic disaster films are not strangers to these fluids. They ooze in all sorts of ways and add their own viscous matter to this taxonomy: guts, slime and some good old-fashioned goo. According to cinema at least, the end of the world tends to bring out the worst in us, and the undead, our alien neighbours, Mother Nature and so on, whilst turning us on.[4] Who, after all, wants to die alone?

Time of the Wolf, Michael Haneke's seventh feature film, is rife with these fluids and impulses. Indeed, according to the bodily fluid index, *Time of the Wolf* is a bona fide disaster movie: blood, tears and vomit – a digestive, gustatory ejaculate – all make early appearances. Following the unexpected, and off-screen, murder of Georges, the claret splash of blood that bedecks Anne's face is the first indicator of the mortal blow; her vomiting confirms the horror and definitiveness of it all, as a sort of deferred bloodshed. These bodily fluids continue to splatter throughout the film's runtime: the horse's blood (sacrificially?) spilt; the tears shed by traumatised families; Benny's inexplicably bloody nose. Yet from its opening minutes, *Time of the Wolf* shows itself to be what Catherine Wheatley describes as a denatured disaster movie: 'an attempt to provide an antidote to the dramatization of disaster in media coverage'.[5] Haneke's antidote, however, lies in making things worse, that is, in exacerbating the apocalyptic idiom further. Haneke, for instance, assiduously applies his irritant to the film's plot by amputating the disaster itself from his disaster movie, despite having originally written a script which examined the fall of civilisation.[6] Post 9/11, however, Haneke believed that audiences would no longer need to witness this collapse and over the course of *Time of the Wolf*'s two-hour runtime we are never privy to what exactly has come to pass. All that is revealed is the slow burn of human existence as it struggles to limp on.

Haneke, however, opens his diegesis with a world which substantially predates even that of the decimated society on display, including excised script segments during the development stage: the bucolic, which, as we shall come to see, arabesques across the film. The uncharacteristic total silence of the opening credits thus gives way to a pastoral world, the brown and green hues of tree trunks and wild grass seemingly accompanied by the sound of rushing water, intimating the lushness of a nearby waterfall. This would-be Arcadia, however, is soon voided, its associative tranquillity intruded upon by the approach of the dark blue, metallic mass of a multi-purpose vehicle. The spritely melody of running water in actuality the rumble of rubber on the forest floor, Haneke's unusually mobile camera, as it tracks the vehicle's movements, redolently echoing the erstwhile imagined watery winding. The car stops and Georges, Anne, Eva and Benny descend. Haneke is, of course, a director who does not hesitate to make flotsam and jetsam of the family (demonstrated in the following chapter), describing it in interview as 'the origin of all conflicts'.[7] Tension, then, for Haneke is the very substance of the family and he quickly sets about dismantling this vessel for received idea/ls by killing off the paterfamilias – (t)his death a marker of the film's adoption of 'a sort of Occam's Razor in which everything possible is removed from a scenario to find out exactly what it is that makes the situation possible'.[8] In such terms *Time of the Wolf* realises a strain of cinema that appeals to a particularly Nancean palate. Georges's death, which the film's title prophesises, constitutes an unusually punctual event within the film, and whilst it hints at generic containment – his murder is essentially the result of a desperate survivalist act native to and endorsed by the disaster movie – it likewise begs obscure questions about the permanence of any doomsday because in narrowly intimating the recent cataclysm, his death becomes a microcosm of the enigmatic catastrophe that drives *Time of the Wolf*'s narrative intrigue. His killing, moreover, asks whether the world, as we know it, ever ends just once, or is always ending, intermittently slipping away from us. 'Georges' is, in fact, just one 'Georges' in a series of many, as are Anne, Eva and Benny, who recedes from view only to return with another face. On film, no one ever really dies, after all, except for the stock itself, complicating cinema's, and Haneke's, relationship to the end of the world.[9]

Wish You Were Here: Postcards to Papa from the Apocalypse

Time of the Wolf is an unusual text amongst Haneke's filmography because, to date, it has garnered very little critical attention.[10] 'Of all the films within [. . .] Haneke's oeuvre', writes Evan Torner, '*Time of the Wolf* has been seen as the most inscrutable and the most impotent'.[11] The small pockets of criticism that do exist home in on the pervasive lack of information to form something of a palindrome with its critical terrain. Tellingly, what little there is leans on a murky constellation – concepts are frequently bracketed off, indicating a caveat: this is perhaps only the end of the world as we know it. Key narrative players, 'the city', 'the train', 'civilisation' and the 'event' itself are all subjected to such rhetorical murk, whilst the conditions that the 'event' itself produces are treated likewise: 'In this post-apocalyptic order', notes Mattias Frey, 'the "necessities" of modern culture have instantly lost all value.'[12] Through 'its extreme restraint with information', resonance could be said to be the film's fundamental structure: 'the event' 'resonates'.[13] Normative (linguistic) codes no longer hold and in her account of the film Wheatley broaches this absence dialectically, judging *Time of the Wolf* to represent, but not to inform: '*information* is what is confined to the off-screen space, prompting not so much a desire to see, as a desire to know. The problem is thus defined in terms not of morality, but epistemology.'[14] Curiously, for both Wheatley and Frey, this lack gives life to nightmares foretold in Haneke's earlier work, *Funny Games* (1997) and *The Seventh Continent*, a suggestion that endows *Time of the Wolf* with a pseudo-spiritualism, as if it (re)incarnates the concerns of these antecedent cinematic efforts. Such a sentiment is akin to the 'return to some sort of animism' that David Sorfa suggests is operative in the film's imagery, its juxtaposition of the horse's spilt blood alongside the coming of the much-needed rain implying as much.[15] *Time of the Wolf* thus flirts with the supernatural and the film fully commits to such otherworldly communion when Eva writes a letter to her dead father.

Eva's epistolary endeavour serves as a backdrop to the information that Haneke does give us in a derisively and delightfully conventional manner – through a news bulletin-style montage. As Eva narrates her letter in voiceover, a series of static images make up this slow-paced synopsis, illustrating the decay and detritus of the film's unspecified disaster. Each still fills the screen and stages a mise-en-abyme-like effect as smaller details pierce the spectator's vision: a key dangling blithely, a camembert hungrily consumed by ants, yellowing, peeling sticky tape. This graveyard of office supplies effectively volumises the film, relaying images of anonymous peoples, landscapes and body parts that culminate in a 'delicate' Dürer watercolour 'with what would appear to be the stem of a mushroom cloud on the horizon'.[16] The apocalypse alluded to, no less. Yet, in framing the recent devastation alongside Eva's epistolarity, *Time of the Wolf* transforms it into consumable, bite-sized chunks, literal clichés like postcard emissaries from another time and place.[17] The film's swollen body metonymically suggests a flood, a plague, a deluge, or some other all-consuming affliction which may have caused *Time of the Wolf*'s rampage, and it is in this manner, through its bloated self, that the film offers a discreet mediatic critique – presenting the spectator with a vivid envisioning of the collapse of civilisation in a visual style that is self-consciously at odds with its pared down reality. Much like the inevitability of its disappearing technologies, then, cinema once again betrays its material limitations when representing the end of the world. Like turning on the television set, we see little bits of the end of the world, yet Haneke achieves such cliché in a markedly arch and mocking fashion, for he suggests that what remains of us is office supplies and leftovers. We are what we don't eat.

Despite its apparent absence of 'normalcy',[18] Eva's epistolary episode is an example of the film's vestigial clinging whereby *Time of the Wolf* is no longer simply about envisioning the collapse of civilisation, but instead becomes a meditation on what would happen were we to continue to maintain the same moeurs if the end truly were nigh: values such as the nuclear family, pets and private property, which it emphatically jettisons during its early stages. Cast out of their holiday home from hell for the next twenty minutes of the film, the remaining members of the Laurent family are pursued by an aesthetic and narrative schema that deftly articulates the breakdown of societal bonds as well as those of the sensory-motor schema where all we are left with is pure optical and sound situations.[19] Sequences are shrouded in darkness, saturated in a white-greyish fog – a visual, material echo of the gunshot, this ether perhaps a remnant of the mystery cataclysm – or detail is swallowed up in long shots steeped in prelapsarian greens. Abstract, shadowy shapes, flickers of faraway movement, black screens, fires crackling, masticating, slurping, sniffing, bicycle wheels turning over and over and over, the near-persistent rustling of synthetic fibres. The film thus proves to be a very slow apocalypse indeed, rhythmically queering critical and societal debates that centre on questions of normative (cinematic) work, waste and worth, that is, productivity and temporality.[20] Disaster movies are certainly no stranger to interminable waiting. There is, of course, no such thing as the timely cataclysm. Fundamentally, the genre relies upon time having run out. The apocalypse always comes 'too early'.[21] The appropriate action is always taken 'too late'.[22] These decalages wend the film towards the temporal-spatial matrix of resonance by means of the false Arcadia the family trudge through and which uselessly blossoms into the verdures of spring: pointless for there is simply no place, or rather no need, for such beauty here. Snow, moreover, would have been more helpful in a water-scarce world. In this way, *Time of the Wolf* deploys the often-overlooked meaning of apocalypse – renewal – which the film's mise-en-scène literalises.[23] Its pretty redundancy quietly, yet palpably, hints at this clinging to superfluous values, for this fertility frames shots or sequences wherein the makeshift vestiges of a pre-apocalyptic world are foregrounded.

These vestiges centre on shelter, companionship, private property, work, funeral rites, community, care, justice and the home. Having lost everything, our bereft trio soon meet a lone and insolent adolescent wanderer, who begrudgingly expands their familial contours, whilst they attempt to reach a railway station from where they hope to catch a train back to the city. Their entire journey to terminus is set against wide pastoral expanses. Upon arrival, incapable of observing the fraught entente of the outpost, the young wanderer steals a pair of glasses and then retreats to the surrounding woods. It is against this ligneous backdrop that Eva and the boy form a tender but tentative companionship – each guaranteed a friend for the end of the world. In the context of this fledgling friendship, private property, in a world without rule, is restored through the return of the stolen spectacles, and following this gesture a return to normalcy precipitates as Eva's epistolarity explains through the use of a work schedule illustrated by scenes of foraging. Horror, though, next erupts with the death of the Romanian child, and while he is laid to rest community literally arrives as flaming torches illuminate the grassy horizon. Care shown to an aged relative is not paid in kind by a subsection of the community where prejudice and accusations burst into fisticuffs. Yet despite these differences, the ideal of home is soon privileged by the film as the station is captured in long shot hemmed by waving ears of corn. With the theft of a goat, any threat to this sense of home is sought to be expelled and community-led justice penetrates the lone wolf's wooden cloak, impinging too on the burgeoning friendship before home is reaffirmed. These events constitute the abovementioned slow burn of human existence, and the steady pulse of the film's pastoral register, which rhapsodises remnants of the pre-apocalyptic world order, forms a woody matrix that limns the entire film. These ligneous textures loop and whorl, they arabesque, the beats of their colours, textures, rustlings string together its episodes where very little else does

Figure 4 *The Time of the Wolf* (Michael Haneke, 2003). Reproduced with kind permission of the director.

and suggest a search for meaning in an uncanny world. When this search, however, appears to be paying off, the film's lignin matrix emphatically derails it.

Time of the Wolf ends just as it began, with a look upon a wooded expanse, which is optimistically shot from a moving train, implying a potential happy ending for the outpost inhabitants (Figure 4). In a final application of the generic irritant, though, Haneke never confirms whether our unhappy few are on the train. We will never know. Does the train predate the (in)action of the film, or follow it, or is it internal to it, endowing the film with a Möbius strip-like structure – an unending loop or whorl?[24] We never find out. Such ambiguity, moreover, exceeds narrativity and takes over the cinematic itself. Kinetic, visual, acoustic, *Time of the Wolf*'s closing minutes embody the cinematic in its most basic form. Kinetic, visual, acoustic, and divested and dispossessed of diegesis, this train tracking shot serves as a placeholder for cinema; it moves, it images, it sounds. Materially and verbally, then, it signifies the work's doing, its manner of doing and making: it makes sense possible and in doing so it literalises Nancean *sens* – sensory, directional, pregnant – as well as the tautological meaningfulness of *sens* and *monde*. Indeed, in the space of the auditorium a meaningful world always literally precedes us and here it relentlessly moves towards it, but never arrives. The cinematised wooden expanse thus resonates, it is the very kernel of our encounter with the film, and it is in this way that it becomes the film's ultimate vestige: of life as we know it, or have been coming to know it in the film, of the happy ending, and of cinema itself, which is always the last thing a film about the end of the world ineluctably and inexorably clings to.

At the Time of Writing: Running Out of Track, Water and Time

Those cited here were not speaking at a time of acute climate change chaos. At the time of writing today, this climate is very different. As in any true disaster movie, time is running out. In just a decade, we are more urgently understanding the damage wrought by single-use plastics, fast fashion, virtual water. We have overindulged in what Barbara Kingsolver breathlessly describes as

> our mass hallucinatory fantasy in which the megatons of waste we dump in our rivers and bays are not poisoning the water, the hydrocarbons we pump into the air are not changing the climate, overfishing is not depleting the oceans, fossil fuels will never run out, wars that kill masses of civilians are an appropriate way to keep our hands on what's left, we are not desperately overdrawn at the environmental bank, and, really, the kids are all right.[25]

Water scarcity is hardly a fantasy, it is a pressing reality and a growing international concern from which the global north will not escape. When the water runs out, the fantasy effectively dries up. *Time of the Wolf*'s critique thus materialises just as the seam between fantasy (or nightmare) and reality dematerialises. Increasingly, this will be the new normal. But are we attuned to the warning signs? Ragnarök will rise, but in resonance we might be able to change the ending – not so much a case of 'are we there yet?', but 'are we listening yet?' Terminus approaching . . . next stop, *The Seventh Continent*.

Notes

1. Michael Haneke quoted in Peter Brunette, *Michael Haneke* (Chicago: University of Illinois Press, 2010), p. 103.
2. Linda Williams, 'Film Bodies: Gender, Genre, and Excess', *Film Quarterly*, 44 (1991), 2–13 (p. 2). See also Brigitte Peucker, *The Material Image: Art and the Real in Film* (Stanford: Stanford University Press, 2006), pp. 129–58.
3. Williams (1991), p. 3.
4. See Wheeler Winston Dixon, *Visions of the Apocalypse: Spectacles of Destruction in American Cinema* (London: Wallflower Press, 2003), p. 2 and p. 4.
5. Catherine Wheatley, *Michael Haneke's Cinema: The Ethic of the Image* (Oxford: Berghahn Books, 2009), p. 148.
6. Nick James, 'Darkness Falls', *Sight & Sound*, 13 (2003), 16–18 (p. 17).
7. Christopher Sharrett, 'The World That Is Known', *Kinoeye*, 4 (2004) <http://www.kinoeye.org/04/01/interview01.php> (last accessed 22 May 2020).

8. David Sorfa, 'Uneasy Domesticity in the Films of Michael Haneke', *Studies in European Cinema*, 3 (2006), 93–104 (p. 100).
9. See Dixon (2003), p. 3.
10. Discussion of the film is also missing from Christopher Rowe's *Michael Haneke: The Intermedial Void* (Evanston: Northwestern University Press, 2017) as well as Elsie Walker's *Hearing Haneke: The Sound Tracks of a Radical Auteur* (Oxford: Oxford University Press, 2018).
11. Evan Torner, 'Civilization's Endless Shadow: Haneke's *Time of the Wolf*', in *A Companion to Michael Haneke*, ed. by Roy Grundmann (Oxford: Wiley-Blackwell, 2010), pp. 532–50 (p. 532).
12. Mattias Frey, 'A Cinema of Disturbance: The Films of Michael Haneke in Context', *Senses of Cinema* (2010) <http://sensesofcinema.com/2010/great-directors/michael-haneke/> (last accessed 9 May 2013).
13. Ibid.
14. Wheatley (2009), p. 148.
15. Sorfa (2006), p. 101.
16. Wheatley (2009), p. 139. See also Frey (2010).
17. See Lauren Elkin, *Flâneuse: Women Walk the City in Paris, New York, Tokyo, Venice and London* (London: Chatto & Windus, 2016) and Susan Stewart, *On Longing: Narratives of the Miniature, the Gigantic, the Souvenir, the Collection* (Durham, NC: Duke University Press, 1993).
18. Torner (2010), p. 534.
19. See Deleuze (2005) and Gilles Deleuze, *Cinema 2: The Time-Image*, trans. by Hugh Tomlinson and Robert Galeta (London: The Athlone Press, 1989).
20. See Karl Schoonover, 'Wastrels of Time: Slow Cinema's Labouring Body, the Political Spectator and the Queer', in *Slow Cinema*, ed. by Tiago de Luca and Nuno Barradas Jorge (Edinburgh: Edinburgh University Press, 2016), pp. 153–68.
21. See Williams (1991), p. 9.
22. Ibid.
23. See Kirsten Moana Thompson, *Apocalyptic Dread: American Film at the Turn of the Millennium* (Albany: State University of New York Press, 2007).
24. See Scott Loren and Jörg Metelmann, *Irritation of Life: The Subversive Melodrama of Michael Haneke, David Lynch and Lars Von Trier* (Marburg: Schüren, 2013), p. 80. Loren and Metelmann suggest that the final scene of *Caché* 'create[s] a Möbius strip, as it might be inserted meta-leptically before the opening sequence'. See also Thomas Elsaesser, 'Performative Self-Contradictions: Michael Haneke's Mind Games', in *A Companion to Michael Haneke*, ed. by Roy Grundmann (Oxford: Wiley-Blackwell, 2010), pp. 53–74.
25. Barbara Kingsolver quoted in Bennett (2010), pp. 50–1.

Teenage Dreams in *The Seventh Continent*

– but there are only six continents.[1]

From the end of the world as we know it in *Time of the Wolf*, we move into a world that is all too familiar. Released in 1989, Michael Haneke's first feature film, *The Seventh Continent*, distils three days in the life of a bourgeois family of three, Georg, Anna and Eva – who else? – across three consecutive years, 1987, 1988 and 1989, to produce a synecdochic representation of their diurnal routine. Their 'rote activity',[2] rhetorically imitated by many existing responses to the film, which habitually address the austerity, sterility and superficiality of the Schober family's daily lives that results in the collapse in communication amongst them.[3] Scott Foundas, for instance, highlights how the 'superficial sterility, of meticulously organized surfaces stifl[es] human individuality',[4] while Haneke likewise attaches such depthlessness to his on-screen subjects whom he considers as 'less characters than projection surfaces for the sensibilities of the viewer'.[5] Outwardly ordinary on the surface of things, then, as the film unfolds the family clandestinely resolve to take their lives – school-age daughter included – marooned within the suffocating sanctuary of their home and surrounded by the ruinous landscape of the worldly possessions that they systematically destroy in the hours before their deaths. Their collective suicide is thus widely interpreted as an act of rebellion against the 'narcotizing'[6] panopticon of modernity wherein the objects they ostensibly own, but which arguably own them, unflinchingly scrutinise them, and which transforms them into 'mere appendages to th[is] object world'.[7]

As his first feature film, then, *The Seventh Continent* starts the big freeze typically associated with Haneke's initial trio of German-language films: the glaciation trilogy (*The Seventh Continent*, *Benny's Video* [1992], *71 Fragments of a Chronology of Chance* [1994]). Although Haneke himself introduced critics to this affective climate, discussing his work in terms of an 'emotional glaciation' (*emotionale Vergletscherung*),[8] the director reportedly 'disdains' this nomenclature and, likewise, I find such a designation excessively cold.[9] For despite the crises of isolation and abundance they recount, even in its title *The Seventh Continent* hints at thaw because, depending on your perspective, the seventh continent is itself a figment, a work of geographical excess: implicitly nodding towards the diegetic senses of emptiness and abundance that cause the family's alienation, whilst intimating the potential for fantasy. Indeed, even as the family seek to purge themselves of matter, they create more, their efforts to cease their (over-)consumption requiring a trip to the hardware store. This chapter will therefore thaw the stylistic, critical and authorial coldness almost automatically ascribed to *The Seventh Continent* by recalibrating the autonomy of objects within the film – a soapy windscreen, a polychromatic child's drawing, a touristic billboard poster, a placid fish tank – and tracing how water, what we will come to understand as Haneke's own cinematic material *par excellence*, percolates the film's imagery and where its viscosity returns in a juvenile form.

Three Lost Souls Living in a Fish Bowl Year after Year

Introducing us to what has variously been described as the cage, tank, tomb or cave-like structure of the Schober family car, the first moments of *The Seventh Continent* are conceived as quintessential and systematic hallmarks of glaciation. Pessimistically understood as instilling a 'deathly stillness' through a style characteristic of Haneke's putatively frigid filmmaking[10] – static camera, unforgiving long shots, spare mise-en-scène, automatous human subjects – the sequence has also been said to show a 'cleansing ritual' akin to rebaptism.[11] At nearly four minutes in length, and almost exclusively shot from one position, sandwiched somewhere between the two sets of car seats, the wet viscera that squirm about counter this stillness. The human body, however, is not the site of this discharge, the eruption of the inside outside, but an observer to, or even a part of, these writhing guts, for our family is resident in the bowels of a machine: a carwash. These mechanical entrails whizz and whir about the car's exterior, covering it in a white, soapy, ghostly substance. A number plate, a headlight, a tyre and finally the windscreen are all individually displayed, the sight of each organ scored by the fluid drone of a pressurised jet of water. The car is thus catalogued as a *corpus corporum* which is soon succeeded by a *corpus imāginum* thanks to the water that sloshes about its exterior. Lathered up, the soapy cloak that bedecks the car graphically hints at the tapered spikes of icicles, the effect of this microcosmic ice age accentuated once the camera penetrates the vehicle's metal shell via the mottled, white expanse that stretches across the image and the icy tracks it suggests. Despite first appearances, however, this plashy precipitate is not frozen, but slowly flowing, trickling and then suddenly gushing down the windscreen's glass pane. The sounds of the automated water hasten this melting, for throughout the sequence we hear it splashing about the car, acoustically, kinaesthetically and materially drawing up its contours as its jets ricochet around the (unseen) space of the carwash. Much like Nancy's thinking, then, from the film's outset we are immersed in listening to a set of insides, and all the corporeal, orificial and sensual stakes such listening entails. This immersion marks the first warming of the big thaw.

Alongside the car(wash), however, the sequence likewise houses a bleakly aestheticised sentimentality, for it recalls one of Haneke's first experiences of film where he somatically remembers the theatre 'like a car'.[12] Indeed, rather than a tomb, tank or cave, *The Seventh Continent* could be said to open onto a cinema: the darkness and stillness that reign alongside the immobile audience not deathly, but cinematic. *The Seventh Continent* steers us further towards this impression by means of the Schober family car windscreen, which operates as a second cinematic screen. Whereas the image immediately before us, the car-cum-cinema, remains unchanged – camera position is constant; human figures statically frame the scene, planted on opposite sides of the car throughout; the hum of the carwash continues – different images effloresce upon the windscreen. These images further embody what is variously cast as the internal multiplicity, or resonance of Nancy's account of the image, owing to water's consonant material multiplicity comprised of visual, kinaesthetic, tactile and sonorous elements. Here, then, it is water, not light or wood, which sustains the image. Sprayed and scattered across the glass outer plane, the image fleetingly flowers there until it trickles or washes away to reveal another fluid surface, water's materiality the register upon which the image continues to appear. In this way, the windscreen, and by extension the Schober family car, 'serv[e] as image catchers'.[13] This drives us further towards a key Nancean cinematic trope, for the car, and its particular relationship to cinema, enjoys an especial privilege in the work of Nancy and his observations of and conversations with Iranian filmmaker Abbas Kiarostami. Here the car emerges as a double agent: as an 'actant' in both the waning and securing of the cinematic image in all its resonant materiality, a contradictory gesture which recalls cinema's bifurcating worldliness. Complicit in its disappearance through the image's ricocheting off the car's many glossy surfaces, whereby it 'lose[s] focus, becoming aimless and blurred in the thick traffic and reflections bouncing from windshield to rearview mirror',[14] these same surfaces are operative in 'the tireless picturing of cars, car windows, windshields, and rearview mirrors that act as the capturing agents of various *views*'.[15] Nancy crystallises this tension with the following:[16]

> The capturing of images in a film [. . .] captures nothing if it is not to let it go free again. The framing, the light, the length of a take, the camera's movement contribute to free a motion, which is that of a presence in the process of making itself present.[17]

It is thus the internal multiplicity, the resonance of the image that frees this motion, this movement, and what Nancy calls 'kinematic truth'.[18]

Accordingly, Peter Szendy considers how Nancy conceives the car 'as the *clutch* of [. . .] film – of every film in which it appears – [. . .] in terms of the *routing* that directs and regulates cinematic experience as such'.[19] Cinema as clutch iterates a sense of discontinuous motion, mirroring the motility of *sens*, and its distribution in distinct articles; it reiterates the evidentiary's grasping without seizing, reminding us that to film the world is only ever to approach it. Indeed, according to Nancy, the windscreen (re)doubles the presence of cinema in film through what he calls 'the rhetoric of a "show within a show"', loosely naming this cinematic doubling 'the "filmic" element'.[20] This filmic element distils cinema from film, by first mounting an understanding of the latter 'in its most literal, technical, and material acceptation: as film stock',[21] then in terms of its material, technical distinctions from the other arts, and finally in its most resonant incarnation: as image catcher, as signalling device, as antenna, as windvane, essentially as sensitive to waveforms.[22] Pursuing film's etymological depths, and its Latinate roots in (the) skin – a material and linguistic complement to the co-option of the epidermis into Nancy's cinematic *corpus imāginum* discussed in the second chapter – this skin show leaves us with 'thinness and nothing else', which comes to define film's distinct, resistant 'support'.[23] Unless, of course, addressing its sensitivity to light, which it effortlessly yields to, and which engenders a sort of luminous invagination:

> The film support seems akin to light itself, and it is not the sole material support in cinema: a light beam must travel across it and carry with it a picture until a screen intercepts it, which offers yet another kind of kinship with light in order to restore without absorbing or returning it the light it is thus stopping. The support of motion pictures is at the same time a kind of relation of light with light, holding it all suspended in a delicate equilibrium.[24]

Adrienne Janus is again apposite here, describing how '[t]he passage or route opened with the movement of the filmic image is without ground, but with "sol" [. . .]: "sol" as the fluid suspension of a colloid solid in a liquid as the chemistry of "film"'.[25] She positions Phillip Warnell's *Outlandish* as emblematic of this chemistry where

> the 'Sol' of Nancy's filmic image, as the fluid suspension of a colloid solid in a liquid, is doubled by the suspension in a raised aquarium constructed on the deck of a boat 'of that most inside-out of creatures', an octopus.[26]

Warnell's film effectively 'dramatize[s]' the "inside" of philosophical thought', transforming Nancy's thought into an octopus.[27] In *The Seventh Continent* Haneke becomes something of a teuthologist, dramatising the inside of philosophical thought via the inside of the Schober family car, via the windscreen. Its glass pane acts as sol, its effervescing images colloidal, which doubly dramatise the insides of Nancy's thought through their hydrous production, rather than by invaginated light. Cinema, however, need not be so excoriating in its adoption of theory's textures,[28] it need not transform Nancy's thought into an octopus, and as such 'the "filmic" element is present in a much more intimate way, in the very texture of [its] images'.[29]

Operative within the texture of *The Seventh Continent*'s images here is water, and, together with the car, it constitutes its kinematic truth, its clutch, and accordingly, it echoes the resonant listening that Nancy's philosophy demands of its readers because akin to Nancy's thought, we must attune to its material specificity. This demand is encountered in *The Evidence of Film* when (in parenthesis) Nancy asks that we 'try to hear the verb "to film" also as if we spoke not of recording a picture, but of *fluidifying, jellifying,* or *crystallizing* what the lens "catches"', as if coating the verb, and its issue, in a thin viscous membrane.[30] We can sense this parenthetical demand at work in Nancy's account of the (cinematic) car as an image catcher:

> A ribbon (like the roads travelled), a gel, pane of glass and water, all at once, it is a sort of capturing fluid that grips the living and holds it in twenty-four discrete pictures each second, only to fluidify their sequence instantaneously in a continual look.[31]

Indeed, like *sens* and the auditory, to film/*filmer*, in Nancean terms, is shot through with a linguistic and conceptual multiplicity and each time that we 'hear' it, we must recalibrate its frequency. Already, then, we can see how to film/*filmer* can be(gin to be) catalogued as *corpus imāginum*, as fluidifying, jellifying, crystallising. Laminar and decidedly liquid, to film/*filmer* oozes subtleties in meaning and, moreover, in materiality, espousing fluidity, viscosity and clarity, and thereby channels Janus's thesis on water as the elemental source of the image across Nancy's writing. According to Janus's taxonomy, this lubric undercurrent can be sensed, and is 'secreted', as or at the 'watery ground' of the material multiplicity that the visual, musical, poetic, tactile, olfactory, gustatory, kinaesthetic image is.[32] In 'the liquid sonorities (sound waves) of music and poetry',[33] in 'the humidity in the breath'[34] as these are sung, spoken or hummed along to, 'in the viscosity of the surface of an oil painting',[35] in 'the "luminous chemistry" [whence] the filmic image is born'[36] and in the swell of 'flocculations of sensual material' that touch, envelop, penetrate us.[37]

These secretions, moreover, are not exclusive to Nancy's thinking on the image. Like holding up a seashell to the ear, through which our body and environment resonates, rushes that we mistake for the far-off ocean, the inherent curiosity of water's materiality dovetails many facets of Nancy's materialist ontology. Water, for instance, insulates in the same space-time that it immerses, and as such when submerged in a body of water we only ever feel ourselves indirectly, ultimately reminding us of the unbridgeable distance, yet 'ambiguous proximity', of bodies characteristic of Nancean philosophy which resonance exacerbates.[38] Likewise, its rushes serve as a watery microcosm of Nancy's noisy account of being, of the sonority of being-with, and it embodies our singular-plural existence because it comes in many forms which unproblematically co-exist: its liquid, solid and gaseous states able to occupy the same landscape. Water, and seashells, thus attest to a mineral technicity that articulates and reticulates our compound mode of being, as well as to our adventuring into and with the sense of the world.

For Nancy, this laminate, liquid understanding of to film/*filmer* originates in the 'gelatinous mass of photosensitive grains'[39] that make up film's sensitive skin and upon which 'secretions of visual-tactile-kinaesthetic sense' once caught pool;[40] and it is reflected in Nancy's wider encounter with cinema, describing how we 'sense [its images] flow before our eyes like the surface of a great glistening river',[41] doubling the aqueous airs of this stream of images in detailing how they are whispered towards us in the dark.[42] Evocative of the whole articulatory cinema of the mouth – 'o', 'o', 'o' – and of cinema as an epic of the mouth, what whispers in the dark here is the (interior of the) Schober family car: (sensitive) film (stock), cinema(tic movement), kinematic truth, water, glass, metal, secretions of visual-acoustic-tactile-kinaesthetic sense that fluidify, jellify, crystallise. It is the windscreen that does the work of these verbs, fluidifying, jellifying, crystallising the world, only to relinquish its grasp on it once more, fluidifying, jellifying, crystallising over and over again. Indeed, the windscreen immerses us in the omnipresent, wave-like swell of sonority, that is, the temporal-spatial matrix of resonance, thereby attenuating the thrust of succession.

Any deathly stillness is therefore misplaced, for this space sprouts a multiplicity of images. Death does not reign here, renewal does. We might, then, reconceive water as the vital, life-giving force that flows through *The Seventh Continent* – and, as we shall see later, throughout Haneke's oeuvre – rather than the film's freezing agent, that is, the raw material of glaciation. It is therefore not so much glaciation that occurs between spectator and film during the opening moments of *The Seventh Continent*, but rather condensation: our encounter with its imagery visually, aurally and kinaesthetically filtered through a body of water. Thus, we do not simply gain a metaphorical sense of water – the image flows with water, a flow reflected by the actual flow of images whereby our eyes and ears are then filled with this current – or a mimetic one whereby our bodies imitate its torrent as full-bodied undulating shudders, as moist brows, as tears. Instead we enjoy a resonant one where water precipitates an alternative economy of attending to the film's imagery. In these opening minutes, then, water is the film's clutch, directing and regulating cinematic experience: its very textures coterminous with its exercise and this exercise coterminous with its very textures, sounding out upon its different material registers – visual, acoustic, kinetic – like *La Pointe Courte*'s wooden matrix. In *The Seventh Continent*, however, this exercise pools and this hydrous clutch lends its aqueous architectonics to another watery body which in turn comes to operate within the very texture of the film's images as an altogether more intimate, more discreet filmic element: Eva, the Schober family's school-age daughter.

Fluid Vicissitudes

Any initial appeal for understanding water as Haneke's cinematic material *par excellence*, or Eva as *The Seventh Continent*'s filmic element, however, might at first risk reading like a serious misapprehension of the film. After all, upon first encountering the Schober family car we are unaware of Eva's presence within it, and, moreover, within the film, whilst structurally and narratively, the film defies the transitory, flow logic of water through its repetitious vignettes, and could convincingly be read as a tale of stagnation.[43] The abovementioned pooling of multiply material secretions thus risks not producing the dynamism of rivers, streams and ocean currents, or indeed the fluidifying, jellifying, crystallising of film, but rather the repulsiveness of polluted water. Water, though, floods the visual, acoustic, tactile, kinaesthetic textures of *The Seventh Continent*.

What's more, historical and contemporary debates about water, its uses, abuses, ownership and meanings, perfectly align with Haneke's filmmaking project. Fears and frustration over scarcity and abundance, for instance, specifically how modern water management systems consistently create scarcity out of abundance, parallel Haneke's tales of alienation born from excess. Increasingly, too, we partake in 'an atomized relationship' with this resource.[44] It arrives in the home, and marketplace, via taps, toilets, showerheads, washing machines, exoticised single-use plastic bottles, and we are largely ignorant of the actual water content of much of our daily lives – what Tony Allan calls virtual water. If, for example, you indulge in a hearty breakfast before washing, you have already consumed three baths' worth of water before you have dipped your toes in the tub. Even a solitary slice of dry toast will set you back 80 litres.[45] Virtual water is, then, the hidden hydrous cost of human consumption, and such practices, or rather forgetting, involute 'turn[ing] [...] threats into new opportunities for capital accumulation', much like the Schober family's predicament: their apparently anti-consumerist rampage produces, and requires, more stuff.[46] Our watery estrangement thus mirrors Haneke's film worlds: the commons ever more enclosed.[47] The private (urban) swimming pool perhaps aphorises such abundance and enclosure and, as Christopher Brown and Pam Hirsch note, cinematic pools 'are often deployed in critiques of the idle rich'.[48] In life, as on film, though, water resonates. '[S]imultaneously an economic input, an aesthetic reference, a religious symbol, a public service, a private good, a cornerstone of public health, and a biophysical necessity for humans and ecosystems alike', its resonances operate discursively too.[49] Too much water, in the form of the deluge, delivers devastation and death.[50] Too little water, specifically the desert, constitutes 'a locus for cultural critique',[51] in particular capitalism, becoming an especially savage attack when considered alongside California's position as one of the world's biggest exporters of virtual water, the home of Hollywood transformed into the scorched earth of countercultural renewal, and making Haneke's *Time of the Wolf* a formidable hydrous parable.[52]

The water giants that populate Haneke's diegetic universes are not, then, the urinators of yore, but the no less deistic sounding Veolia and Suez, and the less august Thames Water.[53] These giants flow through the Schober family's domestic routine, illustrated by running taps, teeth brushing, gargling, showering, bathing, feeding the fish, whilst in the rare glimpses we get of the outdoors it is often raining, including as the Schober family car exits the carwash, droplets caught in the flicker of its headlights, demonstrating the futility of their bourgeois outing. Significantly, water also flanks the Schober family's scenes of destruction – their anti-montage sequence prefaced by Anna filling the coffeemaker and concluded with her and Georg flushing their life savings down the toilet – and it is there at the very end, its final task to liquidate life itself.

Indeed, water, that life-giving, vital fluid, floods a diegetic universe riddled with death, dying, suicide and murder, and we can likewise plot the recurrence of watery spaces within Haneke's films. Love affairs, for example, start out on the floor of public restrooms. Affective bursts take place amongst the aisles of a supermarket in front of bottled water, whilst intergenerational confrontations are forced in the office bathroom. Children play, and compete, in swimming pools, by swimming pools and fresh water before something all the more sinister replaces the ludic quality of these moments. Just what, for instance, is Martin in *The White Ribbon* playing at on that ledge? More banally, the domesticity implied by kitchens with their sinks and taps abounds and, as we saw above, Haneke's entire cinematic cosmos is inaugurated by a very watery space: the cleansing carwash. David Sorfa echoes this faith-based logic when discussing the coming of a much-needed deluge in *Time of the Wolf* – its arrival juxtaposed with the horse's spilt blood. Yet water here is equally and powerfully caught up with the consumerist and capitalist concerns of Haneke's first feature film, for it is an expensive, exploitative commodity. Rain again enjoys a powerful agency in the final moments of *Code Unknown* (2000) as a heavy downpour beats down on Paris whilst an incessant drum beat dominates the soundtrack: a pulse that lends collective contours to a film dedicated to social fragmentation. Water, then, witnesses extremes of sentiment, it prompts fear and desperation and it binds us together as well as to our daily routines.

Filling and flushing, the Schober family's bodies, moreover, are always limned with the mundane, in common (hydrous) sounds of the everyday, as Lisa Coulthard carefully describes in a reading attuned to Nancean listening and the 'reshaping of the soundscape toward the resonant – to the sounds themselves rather than the meaning they carry':[54] 'we hear the acoustic details of the sounds of a polyester sock being pulled over skin and body hair with a precision and volume that makes palpable the unbearable, oppressive routine of the family'.[55] This sonorous portrait that skims the outer body is reminiscent of Haneke's approach to filming the Schober family car, suggesting a material equivalence between flesh and metal, the visceral and the mechanical. With the car cleaned, it is in these moments that we see Eva for the first time, occupying the space in the car we initially assumed Haneke had reserved for us. Instead we find ourselves likely imbricated with her point of view, which retrospectively enables our own.

The car passes a billboard that displays the lush promise of the far away: Australia. If we fast-forward to the film's cataclysmic end, its visual mention here chillingly rings out because Australia is the destination our family claim to be departing for when withdrawing their life savings. Whether or not the Schober family witness this haven remains unclear. Yet its recurrence throughout *The Seventh Continent*, abrasively puncturing the misery on show with a utopian vision, indicates that they at least glimpse it, and if we look very closely it may be that we spy Eva turning her head towards its vivid pane.[56]

In an unusually frank acknowledgement from the director, Haneke suggests that this visual metronome is a memory of the advertising image – though he stresses that its status should remain ambiguous – and in what follows I will consider how it shifts from motif to motive, inducing action and fundamentally communication between the members of the Schober family and indeed the spectator.[57] Indeed, as contemporary Haneke spectators, we may retroactively suspect Eva's presence because the violence and crimes of children feature as central preoccupations in a number of his films, including *Benny's Video*, *Caché*, *The White Ribbon* and, most recently, *Happy End*. Yet Eva never (outwardly) displays the murderous appetite of Benny, the vindictiveness of the young Georges, the steely calculation of Klara, or the morbid fascination of her smartphone-wielding (near-)namesake Eve. Instead the film emphasises the clichéd signifiers of childhood. She dresses in bright colours, she feeds the family fish, she fibs, she draws, and it is through these accoutrements, this ornament, that Eva is *The Seventh Continent*'s filmic element, her tiny frame rendered visual, acoustic, kinaesthetic, essentially a plurality of material registers within the film's imagery. Eva's drawing, which apes these properties – it is kaleidoscopic, acoustic, tactile, kinetic – hints at this altogether more intimate, more discreet filmic element. On three occasions during the film we catch sight of the picture and at first its colourful nebula resembles a vibrant, spirited chaos. Ultimately, however, Eva's tiny, golden-haired frame materialises at its core, re-presenting the image of the first image-maker before the rocky, mineral-rich cave wall (Figure 5). Spying Eva amongst its contours makes its later destruction even more poignant, painful even, as if Eva herself is being torn apart. But Eva's drawing goes much further than self-portraiture; it signals how her corporeality swells and swirls throughout the film's runtime.

Practically universally, however, and whether as a consequence of her belated introduction or simply because she is a child and so, hierarchically speaking, expected to endure a lower status than her parents, Eva is seen by critics as secondary to Georg and Anna.[58] Indeed, there is ubiquitous

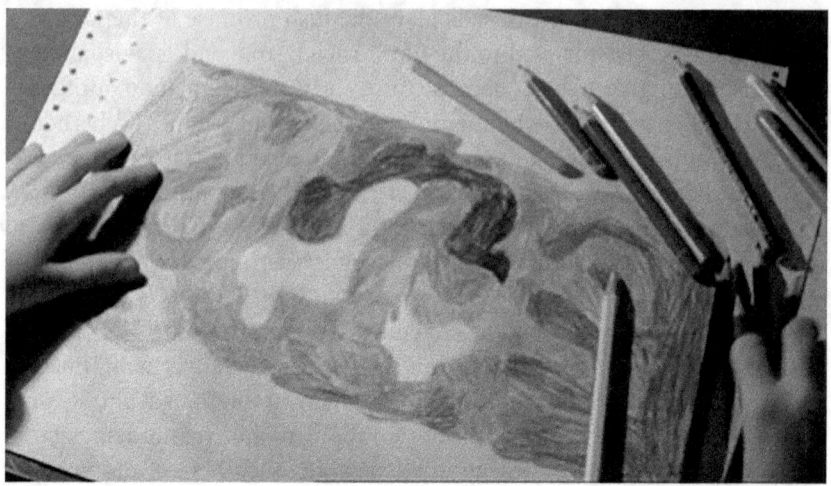

Figure 5 *The Seventh Continent* (Michael Haneke, 1989). Reproduced with kind permission of the director.

accord amongst existing responses to the film regarding Eva's death: that she is monstrously murdered by her parents. In interview, Haneke affirms this societal and familial distribution: 'It is a hierarchy of power [. . .] Men on top, then women, then children, then animals at the lowest end. They are the ones that have to bear it.'[59] Within *The Seventh Continent*, the house pets certainly have to bear it. The swift, shattering movement of an axe roughly ejects the family fish from their aquarium, which leaves them flopping amongst the detritus, making them detritus, and gasping for water, in a sort of microcosmic allusion to the alienating abundance the film thematically ponders, suffocating because there is too much air. Haneke's logic, however, does not quite apply here. No body is spared. Man, woman, child, family pet, money and household goods all meet the same fate. In essence, every body bears it. Such, though, is the critical dismissal of Eva's corporeal significance that despite being the first body to body forth fully, to de-acousmatise as Coulthard describes, ahead of her parents, when she pretends to be blind, Coulthard instead judges this preference disappointing given Georg and Anna's (supposed) hierarchical precedence:[60] 'Thus the suspense of visual discovery built up by the obscured views offered in this opening twelve minutes achieves only partial satisfaction as a somewhat secondary character [. . .] is the first human face to be simultaneously heard and seen.'[61] Rather than a disappointment, though, Eva's fully coincident acoustic and visual presentation in fact offers us vital clues into the significance of her corporeality, that is, as *The Seventh Continent*'s filmic element through its coordination of blindness, auscultation and, of course, water.

Eva's feigned blindness, then, discloses her elemental privilege in a number of ways. In the first instance, it thematises visuality further, and in light of her mother's occupation – optician – this is surely no coincidence. In the only visit we pay to Anna's workplace, a customer recounts a childhood memory. When a girl at the client's school turns up one day wearing glasses, she is taunted by her classmates and wets herself in front of everyone. In her anguish and humiliation, the girl curses her tormenters with bad eyesight. A year later, the entire cohort requires glasses. Upon finishing her tale of youthful cruelty, an uneasiness takes hold. No one in the opticians knows where to look. Inaugurating the authorial collocation of mysterious, even mystical, violence and children, her story of faltering vision can be mapped onto the film's cuts to black, a well-documented characteristic of Haneke's filmmaking where the length of the pause corresponds to the time the spectator should spend reflecting on what has just been seen.[62] In these terms, the black leaders precipitate what Catherine Wheatley 'term[s] a "benign" form of reflexivity, which allows the spectator an extended period of time to reflect upon the image and thus distances them from the action on screen'.[63] Even in the absence of images *per se*, then, these visual and audio silences collapse filming and thinking, whilst risking a cue for carefully managed behaviours by seeking to solicit the spectator in a similar manner to extra-diegetic music in more conventional narrative cinema. Libby Saxton aligns such moments out of narrative time, but very much in 'the film's materiality and constructedness', to blindness, couching this want of sight in 'certain forms [as] a precondition for the cinematic revelation of truth'.[64] Accordingly, then, Eva's faked blindness is structurally thematised, acquiring deeper resonances and establishing sympathy with spectatorial perception. In essence, then, these black leaders cause the spectator to squirm, laying the foundations for imagination and for a different register for the film to play out on.[65]

Another of Haneke's material refrains reflects such viscosity: the bloody splatter. Brigitte Peucker comments on this ichor refrain in *Caché*, foregrounding how it becomes the film's 'constant through multiple mediatic transformations' and how 'blood produces authenticity for representation by way of its strong influence on spectator affect. Perhaps it is for this reason that the "drawing" of blood – represented or metaphorical, imaged as well as elicited – seems the goal of Haneke's cinema.'[66] Peucker plots the migration of this bloody splatter through the film from 'the bloody throat in the childish drawings [...] to the newspaper photograph of Georges, then to the body of the film itself' with the suicide of Majid.[67] In spite of its grisly content, *The Seventh Continent* is almost entirely bloodless, effectively portraying an immaculate annihilation – the blood-splattered corpses of road accident victims the only actual trace we see – meaning that it is not so much a case of mapping the bloody splatter's trajectory or metamorphosis, but rather of observing its primary oscillations which then resonate throughout Haneke's oeuvre in manifold ways. Indeed, its drawing of blood is closely connected to the clichéd signifiers of childhood associated with Eva. More rouge burst than violent spurt, Eva dresses almost exclusively in red, the colour of our internal recesses, and by default of any bloody splatter, and given her redness, and as we shall come to see her viscosity, we might situate Eva as *The Seventh Continent*'s own bloody splatter.[68] Peucker's plotting, however, invests Haneke's bloody splatter with a teleological pragmatism, a goal-orientated need to draw, to show, to expose what generally lies hidden. In essence, Peucker reads the bloody splatter as a hued cue which serves a predetermined spectatorial response, much like the black leaders, whereas Eva's hued cues are far more discreet and, moreover, resonant. In fact, they are discreet touches, each touch constituting a florid tendril along the film's vine, discontinuously stringing out her vitality. Arguably, then, Eva is extravasated, for through these touches of costume and colour we come to listen to her insides, insides which the film has already alerted us to through our immersion in the bowels of the carwash. Entrails which her presumed point of view captures and fluidifies.

Crucially, Eva's crimson, textile confections mark her out amongst Haneke's usual 'study in neutrals':[69] discreet touches that disrupt the overriding timbre of his staid imagery and, like the flower in Nancy's writings, through her distinction from the wan film world, colour effectively sounds out. Eva's red touches are resoundingly louder than their surrounds and their soundings do not simply draw our attention to their rouge bursts but attune us to the material multiplicity of the (film) image, that is, of film as matter in movement, of film as the ultimate resonance form, which creates meaning materially. The clash of red and beige, for instance, highlights the differences between distinct elements of mise-en-scène which in turn point up the differences between its distinct elements. Close-miked sound articulates tactility. Cuts swallow red up or spit it back out and juxtapose it with a washed-out film world. Static cinematography foregrounds it or allows it to recede from view. We of course experience such material multiplicity via Eva's drawing – kaleidoscopic, acoustic, tactile, kinetic – qualities that soon become intimately caught up with Eva, parallels which her discreet touches accentuate further. It is not therefore the drawing of blood that careers through *The Seventh Continent*, but rather a drawing out of the cinematic, which Eva's drawing miniaturises. Material and motile, it is in this way that Eva arabesques throughout the film; her discreet touches swell her corporeality and whilst we might think of her as colloidal, suspended in the film's hydrous matrix, the resistant red ornament of her clothing begins to do the work of ontology for it is through this swell, as we shall come to see, that she infiltrates the very texture of the film, like water, in a far more intimate, and discrete, manner, that is, as the filmic element. Indeed, her syncopated, corporeal rhythm reverberates throughout the film, and in doing so it refines resonance, both theoretically and materially, peeling it further away from sonority by staging, through colour, movement and sound, the noisy choreography of a self and a world in resonance. Her textile tendrils allow sensation to linger longer and like the flower in Kiarostami's cinema, and wood in Varda's first feature film, they recover the beat that Nancy's own thesis on resonance silences and thereby attest to the murmur of sonority, resonantly understood here, that subtends the coextensivity of *sens* and *monde* and which articulates and reticulates our compound mode of being. Decoration thus does the work of ontology, undermining Nancy's own imagistic hierarchy, as well as Haneke's familial equivalent.

The Beaches of Haneke

In his influential responses to the film, Christopher Sharrett also recognises Eva's fundamental relationship to the film's imagery. Sharrett's discussion focuses on the sale of the family car, which undoubtedly centres Eva; the unusual concentration of point of view shots affirms as much, as Adam Bingham comments, by 'draw[ing] us into [her] world'.[70] Bingham elaborates on this perspectival pull, remarking on the changes to the sequence's cinematography Haneke enacts 'by using a slightly longer lens, closer than before to a telephoto (which compresses the planes of action and makes the image flatter)'.[71] Bingham conceives this change in somewhat typical fashion, as 'another visualisation of the shallow modern world and the lives of those within it'.[72] Rather than an anodyne visual commentary on modernity's superficiality, though, this shift in cinematography achieves a corresponding shift in register: diluting the relentlessly realistic fabric of the film by introducing a more fantastical, even oneiric, quality into it when, in a highly uncharacteristic deployment of extra-diegetic music, Alban Berg's 1935 violin concerto *To the Memory of an Angel* plays and endows the episode with a straightforward sense of reverie to promote an alternative approach to (the film's) reality losing its realness that is not predicated on questions of mediation.[73] Whilst Georg finalises the transaction, Eva wanders alone and looks out across the bay. All she sees at first is emptiness until a boat passes by. Sharrett links this sighting to Eva's possession of 'a vision of utopia that her family can't realize',[74] judging it in later writing to be 'one of the many intimations in the film of the thoroughly unattainable utopia',[75] its passing ultimately giving way to the 'tragic summons' of water and the ships and ferrymen of the dead.[76] The recurrent beach images crystallise such complexes, by means of a less ocularcentric and more resonant understanding of Eva, whose swollen corporeality becomes the filmic element and transforms the beaches of Haneke into a cryptic contract between the family members.

Over thirty minutes into the film, then, we are once again welcomed to Australia, when the (utopian) beach image acousmatically reappears. On this second outing, however, the image has undergone a number of minor permutations. Gone are its folds, as well as its advertising paraphernalia, and it is no longer a silent, still image, but 'transformed into a moving [and sonorous] landscape', for implausible waves – apparently originating at the foot of the mountain range – crash onto the shore, whilst invisible wildlife chirps off-screen.[77] Resurfacing here, the beach image's second iteration constitutes the penultimate vignette before the film transitions into 1988, and in its appearance here it could be classed as a dream, for it is succeeded by a dimly lit close-up of Georg's bedside table and lamp which his hand gropes for in the darkness.[78] Something clearly disturbs his usual clockwork slumber and in switching on the light Georg chases this coastal image away. Outwardly wearing no obvious threat, or source of distress to the self, unlike the more recent dream sequences of Haneke's oeuvre (in *Caché* and *Amour*, for instance), the only immediately troubling characteristic of the image is the breaking of the waves. Seemingly, then, it remains a dream, not a nightmare, and as a former advertising image, its re-emergence could be seen as a further indicator of the object-world subliminally imprisoning Georg within the panopticon of modernity whereby traces of his selfhood are cast out of his own unconscious. Yet in deploying this familiar vernacular of the advertising image, Haneke abates any spectatorial speculation of its terms – a likely metonymical warrant for the crimes of the object-world – that have been well asserted by the film throughout 1987. So lethal are these crimes, and so impossible are these waves, that Christopher Rowe believes it is impossible to trace the image 'back to any actual or embodied visual perspective', and, moreover, that 'it is not a vision that is sought out by the characters so much as one that seeks them out and lures them in'.[79] Such enticements will become all the more resonant below; however, its 'asubjective'[80] status is widely refuted by the numerous existing critical responses that anchor this reverie not to

Georg, but to Eva who, in the preceding scene, is shown being tucked into bed by Anna.[81] From off-screen, Anna wishes her daughter 'sweet dreams' and turns out the light before leaving Eva lying motionlessly in bed. The film then cuts to the second incarnation of the beach image which is succeeded by Georg's apparently interrupted repose. His turning on the light, followed by more off-screen dialogue from Anna, establishes equilibrium, a stylistic symmetry between Eva's going to sleep, the beach image and Georg's waking up. Performing a wave-like gesture, there is a subtle structural resonance to the moments that bookend the ambiguous, acousmatic beach image, with one glaring exception: the identity of the dreamer. The pursuit of this estranges the film even further from the already, each time of understanding and channels *The Seventh Continent* towards resonance via the ignominy of the toilet.

What, and whose, enticements does this coastal sojourn therefore share? We edge closer towards its truth upon the image's third outing, seen as Georg and Eva return from the scrapyard. We watch the pair arrive at the house by taxi and enter, followed by Georg successively securing doors, firmly marooning the family within their home. On this surfacing, whilst the sounds of the wildlife have dimmed somewhat, the impossible waves continue to crash against the shore until the film cuts to black once more. Here, then, the beach image preserves acoustic, visual and kinetic properties, an imposed space for thought neighbouring it once more. Still its truth remains oblique, in motion. The image appears again as Eva quivers between life and death, the tools responsible for washing away her vitality successively shown – syringe, dissolved anti-depressants, her tiny limp arm – all basked in the gentian glow of the television. The television is then extinguished and in its place the beach image emerges. As waves continue to move towards the sand, we listen out for the sound of their lapping, we strain to hear their crashing, but they are practically inaudible. Such is the case when we see the beach image one last time, as Georg dying, stares at the television's visual static. Transforming the flashback into a sort of feedback loop, shots seen throughout the film are rapidly fired out and it is not only the film that ties these images together, but a body of water too: a point of view shot in the carwash, the blood-splattered, plastic-covered corpses of the family killed in the accident, the sight of three fish flopping and gasping, Georg's retired boss soaked by rain, Anna's tears in the carwash and finally a rain-soaked road. What we presume are Georg's drenched memories thus doubly fluidify, jellify, crystallise what the lens catches. Visually affirming a material bond between water and the mind, to which we shall return, interlaced with these images and the televisual snow are clustered close-ups first of Anna's face and then Eva's, and as we see the latter one final time the beach image succeeds a moment of static. Editing again indicates ownership. *The Seventh Continent*, however, more discreetly, more intimately reinforces Eva's relationship to the beach tableaux. A trip to the bathroom flushes this out further.

We watch Anna and Georg flush their life savings down the loo, having claimed at the bank that they were withdrawing the funds in order to emigrate to Australia. The flushing of the banknotes and coins proves this claim to be a lie, creating an unexpected link between the beach image, the toilet cistern and their respective flows. The tableaux thus become stubborn images that refuse to be flushed away, clogging up the cinematic landscape with the murky depths of resonance, for Nancy's thought also takes a trip to the toilet. Contemplating the wave-like construction of truth, he writes:

> shouldn't truth 'itself', as transitivity and incessant transition of a continual coming and going, be listened to rather than seen? But isn't it also in the way that it stops being 'itself' and identifiable, and becomes no longer the naked figure emerging from the cistern but the resonance of that cistern – or, if it were possible to express it thus, the echo of the naked figure in the open depths?[82]

Whilst not as dizzying or kaleidoscopic as Nancy's arboreal encounter, in this collapse of (leering) high art nudes and lowly plumbing, Nancy's cistern, and the wave-like construction of truth it illustrates, effervesces with *sens*uous abundance. It observes the structure of resonance, its dispersive temporal-spatial matrix, which reorients our encounter with the quivering sense of the world whereby these cistern sounds are not simply contained therein, but rather constitute the very rhythm of this matrix, of this reorientation, the (porcelain) body beaten by its sense of body, another trunk, another (porcelain) drum, the necessity of emission in its own reception, the essential sonority of being-with. In any search for truth, then, we should not listen to the sounds of the flushing, aural evidence for the mechanised, atomised lives we lead, nor to the lush far away that the crashing waves promise, a cruel counterpoint to this mechanisation, and their respective commentaries on the 'hostile, capitalist social context',[83] but rather we should attune to what escapes easy understanding, that is, to the resonance of the cistern, to the impossible undulations of the waves. Flushes and waves are buccal at best, after all, and thus insist that we are listening 'further upstream' from the oral mouth, that is, to the snores and soughings of sleep.[84]

In the first instance, what escapes easy understanding here is the identity of the dreamer. Material, motile, meaningful and thereby *sens*uous, structurally speaking the beachscape's waves and wildlife hinge Eva's sleeping and Georg's waking and it is likely for this reason that the critical consensus on the identity of the dreamer remains split. Is this Eva's or Georg's dream? More productive is to suggest that it takes place between Eva's sleeping and Georg's waking. Like a kind of bastardised pillow talk, father and daughter share this dream. Material, motile, meaningful, shared and thereby *sens*uous, the original static billboard image surreptitiously acquires the qualities of Eva's drawing and her discreet touches, that is, of the *corpus imāginum* – visual, acoustic, kinetic, tactile – yet with each appearance, as noted above, the soundscape of the dreamscape beachscape quietens. Indeed, the soundscape of the dreamscape beachscape quietens as Eva's life ebbs away. The concomitant loss of Eva's vitality and the littoral soundscape thus establishes a material, even indexical connection between Eva and the waves. In his study of the material imagination and its relationship to water, Gaston Bachelard claims that oneiric 'waves receive their whiteness and their limpidity from an internal matter. This matter is *dissolved maiden*.'[85] In *The Seventh Continent*'s reverie, Eva's swollen, fluid corporeality is this dissolved internal matter, charging the waves with their impossible breaking. Fundamentally, they embody her corporeality, its presence within the film in a much more intimate way, in the very texture of its images, that is, as the filmic element. In so doing, Eva's dissolved corporeality adopts the wave-like structure of resonance; it is this snoring and soughing. Yet we do not see Eva emerge siren-like from the open depths of the impossible waves. Rather, she emerges in the plurality of material registers that make up the beachscape. She inherits water's flow and enables the film's own. Her tiny frame becomes *corpus imāginum*, visual, acoustic, kinaesthetic, that is, the fundamental filmic elements of the beach image.

Eva's intersections with a secondary series of images that function as a veiled pictorial anagram for the recurring beachscape further refine her status as the filmic element: the family fish tank. Like the beach image, we encounter the fish tank on multiple occasions within the domestic setting, the sound of its babbling further inundating the textures of *The Seventh Continent*'s imagery with water. Its murmurings, for instance, feature amongst the family's morning routine, they accompany Eva as she does her homework and become the dominant soundtrack of the brother's breakdown at the family dinner once the music has been switched off. As this veiled pictorial anagram, the fish tank grounds any notion of heaven, of utopia, ever deeper into the terrestrial and it explodes from its decorative function as the family's warpath literally gets into full swing: Georg wielding an axe and colliding it with a computer screen, a glass coffee table, a desk and then the fish tank. Shattering its outer pane, in a reversal of the film's opening carwash sequence, water gushes forth and fills the frame with its confused cascade. Spewing out of the tank, water floods the floor, and as Haneke's camera surveys this effusion we discover amongst its issue the family fish struggling for life. Bringing death and destruction, as the deluge calms, and the water begins to trickle with a light patter, Eva rushes towards the devastation, wailing and crying, struggling against her mother's grasp.

Atypically, Haneke has confirmed that the destruction of the fish tank coincides with Eva's internal death.[86] However, there is something stranger at work here than Haneke's interpretative clarity, which hinges on a convergence between the material pluralities at work across the chapter: the materiality of water and the sonority, ornamentality and (swollen) corporeality of Eva. This peculiarity materialises as Eva quietens and Georg apologises for the slaughter when, between these moments, a ship's horn sounds out. Having seen next to nothing of the area surrounding the Schober family home, we can say with no certainty whether or not the house neighbours a harbour, meaning it could emanate from off-screen space. What is certain, however, is our having witnessed Eva seeing a boat as part of a sequence steeped in possible imaginative play, through the utopic allusions the passing vessel represents and the uncharacteristic use of extra-diegetic music. Just, then, as the scene might signify Eva's internal death, linking her body, her viscera with the inside of the fish tank, the impossibility of ever localising the source of this beacon ties it to her, effectively mooring Eva to water and further anchoring her to resonance. The horn emphasises this resonance, for as its warbled signal rings out, the touch it enacts through the spectator's body touches upon the boat's initial appearance and its particular choreography draw us into Eva's experience, indeed into her body. In doing so, it touches upon the utopian visions present in the Schober family dining room by means of the fish tank's veiled pictorial anagram. Yet now, through the action of the axe, its anagram moves beyond transposition to annihilation: an erupted, extravasated utopia. Violently forced from its original vessel, (the film's) utopia becomes a serous surface spread across the floor of the Schober family home; its supposed promise rendered a flat plane through which one has to wade. Heaven here literally is a place on earth – as well as a part of the familial detritus – and from these fragments we may pick up the pieces of this shattered dream. Ultimately, however, through its links with Eva, the acousmatic siren figures as a literal death knell – another tendril in the complex arabesque of cinematic textures Eva embodies, and it is via this arabesque of touches that Eva splatters forth – prompting the viscosity of water to return in a new, juvenile form – through the configurations her material multiplicity establishes with the car and its usurpation by water as the clutch of (the) film; with water's materiality as it sounds out in her shared dream with Georg and finally with the red that clothes her that is scattered amongst the film's pale palette. Water waves, sound waves, wavelengths of colour prevail and through these modulations, and their flux across the film and flushing through our resonant, cavernous bodies, Eva comes to flow through us and through the film, cementing her swollen corporeality as the filmic element. *The Seventh Continent* thus emerges as a vital body, instead of a glacier, for through our exposure to Eva's swollen corporeality, and the rich arabesque she forms with a plurality of material registers, it exposes us to the tautological meaningfulness of being as resonance and the resonance of being.

Eva's tautology is especially resonant in the altered soundscapes of the beachscape's final two appearances. In its final outing, any local sounds are plastered over by the cacophonous televisual static, whilst in its penultimate appearance the impossible advance of the waves towards the shore is impossibly silent. The vanishing of the waves' breaking from the soundtrack in both instances resonantly utters Eva's loss, for it produces fissures in the film through which our looking becomes all the more resonant. Listening out for the sounds of these lunar-defying waves, we hear only their absence, a silence perhaps momentarily echoed by our own corporeal quiet. But, of course, this silence is no silence at all thanks to our internal rumblings, gurgling and pumping. Indeed, the body's involuntary moans literalise being as resonance and the resonance of being: a body beaten by its own sense of corporeality, whether that body is venturing into far-flung corners of the world such as Australia, or whether these adventures are far closer to home: an empty stomach, a chesty cough, a death rattle. Such resonances stress the mmmmm in âmmmmm, that is, the materiality and corporeality of resonance, and Eva's vital withdrawal from the film does likewise for through this acoustic loss we encounter her swollen corporeality with an even greater acuity: in undertaking a simultaneous listening to a self and to a world we clamour despite this lack of blows. The beachscape's silence thus echoes through us and as we in turn resonate with the internal surfaces left by Eva, with the silence of the waves, we feel her (absence). The truth of the beachscape, then, is that Eva is its source. On this empty beach, she makes a mockery of acoustic and familial hierarchies. On this empty beach, Georg hears Eva's call through the sonic, undulating body of the sea – she is the film's kinematic truth – and it is this realisation that disturbs Georg's slumber and has him reaching for the cord. The truth of the beachscape, then, is that it is Eva who suggests to her parents that they take a trip to the Seventh Continent.

Notes

1. Amos Vogel, 'Of Nonexisting Continents: The Cinema of Michael Haneke', *Film Comment*, 32 (1996), 73–5 (p. 74).
2. Wheatley (2009), p. 57.
3. See Vogel (1996), p. 74, Adam Bingham, 'Life, or Something Like It: Michael Haneke's *Der siebente Kontinent*', *Kinoeye*, 1 (2004) <https://www.kinoeye.org/04/01/bingham01_no2.php> (last accessed 12 May 2020), Sorfa (2006), p. 93, Brunette (2010), p. 13, Russell (2010), p. 6, Benjamin Noys, 'Attenuating Austria: The Construction of Bourgeois Space in *The Seventh Continent*', in *The Cinema of Michael Haneke: Europe Utopia*, ed. by Ben McCann and David Sorfa (London: Wallflower Press, 2011), pp. 141–50 (p. 143) and Lisa Coulthard, 'Ethical Violence: Suicide as Authentic Act in the Films of Michael Haneke', in *The Cinema of Michael Haneke: Europe Utopia*, ed. by Ben McCann and David Sorfa (London: Wallflower Press, 2011a), pp. 38–48 (p. 42).
4. Scott Foundas, 'Michael Haneke on *Amour*: "When I Watched It with the Audience, They Gasped!"', *The Village Voice* (2012) <https://www.villagevoice.com/2012/12/20/michael-haneke-on-amour-when-i-watched-it-with-the-audience-they-gasped/> (last accessed 12 May 2020).
5. Michael Haneke quoted in Frey (2010). See also Bingham (2004) and Russell (2010).
6. See Russell (2010), p. 6 and Coulthard (2011a), p. 45.
7. Oliver C. Speck, *Funny Frames: The Filmic Concepts of Michael Haneke* (London: Continuum, 2010), p. 54 and Noys (2011), p. 141.
8. Andrew J. Horton, 'De-icing the Emotions', *Central Europe Review* (1998) <http://www.ce-review.org/kinoeye/kinoeye5old.html> (last accessed 6 March 2013).
9. Brunette (2010), p. 12.
10. Libby Saxton, 'Close Encounters with Distant Suffering: Michael Haneke's Disarming Visions', in *Five Directors: Auteurism from Assayas to Ozon*, ed. by Kate Ince (Manchester: Manchester University Press, 2008), pp. 84–111 (p. 103). See also John David Rhodes, 'The Spectacle of Skepticism', in *On Michael Haneke*, ed. by Brian Price and John David Rhodes (Detroit: Wayne State University Press, 2010), pp. 87–102.
11. Brunette (2010), p. 12. Speck (2010), p. 79 and Russell (2010) also cast the space of the carwash as a form of symbolic cleansing.
12. Michael Haneke, 'Terror and Utopia of Form: Robert Bresson's *Au hasard Balthazar*', in *A Companion to Michael Haneke*, ed. by Roy Grundmann (Oxford: Wiley-Blackwell, 2010), pp. 565–74 (p. 566).
13. Nancy (2001c), p. 50.
14. Ibid. p. 22.
15. Ibid. p. 38.
16. Ibid. p. 50.

17. Ibid. p. 38.
18. Ibid. p. 28. See also McMahon (2013).
19. Peter Szendy, 'The Archi-Road Movie', *Senses & Society*, 8 (2013), 50–61 (p. 53).
20. Nancy (2001c), p. 48.
21. Ibid. p. 46.
22. Ibid. pp. 46–50.
23. Ibid. p. 46.
24. Ibid. p. 48.
25. Adrienne Janus, 'Introduction: Jean-Luc Nancy and the Image of Visual Culture', in *Jean-Luc Nancy and Visual Culture*, ed. by Carrie Giunta and Adrienne Janus (Edinburgh: Edinburgh University Press, 2016), pp. 1–20 (p. 9).
26. Ibid.
27. Maeve Connolly, 'Outlandish: Introduction by Maeve Connolly', *Vdrome* (n.d.) <http://www.vdrome.org/phillip-warnell-outlandish/> (last accessed 16 April 2019).
28. See Barnfield (2016).
29. Nancy (2001c), p. 48. My emphasis.
30. Ibid.
31. Ibid. p. 50.
32. Janus (2013), p. 75.
33. Ibid.
34. Ibid. p. 74.
35. Ibid.
36. Ibid. p. 76.
37. Ibid.
38. Sherlock (2013), p. 381.
39. Nancy (2001c), p. 46.
40. Janus (2013), p. 75.
41. Nancy (2004), p. 183. My translation.
42. Ibid.
43. See Gaston Bachelard, *Water and Dreams: An Essay on the Imagination of Matter*, trans. by Edith R. Farrell (Dallas: Dallas Institute of Humanities and Culture, 1983), p. 6 and Karen J. Bakker, *Privatizing Water: Governance Failure and the World's Urban Water Crisis* (Ithaca: Cornell University Press, 2010), p. 186.
44. Bakker (2010), p. 216.
45. Tony Allan, *Virtual Water: Tackling the Threat to Our Planet's Most Precious Resource* (London: I. B. Tauris, 2011), pp. 2–3.
46. Bakker (2010), p. 195.
47. Vandana Shiva, *Water Wars: Privatization, Pollution, and Profit* (London: Pluto Press, 2002), p. x.

48. Christopher Brown and Pam Hirsch, 'Introduction: The Cinema of the Swimming Pool', in *The Cinema of the Swimming Pool*, ed. by Christopher Brown and Pam Hirsch (Oxford: Peter Lang, 2014), pp. 1–20 (p. 3).
49. Bakker (2010), p. 3.
50. See Fiona Handyside, *Cinema at the Shore: The Beach in French Film* (Oxford: Peter Lang, 2014), pp. 14–15.
51. De Luca (2013), p. 176.
52. See Allan (2011), p. 30.
53. Bachelard (1983), p. 9.
54. Lisa Coulthard, 'Listening to Silence in the Films of Michael Haneke', *Cinephile*, 6 (2010), 18–24 (p. 19).
55. Ibid. p. 22.
56. See Noys (2011).
57. Michael Haneke quoted in Brunette (2010), p. 12.
58. See Russell (2010), p. 27, Christopher Sharrett, 'Haneke and the Discontents of European Culture', in *On Michael Haneke*, ed. by Brian Price and John David Rhodes (Detroit: Wayne State University Press, 2010), pp. 207–19 (p. 213), Speck (2010), pp. 164–5 and Coulthard (2011a), p. 44.
59. Michael Haneke quoted in Conrad (2012).
60. Coulthard (2011a), p. 44.
61. Ibid.
62. See Brunette (2010) p. 12.
63. Wheatley (2009), p. 54.
64. Saxton (2008), pp. 94–5.
65. Walker (2018), p. 19.
66. Brigitte Peucker, 'Games Haneke Plays: Reality and Performance', in *On Michael Haneke*, ed. by Brian Price and John David Rhodes (Detroit: Wayne State University Press, 2010), pp. 15–33 (p. 32). See also Peucker (2006).
67. Peucker (2010), p. 32.
68. See Georg Seeßlen, 'Structures of Glaciation: Gaze, Perspective, and Gestus in the Films of Michael Haneke', in *A Companion to Michael Haneke*, ed. by Roy Grundmann (Oxford: Wiley-Blackwell, 2010), pp. 323–36. Seeßlen here yokes red and children, suggesting that such a marriage 'represents something like a claim of life and love against the coldness of the environment' (p. 328).
69. Eugenie Brinkema, *The Forms of the Affects* (Durham, NC: Duke University Press, 2014), p. 103.
70. Bingham (2004).
71. Ibid.
72. Ibid.
73. See Russell (2010).
74. Sharrett (2004).
75. Sharrett (2010), p. 212.
76. Bachelard (1983), p. 81.

77. Wheatley (2009), p. 56.
78. See also Bingham (2004) and Rowe (2017), p. 48.
79. Rowe (2017), pp. 49–50.
80. Ibid. p. 59.
81. See Bingham (2004) and Noys (2011).
82. Nancy (2007), p. 4.
83. Walker (2018), p. 17.
84. Ricco (2015).
85. Bachelard (1983), p. 129.
86. See Russell (2010), p. 46.

Le Bonheur:
Happiness Made and Remade

> We were having dinner with the Bigeons and the Benoits. The next time with the Benoits and the Duplats, or the Duplats and Bigeons. They always came in pairs. 'Couples', they're called.[1]

Le Bonheur, Agnès Varda's ebullient, subversive and pseudo-Technicolor 'feminist and anti-consumerist' masterpiece,[2] is a film that knows what it is to touch things in the world, that understands materiality.[3] Saturated with primary colours, as if taken over by the advertising images that limn its diegetic world – a saturation which suggests mechanical and material parallels with Haneke's *The Seventh Continent* where another advert promotes a way of life that is death – the seeing that Varda's film is has a texture and solidity akin to the arboreal matrix of her first feature film. Ostensibly complementing the jobs of the film's lead protagonists, François and Thérèse (carpenter and seamstress, respectively), in light of *Le Bonheur*'s narrative design, such texture and solidity have long provoked concerns over solidarity: just whose side is Varda on here? The film, after all, shows Thérèse, played by Claire Drouot, the on-screen and real-life wife of François actor Jean-Claude Drouot, being seamlessly replaced by Émilie, the latter's lover, following Thérèse's death. Such interchangeability dovetails with the film's easy and sprightly manipulation of the materiality of the world that offends and confounds because it appears to 'line up with things in the right way', that is, with a complex economy of happiness, which is simultaneously moral, affective, social, (phenomenologically) intentional and historical:[4] 'To be affected in a good way', writes Sara Ahmed, 'by objects that are already evaluated as good is a way of belonging to an affective community. We align ourselves with others by investing in the same objects as the cause of happiness.'[5] Happiness is thus exposed as a process that predates our happening upon its causes, effectively draining it of its etymological roots in contingency.[6] Ahmed reads the (murky) 'happy family' as a paradigmatic happy object, a conduit and collocation so compelling that 'we register the connection of these words in the familiarity of their affective resonance'.[7] In this way, *Le Bonheur* is happiness incarnate; it relentlessly pursues such alignment through Émilie's replacement of Thérèse. A racking focus, for instance, transports us through centuries-old stone castle walls with a breeziness that lends the film a momentary breathing visuality to suggest that such substitution is as natural as the movement of air in and out of the lungs.[8] A canny pan switches Thérèse with Émilie at a village dance, one transformed into the other through the apparently rhizomatic qualities of a tree. *Le Bonheur*, then, borders on an embodied mindlessness, and according to Varda, 'it's about fucking and it's about picnics', two resolutely carnal interests.[9] Claire Johnston's fabulous misunderstanding of the film is a telling illustration of the horror such an understanding produces:

> The films of Agnès Varda are a particularly good example of an oeuvre which celebrates bourgeois myths of women and with it the apparent innocence of the sign. [. . .] Varda's portrayal of female fantasy constitutes one of the nearest approximations to the facile day-dreams perpetuated by advertising that probably exists in the cinema. Her films appear totally innocent to the workings of myth; indeed, it is the purpose of myth to fabricate an impression of innocence, in which all becomes 'natural': history is transmuted into nature, involving the elimination of all questions, because all appears 'natural'. There is no doubt that Varda's work is reactionary: in her rejection of culture and her placement of woman outside history her films mark a retrograde step in women's cinema.[10]

Through its very depiction of happiness, however, *Le Bonheur* does not, indeed cannot, place women outside history. Rather, Varda firmly embeds women in its punishing miseries, specifically those unearthed when we stand in the way of socially produced and prescribed bliss. These miseries centre on the home and the promise of happiness that domesticity supposedly brings, and it is thus that Varda's second feature film furthers its kinship with Haneke's first, for the 'visual strategies' of each film foreground the rote rhythms that govern our daily lives:[11] Haneke's vignettes and Varda's deployment of what Rebecca DeRoo terms the ideal of the serving hand.[12] According to DeRoo, these hands, amputated from their bodies, and by extension from any meaningful sense of subjecthood, 'glamorize domestic chores and represent an ideal to emulate' across the pages of women's magazines, including *Elle* and *Marie Claire*.[13] *Le Bonheur* echoes this iconography through a pair of montage sequences where different hands serve the same ideal. In their first incarnation, Thérèse carries out a series of domestic tasks – making the marital bed, kneading and rolling dough, ironing, playing with the children, watering flowers – and in the final five minutes of the film these same gestures repeat when Émilie's hands make the bed, iron, water flowers, play with the children.[14] Like Eva in *The Seventh Continent*, then, whose presence, and absence, we experience in a far more intimate way, as the filmic element, we do not (immediately) feel Thérèse's loss because the film's style appears so intent on lining up in the right way, that is, phenomenologically intending towards happiness-causes.

Drawing on Betty Friedan's *The Feminine Mystique* and its diagnosis of 'a problem that has no name by evoking what lies behind the image of the happy American housewife', Ahmed considers how '[t]he happy housewife is a fantasy figure that erases the signs of labor under the sign of happiness.'[15] '[H]er duty', Ahmed continues, 'is to generate happiness by the very act of embracing this image', a prehensility that the ideal of the serving hand literalises.[16] *Le Bonheur*'s final frames reinforce such alignment as the family enjoys autumn's gold, whilst clad in the season's hues, in exactly the same way they had been steeped in summer in its original configuration at the film's opening. Both in isolation and in parallel, to film/*filmer*, then, here is to make the world flow in a way that is not resistant to happiness, that is, fluidifying, jellifying and fundamentally crystallising its causes and images. Following such flow, then, to film/*filmer* extracts Thérèse and Émilie from the eternal and instead places them into a precarious economy of interchangeability; their work, and affective labour, is reproducible by another and they are thus replaceable by this other.[17] The threat of an embodied mindlessness once again rears its ugly, empty head and it is thus that *Le Bonheur* becomes murky: just whose side is Varda on here? Is she dutiful or wilful? Thérèse's enigmatic death – accident, suicide, economic necessity, Darwinian?[18] – is the overwhelming source of this murk; it is where consensus, where sticky, happy community, falls away.[19]

Indeed, despite such earlier transparency and ease – thickness, texture, solidity, pleasure – in the moments surrounding Thérèse's death, the film's material world refuses to clarify. On one of the idyllic summer afternoons the film depicts, François confesses his affair. He explains the workings of his happiness, which resemble some sort of warped meditation: we're in a field together, you and me and the children, growing happily in neat rows, and then I notice a tree growing outside the perimeter, and I take pleasure in its harvest too. More apples, more flowers, more happiness for everyone, but especially for me. Whilst at first uncertain, Thérèse appears content with, even elated by the news. The pair make love and then nap. François awakes, alone, and searches for Thérèse in an increasingly frenzied fashion until he finds her lifeless body on the bank. He takes it in his arms, an image that repeats over and over again as François draws his ear to her chest. We next see shots of Thérèse in the pond, an arm aloft, an arm reaching for a branch, these images somehow swelling up from inside her corpse, François somehow listening to them, and us in turn doing the same. But is she waving or drowning? (Figure 6).

What is her (formerly) idealised serving hand doing? Is it relinquishing or hanging on for dear life? *Le Bonheur* refuses to confirm either way. Here, then, as it once again toggles between two alternative realities, the film demonstrates a keen loss of material easiness, for whereas formerly hard stone proved to be perfectly penetrable, here water proves impossible to penetrate. It still knows what it is to touch things in the world, it understands materiality, it has a texture and solidity, and yet on the matter of Thérèse's death it is numb. We listen but all we hear is her death – a clichéd holiday snap of François and the children, a further happiness emissary, doubles down on this silence through a watery expanse looming behind the happy family. In spite of the (literal) silence of the encounter, however, we attune to its reiterations, to her corporeality, where meaning gathers, but understanding never crystallises. Fundamentally, then, Thérèse's death resonates. It is resonance itself. It does not give way to understanding. Instead it prompts us to strain towards a possible meaning that is not immediately, if ever, accessible. The film's repetitious handling of Thérèse's body accentuates this sensation for it obliges us to attune to what escapes easy understanding, that is, to the resonance of the cistern,

Figure 6 *Le Bonheur* (1965), a film by Agnès Varda © 1965 ciné-tamaris.

to the echo of the naked figure in the open depths, here encapsulated by the gentle yet disturbing bobbing of Thérèse at the waterline, alongside François's embrace, which repeat, momentarily clogging up the film. Resonance and materiality are hauntingly isomorphic – the film displays sounds and images rich with familiar elements, such as picnics and fucking and trees, and Thérèse herself is likewise itemised: young, blond, female, wearing a blue, flowery dress – yet by killing off the happy housewife this familiar pastoral and carnal terrain suspends the idiom that *Le Bonheur* has apparently been servicing.

To film/*Filmer* thus signifies a failure to clarify, and such opacity gives way to what Delphine Bénézet calls 'Varda's cinema of interpellation' which centres on corporeality and 'resonates' across the director's filmography: 'Like other forms of enunciational address, such as the direct gaze into the camera, an offscreen voice or intertitles, the bodies of the people on screen call our attention.'[20] Thérèse's iterative corporeality certainly calls our attention and in doing so it hinges the film's other repetitions. Indeed, it relieves repetition of its comforts by deploying it to recapture the loss of the happy housewife, that is, to make it resonate. Thus, *Le Bonheur*'s repetitions become affect aliens, 'convert[ing] good feelings into bad', thereby '"kill[ing]" the joy of the family' and placing it firmly at odds with any reading of the film's later repetitions as a seamless usurpation despite the strength of context and causes. Rather, these repetitions precipitate as a gestural elegy.[21] Like Eva, then, we feel Thérèse's absence through the film's later repetitions. For the unthinking flow that to film/*filmer* appears to impose upon *Le Bonheur*'s worldview, which indicates that its two women are likewise isomorphic, in truth carefully dismantles such imagery. Its rote, repetitious displays distil the labour that such happiness-causes entail, which in turn intersect with Ahmed's genealogies of feminist killjoys and female troublemakers[22] – the unhappy housewife being a key spoilsport.[23] In the ruins of such imagery, then, *Le Bonheur* erases all signs of happiness and through their interchangeability Thérèse and Émilie do not bear the promise of happiness but instead kill joy. It is for this reason that *Le Bonheur* makes trouble amongst its audiences, because even the belief in making trouble can be a troubling one. After all, as Ahmed notes, '[i]t is hard to leave happiness for life.'[24] Tuning in to its images, then, we might hear happiness, and appear to understand its causes, but if we listen to its imagery all that materialises is the hap of interpretive labour. This is perhaps, then, *Le Bonheur*'s most radical gesture: the freedom to choose what form your life and death takes, a freedom which endures as resolutely feminist and alienating. What makes you happy?, *Le Bonheur* dares to ask. Make it hap–.

Notes

1. Céline in Christiane Rochefort's *Les Stances à Sophie* (1963) quoted in Kristin Ross, *Fast Cars, Clean Bodies: Decolonization and the Reordering of French Culture* (Cambridge, MA: The MIT Press, 1995), p. 135.
2. Catherine Dousteyssier-Khoze, 'Mise-en-abyme, Irony and Visual Cliché in Agnès Varda's *Le Bonheur* (1964)', in *Agnès Varda Unlimited: Image, Music, Media*, ed. by Marie-Claire Barnet (Cambridge: Legenda, 2016), pp. 97–107 (p. 104). Dousteyssier-Khoze describes the film as a 'manifesto', which (erroneously) suggests that its objectives are programmatically clear.
3. Sobchack (1992), p. 133.
4. Sara Ahmed, *The Promise of Happiness* (Durham, NC: Duke University Press, 2010), p. 37.
5. Ibid. p. 38.
6. Ibid. p. 22.
7. Ibid. p. 45. Murkiness also appears amongst Ahmed's treatise on happiness (p. 39).
8. See Quinlivan (2012).
9. Agnès Varda quoted in Barbara Halpern Martineau, 'Subjecting Her Objectification, or Communism Is Not Enough', in *Notes on Women's Cinema*, ed. by Claire Johnston (London: Society for Education in Film and Television, 1973), pp. 32–40 (p. 38).
10. Claire Johnston, 'Women's Cinema as Counter-Cinema', in *Notes on Women's Cinema*, ed. by Claire Johnston (London: Society for Education in Film and Television, 1973), pp. 24–31 (p. 30).
11. DeRoo (2017), p. 51.
12. Ibid. p. 53.
13. Ibid. p. 55. The Schober family in Haneke's *The Seventh Continent* are also depicted as servient hands attending clock radios, taps, telephones, and so on.
14. Émilie as the 'other woman' returns in *Documenteur*.
15. Ahmed (2010), p. 50. DeRoo (2017) too draws on Betty Friedan's seminal text.
16. Ahmed (2010), p. 53.
17. A continuity error when François visits Émilie at the post office where she works suggests likewise. The shot shows a close-up of Émilie's arms as she writes a coded message to François, but these arms are clad in a pink-sleeved cardigan instead of her blue uniform. We assume these arms belong to Marie-France Boyer, but in truth they could belong to anyone. In terms of function, then, one image quite simply stands in for another.
18. See Mark Lee, 'Re-viewing Varda's *Le Bonheur* (1964): Accident? Suicide? Or the Natural Order? That Is the Question', in *Agnès Varda Unlimited: Image, Music, Media*, ed. by Marie-Claire Barnet (Cambridge: Legenda, 2016), pp. 87–95.
19. See Ahmed (2010).

20. Bénézet (2014), p. 123.
21. Ahmed (2010), p. 49.
22. Ibid. p. 53.
23. Ibid. p. 65.
24. Ibid. p. 78.

The Singular Plural of Seeing in *Cleo from 5 to 7*

Sense never becomes clear, and for this reason it is always rending and heartrending.[1]

A philosopher walks into a French New Wave film . . . sounds like the start of a bad gag, or perhaps a partial synopsis of a Jean-Luc Godard film.[2] *A French New Wave film walks into the bedroom of a philosopher* perhaps sounds less plausible, and predictable, but no less jokey. Coming almost a decade after Agnès Varda's first feature film – discussed in the third chapter – *Cleo from 5 to 7*, her second, facilitates such an overlapping of walking, thinking and sleeping. Indeed, its story of death in life, of an 'imminent mortality', moves us neatly from the domestic somnambulism of *The Seventh Continent* and *Le Bonheur* to what many responses to *Cleo from 5 to 7* consider, at least for its first half, is a solitary sleepwalker.[3] During its ninety-minute runtime the film recounts, in 'real time', a peculiar double life:[4] narrating two-ish hours in a woman's life, as she awaits the results of tests for cancer, whilst documenting early 1960s Paris.[5] This twofold vitality has bred a tripartite vision of the film which examines Cléo, the woman seen, Paris, the city seen and Cléo, the woman seeing. The film's threefold existence views it as a lesson in looking, which charts the 'perambulatory odyssey' of the eponymous female lead – new pop starlet Florence 'Cléo' Victoire – as she journeys through Paris on a voyage of self-discovery and towards a look of her own.[6] Beneath its surface, then, many hearts beat – Cléo's wanderings forming a city symphony-cum-*Bildungsroman* hybrid, her self-discovery mediating the audience's contemporaneous discovery of France's capital – and in *Cleo from 5 to 7* things tend to come in threes, triumvirates which resonate with the aesthetic, political and historical contexts that shape the film. Three mentions of the colour black, cancer and the Algerian war score the film. Three shop floor performances take place *chez* Francine, the hat shop. Three amphibious encounters occur across Paris, and three pairs of sunglasses, and three solitary tears bedeck characters' faces.

If Cléo, though, is our sleepwalker, ineluctably going through the motions, then Nancy is our sleep talker. Following resonance, and gaping itself, John Paul Ricco establishes 'drool' as another gaping Nancean term, that is, a third term without conceptual reconciliation:

> As the liquid fore-speech of the fore-scene, we might say that drool is the pre-cum of a buccal murmur and groan, and imagine that with the lightest of touches, as though with the tap of a finger, this fluid is stretched out and extended, and in its extension (ex-posure without in-tention) traces the tenuous and fragile yet remarkably resilient tensile line of the 'with' of our shared existence, body to body. As though at that sleeping mouth a non-salvific path was opened up by drooling, and in that fall of sleep that is at the same time the fall of speech, one hears the 'with' of being-with or being-together. As exgested substance [. . .], drool is a menstruum universal or 'universal solvent' of sleeping together as being-together [. . .]. We drool therefore I am.[7]

The gummy trace left on the pillow every morning, or afternoon, does the work of philosophy here. It is a gaping reminder of singular-plural being, of being-in-common, that is, of the messy, here mucousy, togetherness that is otherness of Nancy's radical ontology and of the tautological coextensivity of *sens* and *monde* – the mouth's overflow confirmation of the absence of worldly hangover. Its nightly renewal is likewise reminiscent of Nancy's own walking, perhaps a morning or evening stroll to stave off sleep: 'if one day I happen to *look* at my street on which I walk up and down ten times a day, I construct for an instant a new *evidence* of my street'.[8] In Marc Grün's *Le Corps du philosophe* we see Nancy dozing, this *corps du philosophe* encountered in yet another context, adding napper to his singular-plural being. Here we also see the philosopher's duvet. A quotidian object, its banality belies its fruitfulness and its white expanse becomes a complex, dynamic philosophical expanse, almost a map, for Nancy's thinking on aesthetics. Its pocked surface is redolent of the inaugural canvas: the cave wall. Its blankness brings to mind the ground of the image and, in a reversal of Nancy's own proposition, here textile becomes text as we spin these fibres further to produce a resonant assemblage of Nancy's thought.

In the first instance, a duvet spells sleep and what Nancy understands as a reversion 'to the general equivalence in which one sleeper is worth as much as any sleeper',[9] where '"I" do not make a self, for "I" do not return . . . I fall asleep and at the same time I vanish as "I".'[10] Yet Nancy's duvet suggests much more than slumber and subjecthood through its very materiality. Beds, alongside hospitals, cemeteries, factories, are places where bodies reside.[11] Heterotopic, marginal, these places map onto Cléo's trajectory across Paris: her brilliantly white apartment on the rue Huyghens where she greets her lover José, whilst ensconced in bed, as well as a highly parodic style of strings, all coy glances and kittens, part paramour, part patient; the funeral procession she witnesses as she walks; and Pitié-Salpêtrière Hôpital, originally a gunpowder factory, where her journey, and ours, ends. The duvet, moreover, is a site of ordinary turbulence: it edges the white noise of being, the din of soughing, sniffing, snoring, the sonority – the snoronity? – of being-with. There is also something discomfiting about a duvet that has been slept in. It might still be clean, but it is no longer pristine. It subtly but distinctly connotes contact, a touch that has withdrawn, leaving a hollow and a distinctly Nancean touch:[12]

> Without this detachment, without this recoil or retreat, the touch would no longer do what it does (or it would not let itself do what it lets itself do). It would begin to reify itself in a grip, in an adhesion or a sticking, indeed, in an agglutination that would grasp the touch in the thing and the thing within it, matching and appropriating the one to the other and then the one in the other. There would be identification, fixation, property, immobility.[13]

Equally, the duvet draws together the recurrent concerns for and proximity between fabric, flesh and folds that Nancy's engagement with images consistently demonstrates. Sheets, for instance, recur throughout his discussion of the nude with Federico Ferrari in *Nus sommes*, often as a marker of arousal, or skin-to-skin contact, and on occasion of skin itself, recalling Nancy's etymological elaboration of *pellicule* as small skin, as detached skin, as foreskin.[14] These creases that spell caresses coincide with a fabric that froths and foams: warm wrinkles that radiate the heat of exertion and orgasm. Thought with Nancy's drool-encrusted philosophy, pillow and, we might assume, duvet, bodily fluids and textiles acquire a technical, as well as a sensible, dimension – equivalent to brushstrokes, notation, filming, along with pigment, paste, paint and the luminous materiality of light. If, as Nancy contends, truth is in the skin, then its excretions, blood, sweat, tears, surely double down on this veracity and whilst not tear-spattered, or blood-splattered, or especially sweaty, *Cleo from 5 to 7* certainly seeps a little. Cléo sheds tears at pivotal moments. Salty spherules roll down her cheeks during the film's opening sequence and when she sings 'Sans toi' at the midway point, whilst Jean-Luc Godard's (clumsy) cameo, as a suddenly grief-stricken lover in *Cleo from 5 to 7*'s film-within-a-film secretes crystal globules after he witnesses his *poupée d'amour* carted off in a hearse. Godard wipes away his tears with a recently purchased checked handkerchief and in doing so he encrusts its wetness within his *mouchoir*'s textile patterns. And we might assume that Cléo's tears encrust their surrounding textiles too: a carpet-topped table and a feathery peignoir, adding to their textures. Teary testaments to corporeality, the body beaten by its own sense of body, which *Cleo from 5 to 7* plots, these latter tears (wetness) become tears (holes) temporarily drawing the film into alternative narrative spaces divorced from the principal body of the film and which we shall explore in greater detail below.[15] In true Nancean fashion, then, we must reattune to their lexical and verbal resonances whereby bodily fluids and textiles once more acquire a technical, as well as a sensible, dimension, and whilst *Cleo from 5 to 7* only seeps a little, it is full of fabric: Cléo's successive costume changes, superstitious hat shopping, sailors' pompoms, Antoine's soldier's uniform, a black textile triptych. These textiles further attune the spectator to their technical and sensible dimensions – dimensions shored up by what Nancy calls *carnation*, or local colour, which in turn encourages a resonant reading.

Carnation is not incarnation, that is, the flesh infused with Spirit, but instead flesh itself and what Nancy (parenthetically) describes as 'the vibration and the singular intensity – itself changing, mobile, multiple – of a skin-event or of skin as the place for an event of existence'.[16] Blood, sweat, tears and drool are arguably skin-events and Nancy's drooling tautology, and tautological ontology, encrusts textiles with bodily fluids even further thanks to its encounter with Japanese artist On Kawara's *Today* series (1966–2014). On monochromatic canvases, Kawara painted the date of each painting's creation, its format reflecting the location of its production, and he destroyed any efforts that were not completed by midnight:

> With On Kawara, this technique [. . .] may at first seem purely tautological. The date says nothing but itself. [. . .] In saying nothing but itself, the date says nothing of itself: this time it is the date of nothing, of no event. It says of itself only (and it doesn't say it, it isn't visible): that it is painted the very day.[17]

Drool writes a similar nightly, or perhaps post-lunch, nothing. It is an unending, 'literary' note that renews itself night after night in a silvery strand, speaking nothing but the singular-plural sense of the world, effectively another example of bastardised pillow talk, our pillows its canvas. Kawara's date paintings of course submit to a similar logic, but one that sounds out further downstream than drool:

> But a *date* in English is also an encounter. And *to date* can mean: 'go to an encounter'. The date is the possibility of an encounter, with the indication of a place, that is, of the point ordered by the punctuality of the encounter. Here, the place is here. That is, anywhere: in any place *where I am dating here*, that is in any place where a *date painting* can be exposed. On Kawara sets a date anywhere, anytime, he sets a date with 'the date' itself. The painting announces: find me there where I am, and we will meet. You will recognize me by this, that I am only there for the encounter. And I will

recognize you by the same. We will be there, you as well as I, only to find ourselves there. [. . .] We will find each other by each other.[18]

Reminiscent of Eva and Georg finding each other on the beaches of Haneke in *The Seventh Continent*, Nancy's encounter with Kawara is an emphatic reminder of the inherent (pseudo-)spectatorship embedded within the very texture of his thinking on images, and it is such potential that Stephen Barker suggests 'is the central reason why Kawara's work so fascinates Nancy [for] [t]he evocation of a single date [. . .] slides into the *hic et nunc* of both the sensuous and memory'.[19]

Sensuousness and memory crash into view as Nancy frames the abovementioned skin-events with reference to local colour when discussing Kawara's *Viet-Nam* triptych (1965) and how the red magenta used in the paintings is quite literally their local colour because it serves as 'the *datum* of a bloody spatter', that is, a marker of the blood spilled during the war.[20] A terrestrial and canvas claret encrusting thus takes place through the arabesque logic of Nancy's thought and he elaborates further on similar splashes of red in his joint-authored text with Ferrari when describing the rouge burst in Rembrandt's *Bathsheba at Her Bath* (1654):

> A small red, velvet ribbon which ties the hair, and lights up [*renvoie*] the sombre colours that surround it, makes the entire canvas vibrate and draws attention towards *Bathsheba*'s breasts. The left breast is slightly deformed, probably a tumour – a sickness that insinuates itself in her body – an imperfection which renders her nudity all the more singular.[21]

According to Nancy and Ferrari, the gentle tumble of the rouge textile slither illuminates the edges of the obscurity that surrounds it. Indeed, the very texture of resonance encrusts the canvas, for the ribbon enters into a sort of relay with the darkness, which makes the entire canvas vibrate. Otherwise put, it makes it resonate: neither swatch is subsumed by the rhythms of the other, each beats the other into existence. The canvas is thus matter in movement and it further refines Nancy's local colour and what he further refines elsewhere as profoundly sympathetic to waveforms and thus to resonance: 'the vibration, color, frequency, and nuance of a place, of an event of existence'.[22] This red flash is this vibration, colour, frequency, and nuance of a place, of an event of existence, and it is through this local colour that we come to listen right up against the image, that is, to its illumination, its obscurity, its nudity, its rouge dribble, further affirming how within the Nancean vernacular the image is but a placeholder for a *corpus corporum*, that is, a *corpus imāginum*: breath, crease, differential, drool, fabric, flesh, foam, fold, intimate, material, multiple, nude, orgasm, pleasure, plural, resonance, singular, skin, sweat, tactile, textile, visual, warmth, waste, world. It is thanks to its local colour that we resonate. Fundamentally, then, the small, red velvet ribbon enjoys a technical as well as a sensible dimension. For Nancy and Ferrari, however, this resonance centres on sickness – a potential cancer in the left breast that mirrors Cléo's own – which extends the canvas's encrusting of the very texture of resonance, by staging another percussive corporeality, that is, an instance of the body beaten by its own corporeality, which of course recalls Nancy's illness and his subsequent emergence as an artistic subject and his artistic syntax. Indeed, the nude is perhaps the ultimate skin-event for, as Christina Howells details:

> it shows [. . .] that truth and meaning lie not in the depths of our souls, nor yet in the heights of the heavens, but rather on the surface of the skin. This, indeed, is the secret of naked flesh and its images: there is precisely no secret, nothing to discover beyond or beneath the skin itself.[23]

Resonance, however, complicates this choreography – the ears have no eyelids, after all – and the vibration of *carnation*, and its coincident taxonomy of waveforms, which Nancy's own account of cinema is sensitive to, further embellishes its sense of matter in movement, more acutely reorienting us towards the sensuousness of the world that flows through us.[24]

Looking, listening, drooling, lachrymose leaking, sweating, sensuality, memory, nudity: the warp and weft of Nancy's duvet is thus made up of the intimate anatomy, and resonant materiality, that his encounters with the arts foreground – mouth, lungs, ears, (closed) eyes – and it is the collapse between textiles and an encrusting of an embodied, yet ethereal, encounter with the sensuousness and otherness of the world that blows through us realised by Nancy's somniloquy that this chapter pursues. Along with this intimate anatomy and resonant materiality, *Cleo from 5 to 7* also becomes caught up in the warp and weft of Nancy's duvet, for Kawara's date paintings unwittingly nestle Varda's film because alongside its topographical coherence, *Cleo from 5 to 7* is, as noted above, temporally sound too. If, then, we were to imagine *Cleo from 5 to 7* as a date painting, its date would read *21 juin 1961*, while its boxed lining would be constituted from the 'Cléo-realism' that encroaches on our eponymous heroine's (fictional) perambulatory odyssey, that is, its documentary details rhythmed by newspapers, radio news broadcasts, the sights and bustle of Parisian streets, overheard café conversations and the journeys taken in taxis, with friends in cars and on buses.[25] We might mistake these details for the film's local colour. This chapter, however, adopts a more Nancean application of local colour, albeit one disavowed by Nancy himself, by casting *Cleo from 5 to 7*'s *carnation* as a colour, specifically the triptych of black fabric expanses that thread through the film.

Listening to *Cleo from 5 to 7*

Textiles and blackness are certainly no strangers to the reception of *Cleo from 5 to 7*, and the film's clever opening sequence, which depicts our eponymous heroine's visit to the fortune teller Madame Irma, patchworks together, in vivid colour, the warp and weft of the film's narrative with the ornament (and information) of the credits. These moments are frequently read as a space for fantasy. Valerie Orpen, for example, highlights how Varda 'sees the [tarot] cards as an "illustration" of life' which is 'not to be confused with black and white "reality"': the tenuous line between the two colourfully bolstered, where black is principally read as the arbiter of the (now) archival, documentary real, increasingly so as the film becomes further rooted in the past.[26] We have already seen, through Nancy's work, how such a decorative disclaimer risks relegating the tarot cards, and the sequence more generally, to a lowlier pictorial register. Indeed, the sequence is brimming with risky pictorial qualities. Floral forms, the backbone of the arabesque, abound. A textile expanse, the product of a lowly, feminine artistic practice, in the form of a carpet, a very everyday object, is the first thing we see followed by the profilmic female figure, who is always structurally risky and at risk.[27]

At around about 5 p.m. on 21 June 1961, the film starts to take such risks, commencing with a close-up of a pair of hands shuffling a deck of cards. These disembodied mitts are soon joined by a third hand which emerges from the top of the frame and chromatically detaches from the grey-green of the textile expanse above which it hovers. The scene advances by playfully alluding to the fleshy presences beyond the frame for as Cléo is instructed to cut the deck of cards, the film follows suit and cuts from a tight framing of the protagonists' hands to a looser framing which incorporates the arms of each. In effect, the camera too responds to the tarot reader's directions and this 'Coupez, mademoiselle' perhaps addresses Varda as director, or Jeanine Verneau and Pascale Laverrière as editors, as much as it does Cléo. This wider framing reveals the textile surface upon which the tarot cards are spread to be the central medallion of a carpet that branches outwards towards thorny vines of flowers that neighbour still more decorative foliage patterning, with what we determine to be a lamp, thanks to its luminous halo, balanced atop a lacquered wooden table further ornamenting the patterns woven into the carpet. Occasionally, when a hand pauses above the table, it cups into a closed bud, extending the floral vines, their discreet touches embellishing the ornamental qualities of the film's imagery. Encrusted within the carpet is an invitation not to get caught up with the signifying potential of the tarot reading, but rather to relish in the bountiful festoons of the decorative, that is, in the tiny stiches and teased, tensile fibres that make up the vast textile landscape of the carpet's florid desert. Formally speaking, then, on- and off-screen space partake in a shared rhythm. They are in resonance. This cut produces such an effect – a structural and diegetic coincidence reminiscent of Walter Benjamin's approximating the director with the surgeon in a parallel that bears keen critical and contextual resonances in a discussion of Nancy's thought in relation to Varda's celebrated film.[28] Both Cléo and Nancy, after all, find themselves recipients of a physician's punctual speech act. These speech acts bookend Nancy's and Cléo's journeys. Nancy's corporeal disarray starts with such an enunciation, whilst Cléo's ends with one. The linguistic and cinematic breeziness of this latter proclamation, the doctor's matter-of-fact delivery, the camera's jaunty withdrawal, is underwhelming given Cléo's turmoil. She's going to be fine, after all.

These striking cinematic textures seamlessly establish a clash, according to Judith Mayne, between the scientific and primitive, which the film codes as masculine/male and feminine/female, respectively.[29] The doctor's pronouncement born from reason, the fortune teller's prediction from superstition.[30] These textures telescope broader concerns which centre on blackness. Indeed, following the doctor's prognosis, Cléo and Antoine regard each other and then the film quickly cuts to black – to which we shall return at this chapter's close. There are three mentions of black in the film, the only colour mentioned, and all of which limn roleplay – Cléo as widow, Jean-Luc Godard as mourner, Cléo as escapee – and a diptych of existing responses to *Cleo from 5 to 7* from Mayne and Elizabeth Ezra highlight the complex position that blackness occupies in the film. This position is no more apparent than when the playful and parodic silent short – *Les Fiancés du Pont Neuf*, which features a raft of French New Wave stars – is taken 'as a metaphor for Cléo's dilemma of perception'.[31] Like Nancy, then, Cléo goes to the movies and despite her own place within the pantheon of *nouvelle vague* characters, here the film substitutes Cléo's look for that of others, which gives rise to a very real dilemma of perception, as Ezra explains:

> In this whimsical tale, Godard plays a young man whose world changes completely once he puts on a pair of dark glasses. His blonde girlfriend called Anna, turns into a black woman, and an insignificant mishap becomes a fatal accident (complete with ambulance transformed into a hearse). Once the man removes the sunglasses, everything returns to normal and he cries, 'It was because of my glasses that everything

looked black.' Blackness turns out to have been an illusion, a question literally of
outlook. The short film's funereal imagery indicates that the color black is meant
to be interpreted as a metaphor for affect (as in a dark mood), but in the context of
the larger film's exoticist allusions, the short film's use of a black woman inevitably
conjures up certain cultural associations. Judith Mayne has noted the short film's
'unproblematized relation between black and white; indeed, the black remains as the
unexamined projection of the white man's sunglasses or the spectacle of a "primitive
mask"'. The black version of Anna is presented as a disguise covering the 'real' Anna,
who, within the diegetic universe of the short film, appears to have been wearing a
kind of black mask. This notion of blackness as a mask or visual effect can be read
as a kind of reversal of Frantz Fanon's 1952 *Peau noire, masques blancs [Black Skin,
White Masks]*, which argues that colonial subjects of African descent internalise the
worldview of their white oppressors. For Fanon, the white mask was a symbol of the
attitudes and behaviors of a dominant (colonizing) culture that had been embraced
by a dominated (colonised) culture. The performance of blackness, on the other
hand (as epitomised by the wearing of blackface, for example) is a form of cultural
tourism, a temporary borrowing or wearing of a mask – representing not 'black' culture, but the system of domination that insists on polarizing what the terms 'black'
and 'white' represent. In the short film, difference turns out to be a reflection of the
lens through which one looks – in other words, subjective, and culturally condi-
tioned. Cultural tourism commodifies 'racial' identity, making of it something to be
tried on like a hat in a shop.[32]

Ezra here excavates a seam of colonialist domination that the film's rich critical history on roleplaying largely overlooks and, as Mayne's initial teasing of this seam makes clear, this unproblematised polarisation cannot simply be bracketed off within the parodic short, neither can it be reassuringly contained by 'the limited state of Cléo's limited consciousness' when earlier in the film an African mask displayed in a shop window and a black student protester startle her.[33]

Once exposed this seam resonates – hearing becomes impossible, listening is all that remains – and it resonates with discussion of Cléo's successive costume changes, which map her change of address onto the change of a dress.[34] Sandy Flitterman-Lewis aggregates these tropes at length:

She [...] tears off the traditional attributes of stereotypical feminine beauty – blonde wig and feathered satin peignoir – and thereby activates her transformation from object to subject through a change in image. In order to leave the world of those who have defined her as a cliche [...] she now puts on ordinary-looking clothing (a black dress, simple jewelry) and with a violent sweep of a black curtain [...] she emerges, *changed*.[35]

Even syntactically Flitterman-Lewis hints at the interrelation between a change in Cléo's outlook hinged on a change in her look, and this costume change, alongside the addition of a pair of dark glasses, brings with it a constellation of conflicting, and ultimately compromising, characteristics: harmony, invisibility, anonymity.[36] Orpen epitomises this conflict: 'in the black dress, Cléo does become anonymous and is thus better able to observe others and leave aside her former "fake" identity'.[37] However, Orpen quickly negates the affirmative properties of Cléo's more real attire by positing it as 'her final "camouflage" outfit', that is, 'a costume, a masquerade to protect her against the reality of the outside world'.[38] Whilst ostensibly placing Cléo at the heart of their thinking, each of these accounts suggests that Cléo must absent herself from the cityscape to become a rend in their theses and, moreover, in the film itself, lending it a curious orificial structure. It is holes that this chapter will continue to pursue, specifically those tears created by the black textile triptych – tears articulated by a rare visual absence, tears with the immediate environment and black holes, all of which profoundly transform our encounter with the film.

Dressing Up

We encounter *Cleo from 5 to 7*'s first black fabric panel as Cléo, both character and film, playfully, yet unthinkingly, invoke otherness *chez* Francine – the hat shop. Wandering from the Café Ça va Ça vient, Cléo and Angèle approach the shop's window display, and the camera takes up residence behind the glass. Buried amongst the items on show we peer out from beneath the rims of the many textile orbs suspended above. There is something wonderfully cosmic about this image, and the shot/reverse-shot sequence that follows as Cléo and Angèle exchange glances with these floating discs attests to this notion; they speak of a mutual drawing together of pseudo-celestial (hats) and earthly bodies (Cléo). Their ornament, however, constitutes only part of the sequence's roleplaying for the reflective glass surfaces of the mirrors scattered throughout the store, the smooth plastic of mannequins, and the matt, opaque surfaces of fleshy, human others operate as projectors and screens that assist in mediating those Cléo parodies: the bride, the southern belle, the widow and, of course, her capricious self. Cléo's charade thus opens up a space to rethink this consistent focus on her character, and rather than demonstrating an indisputable instance of her image being shaped by the gaze of others, the creation of her fluctuating image could instead be attributable to the encounter between the different surfaces that adorn the shop floor. Her impersonations are, for instance, structured around clever rear projections: the bridal mannequin stands tall behind Cléo as she shows off her imaginary solitaire; mounted officers enter the frame thanks to a strategically placed mirror as Cléo twirls a lace bouquet between her fingers; and finally, the mourning that graphically bordered the image, before dropping into its recesses as the cosmic power of the hats effervesces on its surface, muscularly works its way to the surface of the image once again thanks to a tiny arabesque as Cléo places the wide-brimmed, black veiled hat upon her head, declaring that black definitely suits her. Despite, then, the accent on image-making, such a textile reading of the sequence suppresses the reflective properties of the mirror in favour of the interplay of the film's textile nuclei, indicating an attenuation of the mirror's significance in Cléo's tale that most existing secondary literature foregrounds.[39]

As Cléo scours her choice of headwear from the flying saucers stationed in the window, she passes a black sheet draped across part of the shop's window display, and the first panel of our textile triptych, which momentarily blots out our view of her – a rare visual absence which transforms her into a rend, a tear in the fabric of the film – and plunges us into the matted togetherness of otherness through the brief collapse of shop front and cinema screen. The image that replaces Cléo continues the hats' cosmic disposition, for pinned upon this twilight textile expanse is a series of white ellipses resembling palm-sized galaxies (Figure 7). This familiar disposition recalls the shot/reverse-shot sequence that opens the episode but here the reverse shot is embedded in the frame for, practically imperceptibly, these microcosmic star systems intermingle with the city's reflection that becomes caught up in the diaphanous glass surface of the window, and cinema screen, the social fabric, and (now) archival reality of the city, encroaching upon, or encrusting, the fancy of Cléo's game of dress up. This nestling of shot/reverse-shot realises several frames of Nancean cinema, that is, 'cinema *intensified*, pushed from the inside toward an essence that detaches it to a large extent from representation and turns it toward presence' which works to refine our plunge.[40] Once more, then, pseudo-celestial and earthly bodies conjoin, once more fantasy juxtaposes reality, yet here black simultaneously bolsters and erodes their distinction.

As the camera pans across the shop window, the cityscape temporarily takes over the film and in realising this takeover, textiles here acquire a technical, as well as a sensible, dimension, effectively disclosing the resonant constitution of the film: city symphony, *Bildungsroman*, new wave film – one percussively beating the other into being. Before this first panel of the black, textile triptych, then, and through the profilmic textures, we encounter the texture of Nancean ontology – its singular-plural irreducibility – thanks to the materiality and corporeality at the heart of resonance. Cars, buses, shop fronts and Parisians ripple and pool on the window pane. Momentarily, our eyes function like organs of touch for our look grazes

Figure 7 *Cleo from 5 to 7* (1961), a film by Agnès Varda © 1961 ciné-tamaris.

this glass pane and the urban lining that encrusts it, and through this haptic inclination, the film produces a material, motile look that buds and opens in the middle of ordinary turbulence, indeed that is ordinary turbulence. On the other side of the glass, both commercial and cinematic, is the world before Cléo's cry, both character and film, into it. This, though, is not simply a visual staging of otherness, like resting a hat upon one's head, that is, a temporary, touristic trying on. Rather, it is like resting your head on your pillow and drooling, for through the camera's glide and the city's hum and ripples we come to listen right up against the image. Glide, hum, ripple, these frames form a *corpus imāginum* which traces our shared existence, body to body, both cinematically and corporeally because like the film here, the first panel of its black textile triptych alloys our looking. The film resonates with and between its material multiplicity and we in turn resonate with this material multiplicity. We look, we touch, we listen, we glide whereby *Cleo from 5 to 7* presents not a fixed snapshot of a 1960s Parisian pavement, but a fleeting, material evidence that renews itself with every look, touch, listen and glide.

Swelling Up

Tellingly, roleplaying, that is, a temporary trying on of otherness, extends to Cléo's entourage during the first half of the film: doctors, nurses, frogs, all attend to her before she reaches the Parc Montsouris or the hospital courtyard. Indeed, there is a culmination of such roleplay in the moments leading up to the second textile tablet, which is widely read as the crucial and literal turning point of Cléo's transformation and seen as she sings 'Sans toi' whilst standing in front of a draped curtain. Having changed into négligée, coyly greeted her lover José, smoked a few cigarettes, lamented men and love with Angèle and, finally, embarked on a rehearsal with Bob, who stocks her musical catalogue, the sequence erupts into a devastating musical crescendo. Attuned to a palette which dichotomises black and colour into reality and fantasy, it is surprising that existing responses to the scene read a sense of fantasy and play as centrifugally radiating from this second triptych panel given that it is pitched in black. Flitterman-Lewis, for instance, considers it 'an apotheosis of the fetishized woman's image'[41] and for Orpen it is 'an anti-realistic (and hyper-real) orchestral and reverberating rendition of the song's last few stanzas'.[42] Like the shop window-cum-cinema screen, it consists of a tangle of textures. Cléo is first accompanied by Bob on the piano, but as the camera moves towards her with an encircling, gentle sweeping motion, this diegetic music very soon and (again) almost imperceptibly becomes extra-diegetic as orchestral string music begins to play. Cléo too, seemingly instinctively, becomes aware of this extra-diegetic dimension and turns towards this imaginary concert hall. The film effectively stills and apart from the movement of her lips as she sings, a single teardrop falling down Cléo's cheek is the only visible movement in the frame – a teary testament to her corporeality – until the number is over, and the camera rapidly retreats from her figure revealing her heightened despair. Stilling, crying, falling, the film here recalls an earlier moment in the film: Cléo's departure from Madame Irma's.

Money is exchanged between the pair and as the notes are passed from Cléo to the fortune teller the camera adopts a pointedly angular attitude towards the profilmic; it seamlessly, although jaggedly, joins Cléo's transaction, Madame Irma's refusal to look and Cléo's visual snub with a lateral, vertical and a corresponding horizontal movement. The film then cuts to Cléo's hand turning the doorknob and as it grasps the metal it buds once more. Madame Irma mirrors this gesture and the camera continues its linear style and threads Madame Irma's hand, face, secreted husband and finally her budding right hand, which concludes the scene. Reminiscent of the surgeon's scalpel that incises flesh, bone and the profilmic, such camerawork bears similarities with the peaks and troughs of an electrocardiogram, recalling the ordinary turbulence of Nancy's wasted heart.

Having shed a solitary tear, Cléo departs the tarot reader's rooms and begins her flânerie. Her walking, however, does not commence on the streets and boulevards of Paris, but rather in the narrow corridor and winding stairwell of Madame Irma's apartment building. These first steps are almost as significant to our understanding of *Cleo from 5 to 7*, and the profound transformation of Cléo's entire being, as her entire perambulatory odyssey. At first, her descent appears to be an audio-visual ode to (self-)image, with both the image- and soundtracks dominated by Cléo through a series of overexposed point of view shots, a rearranged version of what we later learn has been a moderately hit song for Cléo, 'La belle P', that plays, and a tightly framed, thrice regurgitated, close-up of her head. Unique amongst the film's editing pattern, this repetition momentarily creates an illusory stasis, producing a phoney still within a film driven by bipedal movement. Arguably Cléo, protagonist and film, enjoys a Kuleshov moment, but the image of the star only ever neighbours itself. Cléo's face becomes a cranial, orificial, stuttering montage, the self-sameness of which seemingly exhausts any logic of what Daniel Fairfax determines as 'resonance-montage' – a 'polyphonic', yet visuality-driven, stitching together of images from across cinematic history whose collisions produce dialectical images 'typified by a "flash-like" coming together of past and present, which form[. . .] a constellation of ephemeral, fleeting duration, whose potential meaning or affect is elusive, shifting, polysemic'.[43] These collisions 'tap into a certain eternal iconography [. . .] the same gestures, the same movements, the same motifs, repeat themselves'.[44] Resonance here, then, is repetition – a reminder of tautology, of a fault in style, as well as Nancy's belief in the ubiquitous flashes of cinema within the everyday. In the case of *Cleo from 5 to 7*, we might suspect that its visual affinities are too exact to offer any flash of eternity, appearing to provide only a momentary visual arrhythmia,[45] or what Nancy would temporalise as 'the simultaneous eternal present' defined by 'self-same sameness' that Kawara's date paintings exemplify: 'Nothing distinguishes one year from another but the difference of a numeral, and nothing presents the perennial but the simultaneity, here, of all these differences.'[46] Resonance inveigles itself into such thinking, once again through repetition, and through the encounter, that is, through spectatorship, because in front of the date paintings,

> One hears oneself saying the date: I see the canvas and I pronounce its date, thus repeating that which makes the canvas itself. With a canvas voice, matte and flat against the wall, each person says the which of the date [. . .]. The voice becomes silent, sticks to the canvas, and this is how it resonates: and its resonance is painting.[47]

Before the date paintings, then, the (spectating) voice becomes encrusted in the canvas – a canvas that announces its desire for encounter and that is made for encounter and is thus irreducibly singular-plural. Indeed, we might consider Kawara's *Today* series as the most basic manifestation of being singular-plural, one singular day lived in different ways, like the many Parisians, spectator included, matted together on the hat shop's window. Matte and flat against the wall, we see the voices that we hear. Predicated on silence, stickiness and solipsism, such a dynamic risks short-circuiting resonance despite Nancy's assurances. Yet again, though, the very texture of resonance encrusts the canvas for voice and canvas are both emitter and receptor, each effectively a sonorous and sonorised body, sounding out the other, defying any supposed silence not least because this encounter buzzes with the hum of worldly sense. This canvas voice, moreover, recalls the whole articulatory cinema (of the spoken text) whereby speech becomes an invitation for spectation – *la voix, c'est du cinéma* – or perhaps, more accurately, spectation becomes an invitation for speech, and this invitation, which hinges on the passing glimpse of the inside of the mouth, is a sort of invagination, a 'self-same sameness', a percussive corporeality produced by a body beaten by its own sense of being a body. A voice that thinks, a body projected into a memory.

Cleo from 5 to 7 here is subject to such a percussive corporeality – its three visual beats accentuating the event of filmmaking – and in spite of such self-same sameness, the image of Cléo's face is falling, a movement intensified by its repetition, like a stone towards the bottom of a well, that is, like another of Nancy's ubiquitous cinematic flashes. Falling, faltering, we might suggest that, like Nancy's wasted heart, it is through the stuttering, vomiting, even rejection, of Cléo's image that the film performs a percussive corporeality: it is a film beaten by (phoney) film stills. It implies a body in disarray, a self that struggles for authorship.[48] Indeed, it indicates a sense of faultiness, much like that detailed in Nancy's account of his heart transplant:

> this thing surged up inside me, where nothing had been before: nothing but the 'proper' immersion inside me of a 'myself' never identified as this body, still less as this heart, suddenly watching itself. [. . .] Something strange is disclosed 'at the heart' of the most familiar – but 'familiar' hardly says it: at the heart of something that never signaled itself as 'heart'. Up to this point, it was strange by virtue of not being even perceptible, not even being present. From now on it fails, and this strangeness binds me to myself.[49]

Nancy continues this thinking with a tragic Cartesian parody: '"I" am, because I am ill', which morbidly, yet melodiously, chimes with Cléo's own confrontation with her body and subjectivity.[50] For at the heart of each text is an awakening of the originary strangeness of ourselves engendered by the faltering and consequent sprouting of an internal organ: in Nancy's case, his heart; in Cléo's, her stomach, or perhaps her uterus.[51] By the time Cléo reaches the atrial space of the building, the film's resonances with Nancy's defective atria are palpable and upon her arrival here, *Cleo from 5 to 7* attempts to restore bodily coherence through a mirrored monologue, but it does not hold. In essence, each body, Nancy's, Cléo's and the film's, experiences a corporeal faltering; the three close-ups materially sprout within the body of the film, much like the sensation of Nancy's irregular heartbeat that put him in 'touch' with 'himself', and, like *Le Bonheur*'s own repetitions, enigmatically politicising and historicising Cléo's, and *Cleo*'s, image(ry).[52] Its enigma is the image of the hysteric. Its enigma lies in its very selfsameness, in its exhaustion, which discloses such eternal iconography. Its three visual beats produce three parallel images, three clichés that recall the photography of the Pitié-Salpêtrière Hôpital – Cléo's final destination in the film, which works to transform the entire film into a sort of slow-motion dialectical image as the present of Cléo's journey comes together with the past of the hospital – their reiterative pictorial technique effectively inventing maladies, such as Albert Londe's 'Baillements hystériques' (1888), a triptych of photographs that give a snapshot of a young woman named Augustine's incessant yawning. Arguably here Cléo, protagonist and film, has a hysterical moment where any sense of faultiness concerns faulty images of women.

During Cléo's performance of 'Sans toi' a similar swelling (up) occurs and she is struck by a similar sense of faultiness. The words she sings speak of a vital existence which she feels is slipping away from her. Standing before the black, textile backdrop, Cléo cuts a desperate and desolate figure, and unlike the first display pinned to black fabric, Cléo here is not situated amongst a constellation of neighbouring galaxies, but rather she is a lonely, solitary planet, a star. Although its music and lyrics may not have been written by Cléo, many suggest that they 'become conflated with her latent thoughts' and act as a catalyst to her consciousness:[53] 'Now that she looks at us, at the camera, as she sings her heart out, we feel that she already knows the music, she *is* the music, and that the music is issuing from inside the character.'[54] Such accounts of the film, however, indicate a tautology of film style, rather than the Nancean variety, whereby once more Cléo, like Augustine, is nothing more than her image, both visual and acoustic – she *is* this anguish – when in fact a very different issue burgeons here. Stilling, crying, falling, Cléo's tears encrust their textile surrounds. Stilling, crying, falling, encrusting, Cléo's performance, arguably a little film-within-a-film that spills 'outside the room, visually and audibly bursting out of the space', transposes Nancy's cinematic flashes.[55]

Style here swells the film's body and Cléo's tears fall like a stone towards the bottom of a well, and this falling coincides with another corporeal failing and the percussive, resonant corporeality to which it gives rise – the body beaten by its own sense of corporeality. Like Nancy's heart and Cléo's head, some thing sprouts. Stilling, falling, encrusting, Cléo's tears literalise this beat and, despite appearances, they signal not an affective outpouring but rather a tear with her immediate environment. Bodily fluids and textiles once again acquire a technical dimension. Instead of temporarily blotting her out, this iteration of the textile triptych suspends and detaches Cléo from the diegesis and takes her into in 'the abstract time and space of [her] performance', potentially placing her at (greater) risk.[56] Cléo is thus exposed. Yet she exposes not her self, and her feelings, but us, that is, our quivering compound being. Cléo, both character and film, take flight, they perform the venturing and return of resonance, and through its swell, realised by its *corpus imāginum*, its stilling, falling, encrusting, it intensifies our encounter with it, complicating the space between us. We resonate, after all. Embodied by the stilling, falling and encrusting of the tear, what sprouts here, then, is not only Cléo's sickness, but equally her disgust with performance, and rather than using this performance as a further disguise, shedding, discarding, redressing, anonymising, Cléo is instead undone by it, which the film's style emphatically embodies. When the number is over, the camera rapidly tears away from Cléo. Cléo then tears into a corner to change before she tears her wig from her head, wishing she could take her head with it. With this second tablet of the textile triptych, then, comes a second tear in the fabric of the film, which prompts a flurry of further diegetic tears.[57]

Tearing Up

Shedding, discarding, redressing, tearing, these gestures are a marker of Cléo's disgust, which her subsequent spectatorship and flânerie makes obvious – the city's sights not projections of her mind, that is, of her worries about sickness, mutilation and death, but rather manifestations of this disgust. Tearing herself from her world, Cléo decides to escape from her apartment and venture into the city, changed. A heated exchange with Bob ensues and, captured in extreme close-up, his head functions as a wipe across the screen. Cléo hurries into a corner and steps behind the black curtain draped there – drawing it in a counter-movement to the wipe enacted by Bob's head. An apparently osmotic darkened drape fills the screen, for Cléo emerges from behind it cloaked in black. With this third curtain we complete the film's black textile triptych, and significantly, this final pane constitutes the only tablet that is the sole perceptible object of the frame. We may, for a moment, suspect an analogue glitch; once again the film momentarily stills. If imagined hinged together, as we move through the black textile triptych, we move from a series of galaxies, to a lone planet and finally to a black hole. In essence, upon every encounter the content of each panel thins out. The first iteration's intergalactic ripple collapses into Cléo's solitary sung soliloquy, which collapses into the most singular image of the entire film: so singular that we could refute its very being there as an image at all, and playfully and formally implying that Cléo's star turn in the preceding tablet becomes a supernova and what remains of it is an abyss, a blank, a nothingness. Indeed, the empty screen could be said to testify to how in the Nancean vernacular the image is but a placeholder for a *corpus corporum*, that is, a *corpus imāginum* and which here risks being understood as a placeholder for the image itself. However, in our being there for the encounter, both in isolation and as part of the film's textile triptych, its existence cannot be denied because we meet and find each other there at the threshold of the screen. Once more, then, the black textile triptych attunes to the transitivity of being singular-plural. Indeed, through these encounters, the noisy, lively charge of worldly sense precipitates where the kaleidoscopic junctures of reality appear to be far more muted (for black is the film's local colour). Nonetheless, the film's textile triptych quivers, for by design the form of the triptych lends itself to the very principles which charge *carnation* because although technically one picture, each separate tablet affords us a different view of a similar theme, making it mobile, multiple, protean and, like being, hinged. If text is textile, here textile becomes text because in these terms we might conceive each black fabric panel as literalising, like drool, the 'series of modifying prepositions and hyphens [that] punctuat[e] the text of *Being Singular Plural*, the dis- and ex- that repeatedly modifies all position and stance'.[58] As Philip Armstrong continues: 'It is these prepositions and hyphens that inaugurate the *com-* or "being with" by permanently remarking the radical exteriority and desedimentation of all ontological and metaphysical presuppositions, by permanently recomposing Being in terms of its singular plurality and plural singularity.'[59] Each black fabric panel, a tiny tear in the fabric of the film, inaugurates such being. They are the very fabric of encounter and each thus embodies not a way of seeing, but of being, which the tears (wetness and holes) of the final moments of *Cleo from 5 to 7* realise.

Following the doctor's anti-climactic, and scientific, assurances, Cléo and Antoine turn towards us, then towards each other, before the film cuts to black. This cut, however, becomes a tear because it is indicative of a faulty runtime. It is not 7 o'clock, but rather a little after 6.30 p.m., yet the film appears to be over. According to Roy Jay Nelson, Varda 'seems to be encouraging us to shatter the mirror: from 6:30 (Cleo's time), when the screen goes black, until 7:00, the hour promised by the title, we are on our own, without a mirror, in search of our natural selves'.[60] This reading of the film wholeheartedly shatters the mirror, preferring the mattness of textiles to its tain. Somewhat eerily, though, the mortal bounty its narrative places on the head of the figure of the female star becomes fundamentally caught up with the 'real life' in which Cléo's perambulatory odyssey is embedded, that of 21 June 1961, through the October 1963 death of Edith Piaf, who garners audio and visual mention on three occasions throughout *Cleo from 5 to 7* and thus accentuates the 'tenuous line between art and "reality"'.[61] For just as the tension between art and reality exposes the sometimes flimsy juncture between the two, as the reality of the film (five to six-thirty) tips over into our own corporeality (six-thirty to seven and beyond), we experience a further tear as the film emphatically trails off not into nothingness, but into ourselves. It demands to be listened to once more and attests to the kaleidoscopic nature of being despite its muted colour, as does a more discreet percussive corporeality: the potential solitary tear that runs down Cléo's face.

During some viewings I am sure that I see it. During others I am doubtful. Sometimes I see it on Antoine's cheek. Why, then, does this tear that occasionally drops, that has two bodies, and that may not exist at all, and which neighbours the film's biggest tear, appear at all and only sometimes? In *The Forms of the Affects* Eugenie Brinkema places one of cinema's most famous tears 'under suspicion' – Marion's post-mortem pendeloque in Alfred Hitchcock's *Psycho* (1960):[62]

> that tear that may just be a drop, that tear that does not fall but sits thickly next to the eye without revealing its source or its embodied secret: whether it was secreted at all. This tear that may not be a tear is an enigma, but historically it has not been treated as such.[63]

Cléo's tear shares neither the canonicity or certainty of Marion's, and Brinkema's thinking decouples, or tears, the tear from the heart and from the subject. It 'is neither *from* Marion nor *for* us', she writes, it 'no longer has a body' and thus inspires Brinkema's formal affectivity, that is, 'a possibility for reading',[64] 'a visible shape on the face; a distortion or culmination of pattern; a heaviness or a lightness of weight'.[65] Otherwise put, it is a resonant *corpus imāginum* in the extreme and through their mutual estrangement from interiority we can certainly read some sympathies with Nancy's ontology here, which *Cleo from 5 to 7*'s black textile triptych echoes, and which resonance of course complicates for it hovers between the inside and the outside. The mysteries of Cléo's(?) tear, however, lie elsewhere. Yet it is bound to Marion's(?) in relation to whether it was secreted at all, and by whom, not least because it may be shed by the spectator and the spectator alone. However, I do not weep, but my spectatorship tears up, and it does so thanks to the film's local colour. For this tear bears the hallmark of each tablet of the textile triptych. Matted, through its ambiguous corporeality, (quintessentially) falling and (im)material, through the uncertainty that pertains over its very being there at all, and it is thus that my vision comes to embody the falling, stalling, encrusting, tearing of *carnation* and that this tear takes on a technical, sensible dimension. Falling(?), stalling(?), encrusting(?), tearing(?), it charges these final images of *Cleo from 5 to 7* with what we might call a singular-plural of seeing – an economy of looking realised by the film's textile triptych through its intensification of the noisy charge that hinges being embedded in the very materiality of the film. It is therefore not significant whether or not the tear is there at all, and moreover which cheek it trickles down. Rather, what matters is my inescapable and irreducible being there with the film to which this tear testifies. Like sleep, the tear intertwines us and is shared equally without full knowledge of where we go, but we must go together – a togetherness which is the very foundation of resonance.

Notes

1. Nancy (1997b), p. 81.
2. For example, Jean-Pierre Melville as Parvulesco in *Breathless* (1960) and Brice Parain in *Vivre sa vie* (1962).
3. See Barbara Koenig Quart, *Women Directors: The Emergence of a New Cinema* (New York: Praeger, 1988), Flitterman-Lewis (1996), Mark Betz, *Beyond the Subtitle: Remapping European Art Cinema* (Minneapolis: University of Minnesota Press, 2009) and more recently Elkin (2016) and Thomas Deane Tucker, *The Peripatetic Frame: Images of Walking in Film* (Edinburgh: Edinburgh University Press, 2020), pp. 111–20.
4. François Penz, 'From Topographical Coherence to Creative Geography: Rohmer's *The Aviator's Wife* and Rivette's *Pont du Nord*', in *Cities in Transition: The Moving Image and the Modern Metropolis*, ed. by Emma Wilson and Andrew Webber (London: Wallflower Press, 2008), pp. 123–40 (p. 126).
5. See Valerie Orpen, *Cléo de 5 à 7* (London and New York: I. B. Tauris, 2007) and Steven Ungar, *Cléo de 5 à 7* (Basingstoke: Palgrave Macmillan, 2008).
6. Flitterman-Lewis (1996), p. 38. Flitterman-Lewis's work on the film paradigmatically summarises this reading.
7. Ricco (2015).

8. Nancy (2001c), p. 68.
9. Jean-Luc Nancy quoted in Simon Morgan Wortham, *The Poetics of Sleep: From Aristotle to Nancy* (New York: Bloomsbury, 2013), p. 131.
10. Ibid. p. 141.
11. Nancy (2008a), p. 6.
12. See McMahon (2012) for how cinema's technicity mechanically reproduces Nancy's understanding of touch.
13. Jean-Luc Nancy, *Noli me Tangere: On the Raising of the Body*, trans. by Sarah Clift, Pascale-Anne Brault and Michael Naas (New York: Fordham University Press, 2008c), p. 50.
14. Federico Ferrari and Jean-Luc Nancy, *Nus sommes: La peau des images* (Brussels: Yves Gevaert, 2006), p. 46. See, for instance, '*Acéphale*' (pp. 13–15) and '*Caresse*' (pp. 25–9).
15. See Brinkema (2014).
16. Nancy (2008a), pp. 15–17.
17. Jean-Luc Nancy, 'The Technique of the Present', *Tympanum* (2000b) <http://www.usc.edu/dept/comp-lit/tympanum/4/nancy.html> (last accessed 24 June 2012).
18. Ibid.
19. Barker (2012), p. 179.
20. Nancy (2000b).
21. Nancy and Ferrari (2006), p. 21. My translation.
22. Nancy (2008a), p. 15.
23. Christina Howells, 'Jean-Luc Nancy and *La Peau des images*: Truth Is Skin-Deep', *Body and Society*, 24 (2018), 166–74 (p. 172)
24. Ibid. p. 173.
25. Stanley Kauffmann quoted in Ungar (2008), p. 102.
26. Orpen (2007), p. 95.
27. See, for instance, Mulvey (1975), Rosalind Galt, 'Pretty: Film, Theory, Aesthetics, and the History of the Troublesome Image', *Camera Obscura*, 24 (2009), 1–41, Marks (2010) and Anna Backman Rogers, 'Lena Dunham's *Girls*: Can-Do Girls, Feminist Killjoys, and Women Who Make Bad Choices', in *Feminisms: Diversity, Difference and Multiplicity in Contemporary Film Cultures*, ed. by Laura Mulvey and Anna Backman Rogers (Amsterdam: Amsterdam University Press, 2015), pp. 44–53.
28. Walter Benjamin, 'The Work of Art in the Age of Mechanical Reproduction', in *Illuminations*, ed. by Hannah Arendt, trans. by Harry Zohn (New York: Schocken Books, 1985), pp. 217–51 (p. 233).
29. Judith Mayne, *The Woman at the Keyhole: Feminism and Women's Cinema* (Bloomington: Indiana University Press, 1990), p. 202.
30. Ibid.
31. Claudia Gorbman, '*Cléo from 5 to 7*: Music as Mirror', *Wide Angle*, 4 (1981), 38–49 (p. 40).

32. Elizabeth Ezra, 'Cléo's Masks: Regimes of Objectification in the French New Wave', *Yale French Studies*, 118/119 (2010), 177–90 (pp. 181–2).
33. Mayne (1990) p. 199.
34. Roy Jay Nelson plots the briefer permutations Cléo undergoes as reflected in her costume changes, for instance, the 'female clown' (in the hatter's) (p. 738) and 'the sex kitten' (in her apartment) (p. 739), whilst Jenny Chamarette (2012) notes how she becomes an angel whilst swinging in her apartment (p. 114). See Roy Jay Nelson, 'Reflections in a Broken Mirror: Varda's *Cléo de 5 à 7*', *The French Review*, 56 (1983), 735–43.
35. Flitterman-Lewis (1996), p. 275. My emphasis.
36. See Nelson (1983), p. 739 and p. 740, Ungar (2008), p. 71 and p. 74, Flitterman-Lewis (1996), p. 274 and Orpen (2007), p. 75.
37. Orpen (2007), p. 75.
38. Ibid. p. 76.
39. See Nelson (1983), p. 735, Flitterman-Lewis (1996), pp. 272–3 and Orpen (2007), p. 95.
40. Nancy (2001c), p. 30.
41. Flitterman-Lewis (1996), p. 276.
42. Orpen (2007), p. 37.
43. Daniel Fairfax, 'Montage as Resonance: Chris Marker and the Dialectical Image', *Senses of Cinema* (2012) <http://sensesofcinema.com/2012/feature-articles/montage-as-resonance-chris-marker-and-the-dialectical-image/> (last accessed 15 July 2019).
44. Ibid.
45. Ibid.
46. Nancy (2000b).
47. Ibid.
48. See Flitterman-Lewis (1996), p. 38.
49. Nancy (2008a), p. 163.
50. Ibid.
51. Most accounts of the film give the location of Cléo's suspected cancer as her stomach (*le ventre*); however, Orpen (2007) astutely notes how *ventre* may also translate as uterus (p. 88).
52. See Flitterman-Lewis (1996).
53. Orpen (2007), p. 37.
54. Claudia Gorbman, 'Varda's Music', *Music and the Moving Image*, 1 (2008), 27–34 (p. 29). Original emphasis.
55. Janice Mouton, 'From Feminine Masquerade to Flâneuse: Agnès Varda's Cléo in the City', *Cinema Journal*, 40 (2001), 3–16 (p. 6).
56. Ungar (2008), p. 68. See also Mulvey (1975).
57. Through these tears Cléo appropriates Death's gesture in Hans Baldung Grien's *Death and the Maiden* (1517), which Varda identifies as an inspiration for the film. See Varda (1994).

58. Philip Armstrong, *Reticulations: Jean-Luc Nancy and the Networks of the Political* (Minneapolis: University of Minnesota Press, 2009), pp. 125–6.
59. Ibid. p. 126. Original emphasis.
60. Nelson (1983), p. 742.
61. Quart (1988), p. 142.
62. Brinkema (2014), p. 2.
63. Ibid. pp. 1–2.
64. Ibid. p. 20.
65. Ibid. p. 15.

Caché:
If These Walls Could Talk

Denial ain't just a river in Egypt.

Much more than a bad pun marries Agnès Varda's *Cleo from 5 to 7* and Michael Haneke's *Caché*. Despite almost half a century separating their respective productions, little more than a season separates the two films. With Cléo receiving her cancer diagnosis in June 1961, by the autumn of that same year the tragedy at the heart of the latter film and the inciting incidents of both have passed. *Caché*'s silences, however, exceed *Cleo from 5 to 7*'s missing half an hour; indeed, they self-censoriously span the entire forty years that separate the films, and beyond if we include *Caché*'s continuing time of reception.[1] Like *Cleo from 5 to 7*, a great many responses to *Caché* cast it as a lesson in looking on the aptly named rue des Iris where, again akin to Varda's film, the unspoken weighs heavily on what can be seen.[2] In the latter film, for example, Antoine's uniform tells us of the war in Algeria, but barely anything is or can be said about it, whilst there is a whole corpus of work dedicated to the silences of *Caché*.[3] Whodunnit?, Haneke's film asks. No reply. Indeed, if we were to transform *Caché* into a date painting, we would be obliged to place it inside a blank box because the event which resonates here, the Paris massacre of 1961, was long forgotten. The film's silence thus apes Georges's, which in turn echoes the State-sanctioned silence that suppressed the massacre. The pinnacle of Georges's silence can be found in the solace he seeks in the 'moral oblivion' of sleep towards the film's close, a refuge with decidedly cinematic resonances.[4] Georges effectively shuts himself up in a dark room to escape the real world. His doing so mundanely pivots us towards the sonorous modesty of rustling via the comforts of the duvet, as well as a set of curtains that are sweepingly reminiscent of theatre drapes, which once again choreographs a Nancean corpus. Rustling, after all, is a marker of touch and its withdrawal – an acoustic index of fabric moving past itself.

There is an entire work to be written on rustling in Haneke's cinema, although this is not it.⁵ Rustling, if we recall, successfully turns us towards the sense of the world and its inherent noisy charge that articulates and reticulates our singular-plural being, and through a sort of sideways listening it reorients us to the sensuousness of the world. There is a ritualised, homely rustle to everything here as Georges prepares for slumber following his confrontation with Majid's son. He returns home, keys jangling, and scrapes off his shoes. He then rummages in a drawer for sleeping tablets and dunks his head beneath a running tap. The familiar 'pop' of a pill bottle punctuates this scene and next Georges is on the phone to Anne. He's off to bed and shouldn't be disturbed. Denial flows. In the next shot he is in his dressing gown and sets about closing the curtains and putting himself to bed with a listless exhalation that he sighs out across the duvet. Stock birdsong anticipates Georges's oneiric escape. We hear chirping in the darkness and then Georges's childhood home comes into view. We never see these birds, although chickens abound, but we do see a young Majid forcibly removed from the Laurent family farmhouse. Here, the sanctity of home is sonorously stripped away. Tyres and footsteps on gravel connote arriving, fleeing, struggling and departing. From a safe distance, although as the film's central intrigue attests never safe enough, we are absorbed into Georges's dream and Majid's nightmare. The dreamscapes of Haneke's film worlds once again operate as connective tissue and its fibres once again extend to us. We appear to dream lucidly the scene along with a sleeping Georges. This is nothing new, though, for throughout its runtime *Caché* primes us for the theatricality, absorption and mindfulness of the bedroom.⁶

Absorption, Theatricality and Mindfulness on the rue des Iris

Curiously, *Caché* appears to pick up where *Cleo from 5 to 7* leaves off: the mysterious video missive that Anne and Georges are watching effectively places us on the other side of the critical, reflective mirror once again. *Caché*'s opening credits absorb us. Unfashionable, and perhaps unfathomable when discussing Haneke's cinema, this sequence arguably achieves the overt joy or polemical pleasures that prompt Richard Rushton to shut himself up with films:

> When I am in front of a film the thing I want most is to enter the film's world; it is the possibility of doing so that makes films worth going to for me. Though of course the process of spectatorship is egocentric, dare I say 'transcendental', the moment

that the viewing and writing about cinema are always waiting for is that of being *in the film's place* – within the structure of experience the film opens up for others to inhabit.[7]

For Rushton, this structure of experience constitutes (narrative) absorption – the much-maligned other to spectacle and theatricality characterised by film's active acknowledgement of its purpose, to be seen.[8] Momentarily at least, or perhaps retrospectively, during the opening minutes of *Caché*, we are classically absorbed, 'drawn into the drama'.[9] Yet this is something of a belated realisation and, moreover, one that occurs only once any absorption is 'smashed to' pixels as scan lines – a minor aesthetic trope of Haneke's filmography – cut across our look onto the film.[10] These eminently theatrical lines, which ostensibly save the spectator from the threat of narrative absorption, position us directly alongside, they even attune us to, Haneke's on-screen avatars, Anne and Georges, when we discover that we are in their, and the film's, place, very much a part of its and their structure of experience. In effect, these scan lines affirm and refute our absorption. They reveal to us how deep inside the apparatus we really were, cast us out from it, and ultimately reinsert us back into it. Fundamentally, then, Haneke 'takes neither absorption or theatricality for granted' and, according to Rushton's taxonomy, *Caché* is anti-theatrical.[11]

Rushton's thinking also broaches a further dimension for his mention of viewing and writing diagnoses a 'bad epistemological habit', that is, a certain tendency in film studies towards bad faith – 'Game over: support narrative absorption and you lose; enthusiastically advocate spectacle and you win. The game of film studies has never been easier' – a tendency film studies apparently shares with Georges Laurent.[12] Film studies' bad faith hierarchises; Georges's bad faith stems from his refusal to recognise his role in the removal of Majid from the Laurent family home. Georges's childhood lie (likely) changed the course of Majid's life, but life is not done with these would-be brothers and the film's enigma forces them together once again in adulthood: Georges the bourgeois Haneke archetype, in this incarnation a rather nauseating host of a literary programme with a wife and teenage son, and Majid a single parent(?) with a teenage son living in a rundown social housing apartment.

Domestic settings are fatefully revealing in *Caché*. They do not simply represent different social milieus but narrate entire psychodramas upon their walls. Elizabeth Ezra and Jane Sillars, for instance, understand the Laurent family home as a 'fortress' – a coding that 'is driven home visually and sonically: the composition of shots of its exterior puts its vertical barred windows centre frame; horizontal bars cut across shots; the iron gate clangs'.¹³ In this way the Laurent apartment operates as a sleek extension of Georges's mind, as Catherine Wheatley argues:

> the carefully decorated bastion of good taste that the Laurents inhabit might well represent Georges's ego, while the seemingly endless, Lynchian corridors he moves down take us into the dim, messy space of the id (Majid's flat), and a long-repressed secret.¹⁴

In *Caché*, then, it is not so much a case of if these walls could talk, but when they talk. One wall that incessantly chatters away is the TV, fostering a parallel between it and Georges's job as a talk show host, and which beams in images from far away, as well, of course, as those from just outside the Laurent family home door. Early on it speaks the film's title – *caché*, it says in a rare moment of quiet between the couple whereby the TV's chattering can be heard uninterrupted; *cachés*, which Georges later echoes to draw them further together. The film's loudest wall, though, follows Majid's suicide; the neutrals of his kitchen are shockingly and suddenly bedecked by a bloody splatter that traces its entire height, its verticality menacingly looming above Majid's collapsed, lifeless body. So loud and stubborn are these mural markings that they were used to market the film worldwide and they recall Nancy's *carnation*, or local colour, which blood once again literalises. Akin to Kawara's date paintings, this blood (theatrically) beckons us in to an encounter with the film, reminding us of the inherent (pseudo-)spectatorship embedded within the very texture of Nancy's thinking on images, whilst transposing 'the topography of surface and secret', which Jonathan Thomas has identified as the fundamental structuring principle of *Caché* to a topography of surfaces, secrets and secretions.¹⁵

Surfaces, Secrets and Secretions

Caché encrusts such spectatorship into its very fabric through its exploration of shame. Like guilt, shame is a social phenomenon.¹⁶ Like nostalgia, it's catching, and Haneke certainly desires to implicate us all in the film's crimes.¹⁷ Yet unlike guilt, shame necessitates not a victim but a viewer, 'either actual or imagined', self or other, or indeed both.¹⁸ As Christopher Rowe explains:

> Ultimately, shame exposes us not only to the inescapability of the visual regime for the embodied subject but also to the inescapable immediacy of the event for the temporal subject. Georges's shame as a witness to the event of Majid's removal to an orphanage, as a witness to Majid's death, and as a witness *in effect* to the Parisian

massacre, is made accessible to the viewer of the film, who is also called on as a witness, retaining an important role in the film's economy of surveillance. The spectator, in this sense, arbitrates between the *fictionality* of what is visualized on film and video and the *reality* of the unrepresented and unrepresentable event itself, which is summoned forth by the indiscernible but unavoidable void between these two media, and colored by the shame of its remaining hidden.[19]

Shame thus generates the missing event. Arguably, then, we are 'given a glimpse into [Georges's] mind and memory', an 'unusual' although not unique episode within Haneke's filmography.[20] Such is its absorptive power that it has inspired a steady stream of responses to *Caché* that identify Georges as the source of the mysterious missives; they issue from his guilt and shame.[21] The topography of surfaces, secrets and secretions that structure the film, emblematised by Majid's extravasated blood, supersede any search for this source.

However, blood, is not the only fluid that flows through Haneke's filmography. Water, after all, is Haneke's material *par excellence* and through its diegetic presence the film more literally absorbs us into Georges's mind, while a wider serous survey of Haneke's oeuvre reveals a confluence between water and the oblique look into a protagonist's mind such moments facilitate. The beach images in *The Seventh Continent* start this tendency thanks to the dream of a better life they seemingly illustrate – a dream literally shared by father and daughter. More discreetly, this coincidence is staged in *The Piano Teacher* as Walter gets himself a glass of water and asks Erica whether she feels responsible for his brutality. '*Oui, Walter*', she replies with a shudder. When ironing, 'the amplified sound of water and steam' heard on the soundtrack, Juliette Binoche's Anne in *Code Unknown* drowns out the cries of a suffering child by turning up the volume on the TV, whilst in *The White Ribbon* Klara crucifies poor Peepsie with sopping wet hair, foregrounding the possible relationship between the village's children and the violent acts that take place there without actually fixing them as their source.[22] *Amour* furthers the link between the mind and water with Jean-Louis Trintignant's Georges's nightmare of a flooded hallway, through which he slowly wades, until a disembodied hand grabs him from behind. Later he apparently disappears (into an imagined episode) with his reanimated wife who reappears doing the washing up. Most recently, the Calais-set *Happy End* epitomises bourgeois indifference to the humanitarian crisis on the littoral doorstep, as we shall see in this book's conclusion.

Such secretions inundate *Caché*. A video recording shot through a rain-lashed windscreen of this particular Georges's childhood home, for instance, figures amongst the anonymous and source-less missives that terrorise the Laurent family. A head dunked under a running tap washes down the sleeping tablets that usher in slumber and sub- or unconsciously return us to the (repressed) scene of the crime. Indeed, elsewhere in Haneke's oeuvre, images of water are subbed in to block out the grisly truth. In *Benny's Video*, for example, the eponymous son and his mother holiday in Egypt while his father disposes of Benny's victim's corpse – views of the Nile are seen as mention of dad at home (not) doing just that is made. Whilst in *The White Ribbon* Garrett Stewart posits how 'it is history itself that looms at [the] vanishing point' of the 'unpeopled' snowy landscape seen in the film; a 'history [that] silences mystery' by means of the 'mass death' and 'killing fields' these shots parabolise.[23] It is history too – a history of mass death and of an urban killing field – that lingers at the vanishing point of *Caché* where a real-life watery grave lies to succeed the endgame of the young killers in *Funny Games* as they dump a terrified Susanne Lothar into the lake: Paris's Seine river. Despite decades of official silence, it is known that on 17 October 1961 approximately 200 FLN (National Liberation Front) protestors of Arabic origin were killed, their bodies thrown into the Seine, an atrocity during which Majid's parents disappeared. Georges ventriloquises this official silence through his continued refusal to acknowledge his involvement in Majid's fate. Georges's macro- and microcosmic complicity, however, is betrayed by the clean lines and minimalism of the bourgeois decor of his Parisian home that at first sight appears to insulate and differentiate him from Majid and his social housing living space. Indeed, evidence of his complicity exceeds Majid's invitation to be present (at his death) and it is in fact ever present in the supposed sanctuary of his fortified mind and residence, manifested by secretions that carry secrets and which pool on the surfaces of the Laurent family home, in which a picture of a waterway is a central feature. Essentially the negative of the televisual image, silent, static, unchanging, we first spot the painting, seemingly blithely hanging in the background, when Anne receives an anonymous phone call at home. Whoever is on the end of the line wants to speak with Georges. They refuse to give their name and an agitated Anne slams down the phone. We see it again as Georges and Anne host a dinner party – a longer stretch this time that peeks out from behind Daniel Duval's head as the group discuss a friend's divorce and budding film script. Just as the painting comes into view the doorbell rings, signalling the arrival of another anonymous delivery. Next, we see it as Anne and Georges argue about another video missive – this time of the journey to Majid's flat – during which Georges confirms his hunch about the perpetrator, whilst its most sustained appearance occurs following Georges's first visit to Majid. Having falsely claimed to Anne that nobody was home, a further video – of his confrontation with Majid and the latter's devastating breakdown afterwards – proves this to be a lie. In this scene the painting dominates the space behind Anne as she listens to Georges's partial disclosure about the events of the massacre and Majid's removal, whilst he desperately clings to how normally his six-year-old self behaved (Figure 8). Our final encounter with it neatly bookends these appearances when Georges calls Anne to say he needs to sleep.

An apparently innocuous element of the film's mise-en-scène, as the summary above makes clear, its outings coincide with an intensification of the epistles' arrivals, and their consequences, as they infiltrate and record a greater number of places – Georges's workplace and childhood home, Majid's residence – and relationships: spousal, collegial, personal and parental. Yet this is all misdirection. The missives, and their meaning, are entirely moot and the painting's esteemed innocuousness exposes the film's central enigma to be a lure, for its watery winding is reminiscent of the Seine, and in the context of *Caché* we cannot think of this body of water without thinking of the Algerian bodies thrown into it. This painting thus illustrates that Georges's guilt, responsibility and shame penetrate the Laurent familial space long before the anonymous missives' arrival, for the secret of his boyhood crime is literally secreted by the walls of his home – a crime of infancy that ebbs and flows with the past of the massacre and the present and future of his denial – beating beneath his subconscious and obliquely absorbing us into his mind. Michael, like Majid,

Figure 8 *Caché* (Michael Haneke, 2005). Reproduced with kind permission of the director.

wants us to be present; and in resonance with the waters of *Caché*, and the pulse they form with his other film worlds and their respective intersections with mindfulness and morality, to form something of resonance's dispersive temporal-spatial matrix, we cannot help but be so, rendering any equivalent spectatorial denial impossible. Through a sort of sideways listening, then, water and the mind are inextricably drawn together, giving a heretofore unexcavated depth to the well-established superficiality of Haneke's protagonists. The solution to *Caché*'s mystery was thus there all along – all along the perimeter of the living room wall and all along Haneke's oeuvre – not so much hidden, and even closer to home than the doorstep, but there at the seam between listening and understanding, right up against the unstoppable, worldbuilding hum of background noise which articulates and reticulates our compound mode of being. The walls are talking, and they are calling out to you.

Notes

1. See Mary Ann Doane, *The Emergence of Cinematic Time: Modernity, Contingency, the Archive* (Cambridge, MA: Harvard University Press, 2002) and Mroz (2012).
2. See in particular the *Screen* dossier on *Caché* (2007).
3. Examples which focus specifically on the 17 October 1961 massacre include: Nancy E. Virtue, 'Memory, Trauma, and the French-Algerian War: Michael Haneke's *Caché* (2005)', *Modern & Contemporary France* (2011), 281–96, Patrick Crowley, 'When Forgetting Is Remembering: Haneke's *Caché* and the Events of October 17, 1961', in *On Michael Haneke*, ed. by Brian Price and John David Rhodes (Detroit: Wayne State University Press, 2010), pp. 267–79, Mireille Rosello, *The Reparative in Narratives: Works of Mourning in Progress* (Liverpool: Liverpool University Press, 2010) and Asbjørn Grønstad, *Screening the Unwatchable: Spaces of Negation in Post-Millennial Art Cinema* (Basingstoke: Palgrave Macmillan, 2012).
4. Wheatley (2009), p. 165. Directly following Majid's suicide, Georges seeks a similar solace and goes to the movies.
5. See Coulthard (2010).
6. Such mention of mindfulness is obliquely redolent of Thomas Elsaesser's 'mind-games movies' of which he considers Haneke a purveyor. See Elsaesser (2010).
7. Richard Rushton, 'Absorption and Theatricality in the Cinema: Some Thoughts on Narrative and Spectacle', *Screen*, 48 (2007), 109–12 (p. 111). Original emphasis.
8. Richard Rushton, 'Early, Classical and Modern Cinema: Absorption and Theatricality', *Screen* (2004), 226–44 (p. 227).
9. Ibid.

10. Rushton (2007), p. 111.
11. Rushton (2004), p. 230.
12. Rushton (2007), p. 110.
13. Elizabeth Ezra and Jane Sillars, '*Hidden* in Plain Sight: Bringing Terror Home', *Screen* (2007), 215–21 (p. 216).
14. Catherine Wheatley, *Caché (Hidden)* (London: Palgrave Macmillan, 2011), p. 39.
15. Jonathan Thomas, 'Michael Haneke's New(s) Image', *Art Journal* (2008), 80–5 (p. 81).
16. See Wheatley (2009) and Rowe (2017).
17. See Stewart (1993).
18. Rowe (2017), p. 166.
19. Ibid. p. 192.
20. Ibid. p. 164.
21. See Ezra and Sillars (2007), Wheatley (2009) and Rowe (2017).
22. Walker (2018), p. 79.
23. Garrett Stewart, 'Pre-war Trauma: Haneke's *The White Ribbon*', *Film Quarterly* (2010), 40–7 (p. 47).

Bad Resonance in *The Piano Teacher*

The epistolary is thus always already a genre of desire.[1]

From its first moments to its end credits, *The Piano Teacher* tends a giant (cinematic) ear towards its spectators. It is *à l'écoute*; it eavesdrops on its audience. It thus counteracts *Caché*'s failures to listen, and audition constitutes a distinct critical seam amongst existing responses to the film. Lisa Coulthard, for instance, notes that the intercutting of 'audiovisually synchronized scenes of piano lessons [. . .] with scenes of total silence and a black screen', which open the film, issues the spectator with an 'injunction' to listen where 'silences lay bare the act of listening itself'.[2] It is through these silences, she continues, that *The Piano Teacher* 'makes clear [. . .] that it is [. . .] listening to us, that is, reminding us of our own duty and responsibility to' it.[3] According to Coulthard, then, it is during 'moments of *quiet*' that Haneke's spectator is at her most otologically active.[4] Arguably, though, this reminder edges any (Nancean) listening into hearing, for whilst we might hear the grain of the blank film stock, ostensibly devoid of representational material, these black leaders assign us a role that if we do not understand we somehow fail the film. In essence, we must submit to its terms with little regard for our own. Brigitte Peucker adopts a similar approach when discussing how 'the point of *The Piano Teacher* [is] to remind its spectator that music always involves the body – that, actually, it involves several bodies: the body of the composer, the body of the performer, and the body of the listener'.[5] In spite of the potential for contact, communication and community between these several bodies, however, what is paramount to Peucker amongst them is coldness and control. The music must be 'understood' precisely, to the letter, by all three.[6] Any hopes for intersubjectivity, as Jean Ma summarises, are negated by an implicit injunction to submit to the master's voice – the musical score – shutting down 'the very possibility of reciprocity'.[7] Intention and performance are thus fused, and the putatively prescriptive nature of Haneke's silences surfaces once more. Finally here, David Sorfa highlights how *The Piano Teacher* listens in on us via the 'cut to silence' at the film's end which 'brings [its] action [. . .] directly into the space of the screening since the only sound one can hear is that of the Art House audience shuffling and preparing to leave the auditorium'.[8] Akin to *Cleo from 5 to 7*'s missing half an hour, *The Piano Teacher* tips over into our corporeality and (judgingly) intrudes upon us.

Despite the promise of such encounters, through a stress on silence, music and contiguity, *The Piano Teacher* could be read as profoundly unresonant, that is, as a rebuttal to resonance's coordination of our co-exposure to and co-articulation of the sensible, intelligible world, of our attunement to the shared, corporeal, material contours of life, the very kernel of our encounter with others. A brief plot summary indicates as much. Adapted from Elfriede Jelinek's 1983 novel *Die Klavierspielerin*, *The Piano Teacher* centres on Erika Kohut, a forty-something woman who lives, and shares a bedroom, with her overbearing mother. Cloistered within an ivory tower of ivory tinkling at the film's outset, Erika's almost monastic lifestyle is gradually dismantled as she embarks on a relationship with one of her students at the Vienna Conservatory, Walter Klemmer. Erika, then, has not strayed far (from the womb) and in one of the film's distinctive sexual encounters, Erika, according to Isabelle Huppert at least, seeks a return to the womb, launching herself onto her mother from the neighbouring bed. If we return to the originary natal contours of Nancean resonance, this is some very bad resonance indeed. Indeed, in a reversal of the palindromic resonant matrix that Nancy describes, Walter's visits to the Kohuts' apartment mimics this uneasy return when, on each occasion, Erika's mother is locked out:

> The womb[*matrice*]-like constitution of resonance, and the resonant constitution of the womb: What is the belly of a pregnant woman, if not the space or the antrum where a new instrument comes to resound, a new *organon*, which comes to fold in on itself, then to move, receiving from outside only sounds, which, when the day comes, it will begin to echo through its cry? But, more generally, more womblike, it is always in the belly that we [. . .] end up listening, or start listening. The ear opens onto the sonorous cave that we then become.[9]

Walter's visits tie the womb-like constitution of resonance, and the resonant constitution of the womb, in knots. From outside, Madame Kohut must listen in on the noisy world, thereby transforming the Kohuts' home into a place of anti-resonance, which the presence of the TV exacerbates. From its perch, the TV set becomes a new instrument that resounds, its 'cries' narratively, thematically and stylistically resonant:

> the television clip offers a figuration of Erika's central dilemma as being centered on a lack of means for vocal expression, as it features a (male) patient who clumsily attempts to speak through a mouthful of gauze and bandaged lips in order to

engage in a debate about gender inequality. The film thus simultaneously signals and undermines its own themes, as well as Erika's psychosocial situation, via ironic juxtaposition.[10]

Equally, the television's muffled sounds insulate Erika's room – its orality a pseudo-fleshy, mucous lining to the spaces from which the matriarch is excluded. If not unresonant, or anti-resonance, then, arguably, the Kohut family home reconfigures resonance, it does violence to it by reversing its originary natal contours. Such violence is critically resonant here for my thinking throughout this chapter will be done in concert with Nancy's account of violence that reconfigures, rather than assaults, what it encounters. It will do so through the letter and examine how its notation becomes cinematic and whereby *The Piano Teacher* schisms further, rendering conclusions about its denouement, and whether or not a rape has taken place, all the more radical and impossible.

An Epistolary Filmmaker: Missives, Melodrama and Masochism

We might consider Haneke an epistolary filmmaker, for letters recur across his films. The most famous example is surely *Caché*, where a series of anonymous missives, including video recordings, postcards and childlike drawings, disrupts the Laurent family's daily life. Unsigned epistles and the child are again interrelated in *The White Ribbon* wherein the phantom perpetrator(s) leave(s) a cryptic note attached to Karli's beaten body. *Time of the Wolf* extends this link when we see Eva writing her postcards to Papa from the apocalypse, with the film in turn aping her epistolary impulse through its bite-sized presentation of the end of the world as we know it. In *Code Unknown*, Juliette Binoche once more receives disturbing correspondence: an anonymous warning she fails to act upon and others from her war photographer boyfriend. Before taking their lives, the family in *The Seventh Continent* leave behind a letter for their loved ones, and Jean-Louis Trintignant in *Amour* is seen scribing to an unknown recipient. Following the decline in his ailing wife's health, Trintignant's letter details his capture of a pigeon that enters the Laurent apartment on two occasions and, unusually for a Haneke film, the bird doesn't get it![11] What binds the remaining epistolary episodes, however, is violence, with each missive explicitly bound to implicit or inexplicable violent acts: suicide in *The Seventh Continent* and *Caché*; warfare and physical assaults against children in *The White Ribbon* and *Code Unknown*; murder in *Time of the Wolf*. However, whilst these letters attend to violence, they do not detail frenzy, nor are they hastily devised. Instead they are carefully composed and accompany slow suicides, slow familial, relationship and mental breakdowns and even slow apocalypses. Like musical composition before it, then, letter writing could be deemed a metaphor for Haneke's filmmaking, not least because the questions of guilt, intergenerational responsibility and animal rights addressed to the spectator that permeate his films tacitly acknowledge the dialogical character of epistolarity.[12] Despite such discomfiting probing – who should have acted? Who deserves their punishment? – these questions are not returned to sender. Time and time again, and to the imagined delight and rhetorical tastelessness of their author, Haneke's films rape spectators into independence and confront them with the unbound wound of obscenity.[13]

Although distasteful, this authorial desire productively hinges violence, the letter and resonance, as well as the work of Haneke and Nancy. Such mention of an unbound wound, for instance, recalls Nancy's gaping chest cavity and its coincidence with the aesthetic turn of his thought and his emergence as an artistic subject, whilst Coulthard helpfully sanitises Haneke's desire and furnishes us with a set of rules for reading his cinema in general and *The Piano Teacher* in particular: the 'struggle for understanding is meant to *resonate* and be allowed to stand as an ambiguity, rather than be resolved'.[14] We should thus allow uncertainty to sound out, to hang in the air between film and spectator, confirming compromise, rather than Peucker's control, as the condition of the encounter between them. Resonance thus structures reception of Haneke's films; meaning cannot be arrived at complacently for their messages materialise in the 'gaps' between critical responses.[15] These gaps tie *The Piano Teacher* to epistolarity and Hamid Naficy's thinking on the role that letters, as emissaries of desire, play in the counterhegemonic discourses of accented cinema, in particular its assault on synchronised sound practices. 'Exile and epistolarity', for Naficy, 'are *constitutively linked* because both are driven by distance, separation, absence, and loss and by the desire to bridge the multiple gaps'.[16] Reception of Haneke's films is likewise constitutively linked, and elsewhere Coulthard maps their standing ambiguities onto 'the openness, fragmentation, and complexity' of Haneke's narratives, whose film 'titles [. . .] rather simplistically and literally indicate [that], the story is unknown, hidden, or fragmented'.[17] We might, then, perhaps in too twee a fashion, read each title as a brief missive to be pored over by the spectator, their fragments, games, obscurities sent and received. The letter within this juncture emerges somewhat obliquely. However, a return to Nancean resonance readily restores its key stakes, for it houses allusions to the epistolary impulse through *renvoi*.

Renvoi, as *Listening* translator Charlotte Mandell reminds the reader, is another shimmering connotational delight of the Nancean lexicon.[18] Like *sens*, *filmer*, listening itself, *renvoi* translates widely: 'return (as in return to sender, return a gift), send back (a parcel), repeat (a phrase or passage in music), refrain, refer, allude back'.[19] Postal and/or reiterative, in common parlance *renvoi* resonates. Indeed, it structures resonance itself. Sending and receiving are, after all, constitutively linked: 'animal sonorous emission is necessarily also [. . .] its own reception'.[20] Curiously, Haneke's letters are proximate with his soundscapes: with failures to listen, with voiceovers, with off-screen voices. These oto-ethico failures are, of course, epitomised by Georges in *Caché* but their frequencies can be heard elsewhere in Haneke's epistolary filmography. In *Code Unknown*, Binoche's Anne fails to listen to the cries of Françoise, whilst Georg's suicide note in *The Seventh Continent* is not believed by his parents. The supposed fallibility of Georg's final (written) words is at odds with the reassuring power his and Anna's voices draw when heard in voiceover; their respective missives read aloud over mundane montages. Trintignant's Georges in *Amour* likewise narrates his writing, as does Eva in *Time of the Wolf*, whilst, for Elsie Walker, the anonymous voice-off in *The White Ribbon*, that reads the lines from Exodus attached to Karli, reifies Haneke's authorial intention.[21] In one way or another, then, Haneke's epistolary filmmaking aligns with listening whereby each letter tends an epistolary ear to the spectator. Haneke's letters thus serve the same material-ethico function as water does, insistently secreting questions to the spectator, and discreetly insinuating spectatorial proximity to and 'complicity in the cinematic production of desire and illusion' to become something of a material-ethico refrain that miniaturises Catherine Wheatley's aggressive reflexivity.[22] Through such enfolding, this papery ear is caught up with the homology of sound and sense, specifically with the folds that make up sense: 'Sense is first of all the rebound of sound, a rebound that is coextensive with the whole folding/unfolding [. . .] of presence and of the present that makes or opens the perceptible as such.'[23]

Another of *renvoi*'s shimmers, throughout *Listening* these folds accentuate and alert us to the inherent, unstoppable motility and sonority that subtend sense, a refrain that likewise enfolds corporeality and subjecthood into worldly presentation. The murky 'subject' is formed in the fold, and whilst we might add letter writing to these embodied movements – the rhythmical tapping of keys, the fricative rubbing of a hand against paper, essentially, motility, sonority, sense – we can certainly recognise the reception of Haneke's epistolary filmmaking here too: 'there is only a "subject" [. . .] that resounds, responding to a momentum, a summons, a convocation of sense'.[24] Through the *pli*, then, the pinnal joins the papery and subjectivity enfolds the epistolary. It is thanks to such alertness to a momentum, a summons, a convocation of sense, moreover, that we can address the sub-missive resonances of Erika's letter in what is undoubtedly Haneke's most accomplished epistolary endeavour: *The Piano Teacher*. Indeed, the letter guides a critic-spectator through its apparently choicest episodes: meditations on the film, this one included, generally focusing upon Erika and Walter's series of sexual encounters. After an initial sexual tryst in the Conservatory's public restrooms, Erika agrees to meet Walter again, stating that she will communicate her desires through epistolary means. The letter appears soon afterwards as Walter attends a piano lesson with Erika. Here, unlike in *Time of the Wolf* and *Amour*, we do not see Erika scribing, but we do witness the letter's delivery with strict instructions for Walter to read it only when alone. Next, we are present for the disclosure of the missive's contents and the letter garners a fleeting mention when Erika seeks out Walter to apologise for the missive before it re-emerges during the film's penultimate sequence. Narratively speaking, the letter bookends Erika and Walter's series of consummations and it folds a sexual dimension into the violent correspondences that letters score across Haneke's cinema, affirming the epistolary as 'always already a genre of desire'.[25] A gloved eroticism and violence is certainly not alien to readings of *The Piano Teacher*; however, the film distinguishes itself further from Haneke's wider epistolary project because it tracks the missive's inception, delivery, perusal, and the ambiguous undertaking of its illocutionary aims.

Illocution denotes a spoken or written act 'which in itself [. . .] constitutes the intended action', for example, ordering, warning, promising. In essence, the utterance performs the act itself.[26] 'I now pronounce you man and wife', for instance, enacts the union. Illocution thus fuses intention and performance, just as Peucker perceives music does and just as Erika's letter does. Her words sanction acts. However, such seaming of performance and intention proves devastating, and the performance of the letter's illocutionary aims at the film's close erupts into uncertainty. This ambiguity problematises the dynamic that pre-exists Haneke's epistolary impulse because, exchanged between intended lovers, the letter becomes heavy with cliché, that is, a favour, a token of intent and consent between these two individuals, almost courtly in tone. Existing responses to the film echo such thinking, with Erika's missive variously described as a 'contract', a 'scenario', a 'script'; this vernacular suggests a similar contract between spectator and film.[27] Work on the film that reads it as 'a thoroughly modern melodrama' reflects this final contractual encounter between *The Piano Teacher* and its audience.[28] Haneke, of course, exacerbates the generic idiom through sardonic, systematic, yet fatalist, parody: 'the dashing and ardent male positioned to rescue Erika from the strictures of family, culture, and class instead rapes her [...] and even Erika's planned act of revenge against Klemmer is ultimately directed at herself instead'.[29] Erika's missive is the beacon for this disruption and it observes Coulthard's rules to the letter, introducing ambiguity into the very fabric of the film. Indeed, whereas in the rest of Haneke's filmography letters provide more certain contours (for spectators) to uncertain scenarios – yes, we took our own lives in *The Seventh Continent* or yes, you are being punished in *The White Ribbon* – in *The Piano Teacher* the opposite is true. It is open to the standing ambiguities of Haneke's cinema, ambiguities that resonate through slippages that occur materially, and not through the fractures in Erika's psyche, in order to circulate resonant, uncertain afterimages of violence. These ambiguities return us to the violence delivered by Erika's letter and by Nancy's thought.

In *The Ground of the Image*, Nancy narrates the micro-disaster tale of the nail and the wood:

> Violence can be defined *a minima* as the application of a force that remains foreign to the dynamic or energetic system into which it intervenes. Let us take an anodyne example, but one that testifies to violence in the sense of a violent temperament, or in the sense in which one becomes violent in the face of an objective constraint: namely, feeling the need to extract a recalcitrant screw by pulling it out with pliers, instead of loosening it with a screwdriver. Whoever does this no longer follows the logic of the screw's thread, nor that of the material (the wood, for example) that he tears out and renders unusable at that place.
>
> Violence does not participate in any order of reasons, nor any set of forces oriented toward results. It is not quite intentional and exceeds any concern with results. It denatures, wrecks, and massacres that which it assaults. Violence does not transform what it assaults; rather, it takes away its form and meaning. It makes it into nothing other than a sign of its own rage, an assaulted or violated thing or being: a thing or being whose very essence now consists in its having been assaulted or violated. From elsewhere or beyond, violence brandishes another form, if not another meaning.[30]

Here, rather than employing a screwdriver or lubricant to displace the nail, a set of pincers is used: a form of leverage that does not follow the grain of the screw, or the material from which it is ripped. By doing so, the nail's former spot is made redundant. It will not house another screw. The violence of this illogical wrenching thus divests the supporting material of its form and meaning, whilst brandishing another. Where once two things coexisted harmoniously, iron against lignin, fire against earth, suddenly impatience, indifference, insolence wrench this harmony asunder. Fundamentally, violence denatures everything it encounters, and this reckless, shape-shifting violence has an intrinsic relationship to the image. According to Nancy, violence 'is concerned only with its own deafening intrusion'.[31] It cares not for the system it violates; '[v]iolence "doesn't want to hear it;" it has no interest in knowing it.'[32] Violence's sole concern, then, is acoustically conceived.

We might read such self-interest in *The Piano Teacher* via Walter. During his introduction, for instance, he noisily marks himself out as the most vocal on-screen figure, clapping, fidgeting, cheering – the fullness of his acoustic presence especially noisy next to the dubbed bodies of his co-stars – his deafening intrusion utterly unconcerned with the system of respectful reverence and restraint around him. Even when not seated behind a piano, Walter is always somehow louder than his surrounds and ultimately he does not listen (to Erika's letter), he doesn't want to hear it, he seeks understanding which leads to his and the film's undoing. His noisy presence, however, is not just sonorously rendered, because he frequently does violence to Haneke's ascetic aesthetic, disrupting the latter's usual long takes with shot/reverse shot sequences and eyeline matches that situate his desire for Erika at the centre of the film.[33] This inscription of desire into the film's visual track tallies with further reflections made by Nancy on violence and how 'the distinction' between different registers of violence 'is blindingly obvious'.[34] This phrase suggests clarity of vision. Yet in its allusion to sight, blinding evidence deprives the very faculty to which it appeals. Deafening intrusion implies a similarly self-consuming sensory excess, and Nancy shores up the proximity between violence and the senses through 'the worst form of violence' – cruelty – which 'involves a specifically visual desire'[35] to see red, 'to see blood spilt'.[36]

Nancy's broader appraisal of violence, however, is not so discerning and he initially reads this visual desire as relevant to all violence when he asserts how it compulsively 'wants to *see* the mark [it] makes on the thing [it] assaults', for example, a scar, a wound, a burn, a bloody splatter.[37] Fundamentally, for Nancy, violence 'always completes itself in an image', in an enduring afterimage of violence, because it persists as a trace once the violence is over.[38] Nancy's imagistic inscription of violence, then, embeds it into a visual and superficial register, rendering the surface markings of Erika's letter an emblematic manifestation of its superficial imagistic inscription. Images for Nancy, however, are of course not uniquely visual but multiply material – musical, poetic, tactile, olfactory, gustatory, kinaesthetic – and accordingly we can read this material multiplicity at the heart of the image that violence leaves behind. Indeed, through their very constitution and physicality scars, wounds, burns, bloody splatters exceed simple surface markings. Likely formed by touch, and likely sonorous in their coming into being as one surface slips past, cuts through, scalds another, and likely weeping, seeping, scabbing over as they endure, the afterimage that violence seeks out is multiply material.

The film's final sequence, during which Erika stabs herself, demonstrates as much. Removing the knife from her handbag, Erika drives its blade into her shoulder. Blood slowly seeps through her blouse, first as a narrow seam, then forming a classic red blotch. Blindingly obvious, an imagistic, superficial inscription, violence here is visualised as a claret afterimage on Erika's shirt. But despite its blinding evidence, critics have been unable to agree on what this violence means: freedom, escape, (career) suicide, self-harm, self-abnegation, masochistic frustration, a parody of menstruation?[39] Ambiguity thus resonates, and this resonance should not only be understood narratively but materially too for it also makes up the very surface marking of Erika's wound. Her blood flows and effervesces as it rushes through the break in her skin, it patters and sticks as it pools between fabric and flesh, it consists of a dynamic plurality of materiality. In essence, rather than being exclusively understood in a visual and superficial register, the enduring afterimage that violence compulsively desires is itself multiply material.

Sub-missive Instructions

The letter is first mentioned in one of the most widely discussed and reproduced moments of the film: Erika and Walter's initial sexual encounter on the floor of the Vienna Conservatory toilets. It is here, in the contact between their bodies, that Erika's letter is conceived and although not yet written, physical traces of the missive are already palpable through mise-en-scène. Its pure white background is marked only by the dark hues of Erika and Walter's attire, like black ink on a white page. The epistolary is effectively written all over it, upholding some trace of the melodramatic generic contract. At first, Erika acquiesces to the pressure of Walter's embrace recorded in an antithetical manner to the full-frontal nudity shot and its all-revealing and glorious wholeness, for here it is Walter's clothed back, and later his truncated torso, that mediates the couple's clumsy clinch. Walter's rear projection thus occasions and voids our look; the sight/site of his back holds the fullness of the visual image in reserve, like 'the black rectangles that censors often place over genitalia in film', despite the stage very much being set for looking through a surfeit of visual cues.[40] Although explicit in its content – masturbation and fellatio are intermittently practised throughout – this blocking directs spectators' eyes towards the impossible visibility of off-screen space, insisting that they look at Walter and Erika performing mutual sex acts but thwarting any opportunity flirtingly offered up to ocular veracity. In this way the sequence becomes a parody of the European art cinema sex scene – excessive in its restraint.[41] Extending the film's epistolary impulse further, we might read this restraint, as well as the censorious black rectangles, as redaction: an indiscreet editorial technique which judiciously picks holes in documents creating banks of black and white.

Sonically, too, we are bereft. With the familiar sounds of piano playing shut out, Erika and Walter seemingly reside in a vacuum – a space where resonance is impossible. This, however, is impossible which readily proves to be the case as the sound of lips on lips, on necks, of hands on textile, on flesh, of mouths on flesh, of flesh on flesh, of air in lungs, of breath in the air fills the space.[42] Whilst, then, for the most part these touches are shielded from view – captured in long shot or sandwiched between Walter and Erika's bodies – and increasingly forced off-screen as the scene unfolds thorough Haneke's cinematography, they by no means become imperceptible because although not seen, these touches are very much heard. Indeed, the film takes pains to write the fullness of the body into its acoustic and olfactory registers. Full of music, full of breath, bodies in *The Piano Teacher* cough and splutter, expel vomit, blood, semen and urine. The body's insides are, then, well represented and even the surface of the body finds its place here, albeit as something dirty, disgusting and undesirable. Bodies are, then, almost messy and certainly fleshy, and the film extends this cavernous fullness and fleshiness to the spectator for these touches are by no means simply heard: the blind spot Haneke's framing forces them into anticipates the multiply material afterimage of violence that Erika's letter precipitates. Its groans, grunts, sighs point up the inherent carnality of sound, filling the sequence with acoustic and material vibrations, and they charge the scene with space for us, our bodies, even our insides, as auditory and tactile registers are privileged above visuality and as their material vibrations resonate through us. Here, then, these noises do not simply sound out, they sketch out touch too; they are a mark of it, resonantly fleshing out the contours of Erika and Walter's bodies and our own in front of the image as these tactile sounds brush up against our epidermal surfaces and flow through our inner recesses. The image is but a placeholder for a *corpus corporum*, that is, for a *corpus imāginum*, as touch, sight and sound resonate as they move between one sense and another, and where the sounds that emerge from off-screen become touch and touch is articulated as sound. In effect, we tune in to the insistent material vibrations of the image, right up against the corpus of its many parts, right up against it colours, light, sounds, movements. The otology cinema engenders here therefore centres on resonance, which once more involves several bodies because it takes the spectator's resonant body before the bodies of the film, Erika and Walter, to feel the folds of fabric and flesh that are visually unframed. In resonance, we flesh out the unseen as if it were a haptic glory hole.

Once the letter is written, Erika entrusts it to Walter's care. Here, Erika's dry cough replaces the groans, grunts and sighs of frustrated orgasm; her insides are effectively externalised, bodily sounds privileged above dialogue. The constant refrain of her noisy insides consonant with her voicelessness affirms Erika as a cinematic Nancean body through her rendering as an anatomy of orifices: as a set of lungs, a hungry, yet mute mouth, a pair of ears which apparently reject everything they hear. To say nothing of the pleasure she takes in inhaling strangers' ejaculate whilst watching pornography, we only need think of any one of her piano lessons – of which this epistolary episode is an example – to understand how the world for Erika is rejectamenta.[43] Indeed, during another sexual encounter with Walter, Erika emphatically vomits up her world: the swatch of puke speech bubble-like next to her head, a similar shade to her hair and trench coat which draws this effluent into a curious constellation of selfhood and performance where her mouth continues to condemn her to silence. Again, then, Erika involuntarily serves up another delivery to Walter, who once more invokes the putrid upon its arrival, whilst Haneke lays another sicky mess at Huppert's feet and once more these extravasated viscera are swiftly cast off-screen. Tellingly, it is from off-screen space that Walter first declares his lack of interest in the letter and it is in off-screen space that the letter is first mentioned, as Erika kneels before Walter on the floor of the Conservatory toilets. The resonant materiality of film thus binds Erika's letter to off-screen space, for it is on the interior of the relation between cinematography and sound that the letter is cast into this invisibility, suggesting the potential for slippage, even the precarity, between visual and soundtracks, or rather the letter's potential for disrupting the assumed surety between the two. Upon giving the letter to Walter, Erika remains committed to the sensory sanctions she orders during their initial embrace.

Here, she denies Walter touch by instructing him not to make contact with the letter that she has just handed to him, which now lies on the piano. The film concomitantly inhibits and directs our look towards this prohibited contact, which is located (slightly) off camera with Walter's truncated torso once more parallel with the visual field's event horizon. A light tap replaces the frenzied, fricative fumbles of their toilet tryst as the letter disappears from view. Its disappearance, however, is soon superseded by an excessive appeal to vision via a close-up of the letter's unmarked white envelope thrown into sharp relief against the lacquered black of the piano during the scene's closing moments: Walter's name is effectively redacted. With the exception of the television, an object filmed in close-up is a highly unusual shot for *The Piano Teacher* and its use elsewhere in Haneke's oeuvre often spells the apocalypse. His camera, for example, explores the aftermath of *The Seventh Continent*'s destruction, whilst a series of close-ups in *Time of the Wolf* details the leftovers of some indeterminate disaster. In *The Piano Teacher* there are only two such shots: the first of Erika's letter and the second of her clutch bag during the film's final minutes in which she hides a knife – their graphic parallels and complementary shades certainly no accident. We have already seen how close-ups of Walter's face signal 'arousal' and the use of the close-up here might equally indicate desire as the courtly tone of letter writing implies.[44] But if reading the film in reverse, we might also anticipate the violent potential of the letter's contents, that is, its potential to produce an afterimage of violence just as the knife itself later does, casting Erika's letter as a competing deafening intrusion alongside Walter's own, whom Haneke describes as the coming of the apocalypse. The close-up thus folds desire and the apocalypse, sex and violence, into the film's cinematography and mise-en-scène and once more it is in resonance that the film expresses these uncertain sensations and which in its excessive call to vision overspills visuality and issues an alternative injunction to the spectator to listen: a multiply material one.

This multiply material injunction bodies forth following Walter's perusal of Erika's missive. In spite of her strict instructions that the letter only be read once Walter is alone, Erika (mistakenly) breaks her own rule later the same evening when Walter follows her home and forces himself into the apartment she shares with her mother. Once our couple has evaded the matriarch's gaze by barricading themselves in Erika's bedroom they again embrace, Walter once more mediating our access to their intimacy in an echo of the Conservatory toilet scene. Erika quickly refuses Walter any further physical affection until he reads the letter, asking that he do so straightaway. Begrudgingly, Walter agrees and makes light of its 'weighty' substance.[45] However, as he acquaints himself with the missive's contents his jocular tone sours, for he learns that it is not heavy with the weight of courtly cliché but that enclosed within it are Erika's sadomasochistic fantasies. Walter begins to read Erika's letter aloud, essentially ventriloquising her desires, serving as her mouthpiece as she tacitly takes in his disappointment and disgust with the denatured love letter: gag me, blindfold me, hit me, *chéri*. Is this to be taken seriously?, he inquires, and Erika's reassurances that it should merely incite Walter's despondency. Yet while the narrative hints at rupture, the film gestures towards intimacy in deviating from Haneke's well-established interest in the long take, a loyalty to which he believes lessens 'manipulation' of the spectator, whilst bolstering 'responsibility' for what is seen.[46] Within these moments, however, Haneke instead employs a tangle of different shots that gives the film an uncharacteristically rich feel. Here, then, we encounter a keen manifestation of Walter's desire doing violence to Haneke's film form, and whilst 'objective and remote' are most frequently used to describe the film's/ Haneke's cinematography and editing, observations regarding details as sedate as camera height, distance and angle, and the sequence's use of shot/counter-shot patterning show that the filmic body is not remotely objective.[47] Whilst, then, as Wheatley puts it, the film at large 'creates a space for feminine psychology to take centre stage', in some of the most acute moments of its erection Erika's role is somewhat marginalised.[48] Erika, however, regains some unsettling control of the situation when she asks Walter, 'Do I disgust you?' just after he has read the letter. As part of this configuration, her question and look exceed the profilmic, slipping past Walter and consequently inviting a response from the spectator.[49] The film thus forms a schism that will become more pronounced later.

Visibly shaken and unsure how to proceed, Walter recourses to the couple's clumsy, amatory exchange by groping Erika's breast, once more binding touch to the letter, its suspension between his legs graphically hinting at the phallus. Erika is characteristically unmoved by Walter's advances and instead slinks to the floor and uncovers her store of pristine bondage items. When these solicitations also fail, she tenderly invites Walter to 'hit me', and he (cruelly) declines, claiming he would not want to sully his hands. It is during these moments that we physically perceive the letter for the final time: visually, suspended between Walter's legs, and aurally as Walter hurls it at Erika (Figure 9).

The film records Walter's gesture as the rough rustling of the letter's leaves, and as these sounds are woven into the film it realises the resonant afterimage that violence accomplishes: the rushing movement of its pages through the air produces a whisper as they brush against each other. The letter may start out as a set of papery surface markings, akin to the originary surface markings of violence, but when Walter launches it at Erika it becomes an acoustic, kinaesthetic, tactile, visual index of a violent act, its textual origins further sublimated as the film continues to become the enduring afterimage that violence seeks out. Through Walter's violent gesture, then, the letter leaves its mark on what it has violated. It leaves its enduring afterimage of violence as a resonant address, and as this enduring

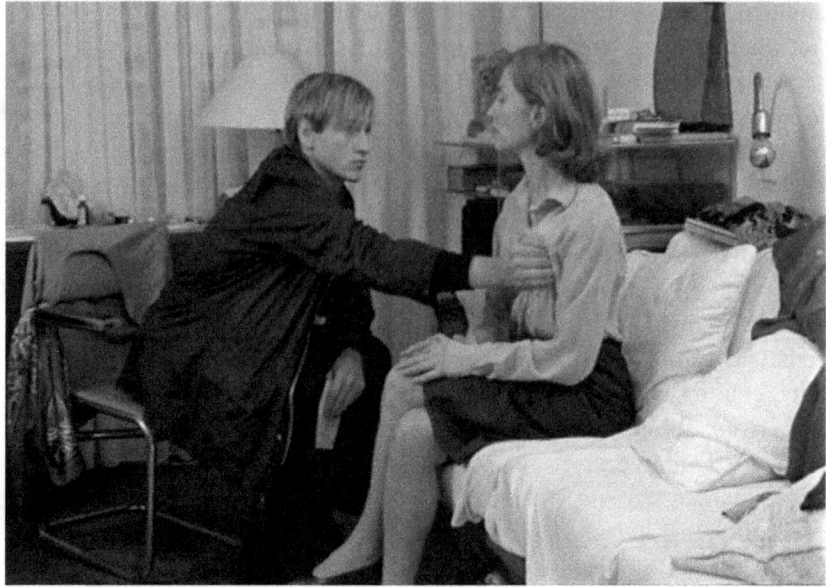

Figure 9 *The Piano Teacher* (Michael Haneke, 2001). Reproduced with kind permission of the director.

afterimage of violence, the letter triggers the ambiguity of any blinding evidence. Yet as this enduring afterimage of violence the letter does not resurface as the tactile sounds of susurrating paper but rather as Erika's ventriloquised words voiced by Walter.

Nancy evokes such decoupling of the subject when reflecting on his heart transplant, asking:

> I (who, 'I'? this is precisely the question, an old question: who is the subject of this utterance, ever alien to the subject of its statement, whose intruder it certainly is, though certainly also its motor, its clutch, or its heart).[50]

Embedded within his thinking here are organs vital to the Nancean cinematic vernacular – a motor, a clutch, a heart – and according to Nancy, the 'I' of the originary enunciation is by design estranged from its originary enunciator, intruding upon and driving the enunciated, yet schisming the enunciator. This pronominal schism opens up a space in which another can become implicated with this enigmatic 'I' so that it comes to be the motor or heart of thought in this other. The 'I', the 'me', then, that originated in Erika's letter, thus lands in Walter's larynx, enters his mouth, passes his lips and into the film. A more cinematic way of considering this phenomenon would be to call it desynchronisation, for it fractures the expected coincidence of enunciator and enunciation. This works to install a distance, or sense of deferral, into the film's soundtrack, precipitating a micro-epistolarity,[51] and recalling Deleuzian 'heautonomy'.[52] Heautonomy sees the visual and soundtrack separate and come to observe their own 'compositional logic'.[53] Sound no longer operates as 'an extension' or 'component' of the visual field and is 'freed' from any dependency on it, and 'off-screen space disappears' because there is simply no more out-of-field to occupy (sonorously).[54] Heautonomy, then, exceeds autonomy. It consists of an extreme estrangement of visual and soundtrack, each circulating its own meaning independently of its traditional playmate. Indeed, such is their alienation that when they do synchronously encounter each other they form a tactile junction.[55] Yet even when in contact these heautonomous images do not inspissate, for their touching only ever stresses their separation. Meaningful contact between the two heautonomous images is therefore always deferred, the 'irrational' cutting that renders them distinct denaturing them beyond the point of formal reconciliation.[56] However, violence here does not show itself in 'savage images' and is not only active as the force which violates the generally synchronous audio-visual image, effectively leaving its mark in this way, but it is equally present in its role as relay: its 'function to circulate between the two kinds of image, and make them connect'.[57]

The 'silent stratigraphy' of Marguerite Duras's *India Song* (1975) is the epitome of Deleuzian heautonomy.[58] Like the letter in accented cinema, desynchronisation here operates counterhegemonically, 'destabilis[ing] hierarchies', that is, Western and patriarchal 'power structures at work within the conventions of filmmaking' which service verisimilitude.[59] 'This non-representational mode of filmmaking', Laura McMahon writes, 'resonates with [Nancy's] deconstructive figuring of presence as interruptive', which the film's form expressly realises:[60]

> Just as the image–sound relation is untied and reconfigured as heterogenous points of contact between body and voice, so the viewer's reception of the film is freed from the homogenous constraint of synchronization to explore different possibilities of being-with. [. . .] Creating multiple points of coincidence and delay between body and voice, the film opens up a singular plurality of positions beyond reified subject–object relations or structures of identification.[61]

McMahon here describes a resonant subject(-spectator) endowed with a verily cinematic look, that is, a look that in no way masters meaning, to portmanteau Nancy. Following Kristin Lené Hole, then, according to McMahon there is a 'literary' quality to Duras's film and to Deleuzian heautonomy; constantly oscillating, out of this latter violence nothing is ever resolved.⁶² Meanings born never settle but circulate and defer to give rise to an uncertain, murky signification. Such murk, however, is not bracketed off, but rather forms the very condition of our encounter with the film. The papery and the pinnal thus insinuate themselves here through *renvoi* which, like heautonomy, is structured by rebounding, resounding, relaying. This sense of Deleuzian denaturation, moreover, complements the Nancean account of violence: a force that reconfigures instead of assaulting what it encounters and emblematised through the illogical wrenching of a nail from a piece of wood. The 'I' that estranges the enunciator and enunciation is so cleaved, and it is in this way that the heautonomous enunciation independently circulates Erika's would-be desire in sound and in doing so becomes Walter's actions.

Yours Sincerely: Dislocation and Desire

The film as a whole suffers such enunciative 'dislocation'⁶³ because, set in an 'impossible Francophone Vienna', its surrounds betray its linguistic displacement through German-language signage, such as the 'no entry to under 18s' sex shop sign or the film posters Erika stands in front of at the drive-in.⁶⁴ Indeed, the dubbing of the Germanic cast realises, and further formalises, this pronominal schism because each body has quite literally been filled with the voice of another, embodying the precarity that Nancy reads at the heart of the subject. *The Piano Teacher*'s penultimate sequence turns up the volume on this dislocation. Here Walter recites a redacted, although verbatim, version of Erika's letter, which cinematically rematerialises in a multiply material admixture of image, sound and rhythm, that is, as *corpus imāginum*: through the banks of black and white that constitute the scene, through costume and lighting, through the gaps and breathiness that make up the soundtrack and through its pace which observes the epistolary to the letter. The scene plays out in the exact time it takes Walter to embody Erika's illocutionary aims. Having raised the Kohuts from their beds, Walter sets about disposing of Erika's mother by locking her, and her voice, her noisiness, out of the apartment's hallway, once more transforming their antechamber into a place of anti-resonance. Upon doing so, Walter quotes Erika's letter, 'As for my mother pay no attention to her', to illustrate that his actions are an accurate manifestation of her desire, that is, a faithful performance of her intention. Paying no further attention to the worried cries of Madame Kohut, Walter confronts Erika further with her estranged 'I', asking whether things are unfolding as she imagined and quoting her once more, 'Hit me around the face and hit me hard', before again acting on the request. Erika intermittently demands that Walter stop his abuse of her. Seemingly, she is experiencing the pronominal schism described by Nancy, her estranged 'I' nosily intruding upon her through Walter – who is this 'I'?, her protestations and silences ask. Walter, however, refuses to relent and despite his own vocalisations regarding his discomfort at playing by Erika's rules, he persists. Reiterative and redactive, then, the entire sequence stages the epistolary imaginary: absence gives way to an all too real presence, the always already embedded scene of the letter's reception in its scene of production crashes into view.[65] What follows has almost exclusively been read as Walter's rape of Erika: her masochistic dream begetting an actual 'nightmare'.[66]

In resonance, though, it is impossible to name this violence in spite of the fact that these moments mark a rare act of on-screen violence within Haneke's filmography. Generally, the violence of his diegetic worlds is carried out off-screen, most emblematically demonstrated in the largely bloodless torture of *Funny Games*.[67] Here, no such attempts to conceal are made. The sequence, including Erika's violation, is all reveal; off-screen space, the former preserve of the letter, shrinks and despite all the blinding evidence, the spectator is left dumbfounded. Nancy would likely disagree with this account, for he writes:

> Violence of violation or of desire? Some would have us believe that the two are interchangeable. That is why there is a certain erotic or pornographic register in which the image of violation (of rape) is so readily invoked. [. . .] It is, however, impossible to confuse the violence of violation with that of desire. The distinction between the two is blindingly obvious.[68]

Rape is not invoked here complacently. However, as we have seen, blinding evidence is far from clear-cut. It annuls by means of its excesses. Filling our eyes, Walter's attack of Erika is blindingly obvious. Filling our ears, Erika's ventriloquised voice contradicts this blinding evidence. Circulating heautonomously, in essence, Erika's audio track detaches from her body, her visual track so to speak, and attaches to Walter's, his visual track, enhancing his noisy on-screen presence and deferring her desire through its expression through Walter. The expected coincidence of visual and soundtracks thereby stresses their separation and how they are denatured beyond the point of formal reconciliation, structurally dovetailing epistolary discourses of desire and counterhegemony. Despite claims to the contrary, then, such dissonance causes ambiguity to sound out and hang in the space between spectator and screen and, threatening even the most certain distinctions, its manner of doing so is undeniably unsettling.

Such dissonance chimes with Nikolaj Lübecker's work on the feel-bad film broadly characterised by 'their deadlock on spectatorial catharsis'.[69] Lübecker argues that these films must be permitted to 'take advantage of the exceptionality of the movie theatre' – as an experiential and experimental space – by 'allow[ing] for an asymmetrical relation between the ethical standards inside the cinema and those outside'.[70] This asymmetry transforms the viewing space into a discomfiting workshop and, moreover, further highlights *The Piano Teacher*'s own state of exception within the feel-bad idiom. In consummating the heterosexual relationship, Walter/Haneke gives the spectator what they want to see, yet in doing so exposes the constellation of violence, submission and control that underpins the romantic ideal. Yet this consummation is not a coming together, but a coming away of sense as signification, that is, of an ability to determine what exactly it is that we see and hear. This dissonance is intimately caught up with resonance, for in the Kohuts' antechamber the papery, the pinnal and the *pli* brutally converge to produce an enduring afterimage of violence. The originary superficial and visual registers of violence's imagistic impulse, embodied by Erika's letter, sublimate and come to affirm the (Nancean) image as a placeholder for a *corpus corporum*, that is, for a *corpus imāginum*. This placeholder moves us from the papery to the pinnal and to a specifically Nancean strain of listening by means of which we do not simply hear dialogue, or the rough rustling of the letter's leaves, but which is rather a resonant listening that attunes to the materiality of sounds, rather than their meanings, and, moreover, to the image's material multiplicity, which in turn takes us to the *pli* and its concertinaing of sound and sense. These wrinkles alert us not only to the inherent sonority that subtends sense, but equally to its motility and corporeality. During the attack sequence, then, what we see and hear create stark conditions for possible meanings, but ultimately, we are denied. These moments therefore open onto an uncertain signification of which we are acutely aware: the sight of Erika's battery endlessly eschewing our full grasp through its carouselling with the heautonomous, resonant afterimage of her desire. As such, the violence expressed between their bodies remains interminably indeterminate, is always amorphous, these uncertain contours rendering the image, and our non-corresponding sense of it, what Nancy might consider the image *par excellence* because it in no way supports signification. We can say with no certainty whether Erika's desire remains unconsummated, or whether our own desire to see has been consummated. All we can say for sure is that violence achieves its compulsive desire to be consummated as an image, an image that resonates.

Notes

1. Hamid Naficy, *An Accented Cinema: Exilic and Diasporic Filmmaking* (Princeton: Princeton University Press, 2001), p. 104.
2. Coulthard (2012), p. 20.
3. Ibid. pp. 22–3.
4. Ibid. p. 20.
5. Peucker (2006), p. 157.
6. Ibid.
7. Jean Ma, 'Discordant Desires, Violent Refrains: *La Pianiste* (*The Piano Teacher*)', in *A Companion to Michael Haneke*, ed. by Roy Grundmann (Oxford: Wiley-Blackwell, 2010), pp. 511–31 (p. 517).
8. Sorfa (2006), p. 101.
9. Nancy (2007), p. 37.
10. Rowe (2017), p. 156.
11. See Matthew Lawrence, 'Haneke's Stable: The Death of an Animal and the Figuration of the Human', in *On Michael Haneke*, ed. by Brian Price and John David Rhodes (Detroit: Wayne State University Press, 2010), pp. 63–84.
12. Naficy (2001), p. 103.
13. John Wray, 'Minister of Fear', *New York Times Magazine*, 23 September 2007, <http://www.nytimes.com/2007/09/23/magazine/23haneke-t.html?pagewanted=all&_r=3&> (last accessed 18 May 2020). Nikolaj Lübecker's recent tome on the feel-bad film, of which Haneke is a key purveyor, points up the emphatically corporeal contours of Haneke's vernacular here via Antonin Artaud. See Nikolaj Lübecker, *The Feel-Bad Film* (Edinburgh: Edinburgh University Press, 2015), p. 38.
14. Lisa Coulthard, 'Interrogating the Obscene: Extremism and Michael Haneke', in *The New Extremism in Cinema: From France to Europe*, ed. by Tanya Horeck and Tina Kendall (Edinburgh: Edinburgh University Press, 2011b), pp. 180–91 (p. 186).
15. Ibid. p. 185.
16. Naficy (2001), p. 101.
17. Coulthard (2010), p. 20.
18. Mandell (2007), p. xi.
19. Ibid. p. xi
20. Nancy (2007), p. 15.
21. Walker (2018), p. 165.
22. Wheatley (2009), p. 78. See also pp. 94–5.
23. Nancy (2007), p. 30.
24. Ibid.
25. Naficy (2001), p. 104.
26. 'illocution', *Oxford English Dictionary* <https://www.oed.com/view/Entry/91498?redirectedFrom=illocution#eid> (last accessed 4 September 2018).

27. See, for instance, Mark Chapman, '*La Pianiste*: Michael Haneke's Aesthetic of Disavowal', *Bright Lights Film Journal* (2011) <https://brightlightsfilm.com/la-pianiste-michael-hanekes-aesthetic-of-disavowal/#.XvCdQpNKhmA> (last accessed 22 June 2020), Harriet Wrye, 'Perversion Annihilates Creativity and Love: A Passion for Destruction in *The Piano Teacher* (2001)', *International Journal of Psycho-Analysis*, 86 (2005), 1205–12 and Jean Wyatt, 'Jouissance and Desire in Michael Haneke's *The Piano Teacher*', *American Imago*, 62 (2005), 453–82.
28. Catherine Wheatley, 'The Masochistic Fantasy Made Flesh: Michael Haneke's *La Pianiste* as Melodrama', *Studies in French Cinema*, 6 (2006), 117–27 (p. 118).
29. Rowe (2017), p. 155. See also Scott Foundas, 'Michael Haneke: The Bearded Prophet of *Code Inconnu* and *The Piano Teacher*', *IndieWire* (2001) <https://www.indiewire.com/2001/12/interview-michael-haneke-the-bearded-prophet-of-code-inconnu-and-the-piano-teacher-2-80636/> (last accessed 22 May 2020) and Saxton (2008).
30. Nancy (2005b), p. 16.
31. Ibid. Translation modified. Jeff Fort's lucid translation of *The Ground of the Image* translates 'fracassante' as shattering. I, however, prefer 'deafening' because it underlines the acoustic refrain that shapes a great deal of Nancy's thought and, of course, it complements my principal critical and conceptual paradigm: resonance.
32. Ibid. Interestingly, Fort's translation turns up the acoustics of Nancy's prose. Violence's wilful deafness is absent from Nancy's original text.
33. Such disruptive, or uncharacteristic centring of Walter's desire is especially apparent during both the recital and rehearsal scenes.
34. Nancy (2005b), p. 19.
35. Eugenie Brinkema, 'How to Do Things with Violences', in *A Companion to Michael Haneke*, ed. by Roy Grundmann (Oxford: Wiley-Blackwell, 2010), pp. 354–70 (p. 366).
36. Nancy (2005b), pp. 24–5.
37. Ibid. p. 20. My emphasis.
38. Ibid.
39. See Brunette (2010), pp. 101–2, Chapman (2011), Robin Wood '"Do I Disgust You?" or, tirez pas sur *La Pianiste*', *CineAction*, 59 (2002), 54–60 and Slavoj Žižek, *Welcome to the Desert of the Real! Five Essays on September 11 and Related Dates* (London: Verso, 2002), p. 20.
40. Wheatley (2009), p. 135.
41. See Morrey (2009), p. 126.
42. I am indebted to Davina Quinlivan's mesmerising *The Place of Breath in Cinema* (2012) for awakening me to the presence of breath and air in the film.
43. See John Champagne, 'Undoing Oedipus: Feminism and Michael Haneke's *The Piano Teacher*', *Bright Lights Film Journal* (2002) <https://brightlights

film.com/undoing-oedipus-feminism-michael-hanekes-piano-teacher/#. XvkBWZNKi9Y> (last accessed 28 June 2020).
44. Ma (2010), p. 519.
45. Fatima Naqvi and Christophe Koné, 'The Key to Voyeurism: Haneke's Adaptation of Jelinek's *The Piano Teacher*', in *On Michael Haneke*, ed. by Brian Price and John David Rhodes (Detroit: Wayne State University Press, 2010), pp. 127–50 (p. 138).
46. Sharrett (2004).
47. Wheatley (2006), p. 121.
48. Ibid.
49. See also Wheatley (2009), p. 137.
50. Nancy (2008a), p. 162.
51. Naficy (2001), p. 111.
52. Deleuze (1989), p. 253. Rowe (2017) also draws on Deleuzian heautonomy when discussing *The Piano Teacher*.
53. D. N. Rodowick, *Gilles Deleuze's Time Machine* (Durham, NC: Duke University Press, 1997), p. 145.
54. Ibid.
55. Deleuze (1989), p. 257.
56. Rodowick (1997), p. 145.
57. Deleuze (1989), p. 259. Translation modified.
58. Gilles Deleuze quoted in McMahon (2012), p. 89.
59. Michelle Royer, *The Cinema of Marguerite Duras: Multisensoriality and Female Subjectivity* (Edinburgh: Edinburgh University Press, 2019), p. 41.
60. McMahon (2012), p. 89.
61. Ibid.
62. See Hole (2016).
63. Charles Warren, 'The Unknown Piano Teacher', in *A Companion to Michael Haneke*, ed. by Roy Grundmann (Oxford: Wiley-Blackwell, 2010), pp. 494–510 (p. 503).
64. Rosalind Galt, 'The Functionary of Mankind: Haneke and Europe', in *On Michael Haneke*, ed. by Brian Price and John David Rhodes (Detroit: Wayne State University Press, 2010), pp. 221–42 (p. 227).
65. Naficy (2001), p. 103.
66. Wheatley (2006), p. 126. Exceptions to this include Champagne (2002), whose use of scare quotes clumsily suggests uncertainty, and Warren (2010) who, when contemplating whether or not Walter rapes Erika, simply states 'I think it is impossible to say' (p. 508).
67. See Wheatley (2009), pp. 78–112.
68. Nancy (2005b), p. 19.
69. Lübecker (2015), p. 172.
70. Ibid. pp. 169–70.

Documenteur:
A Resonant Picture

Vardadian? It's telling that – unlike Godard/ian – Varda does not have an adjective.[1]

Agnès Varda's *Documenteur* is a marginal film full of marginal figures. Like Haneke's *The Piano Teacher* it is structured by a wincing proximity which boldly, and playfully, mulls art's imitation of life, as well as our imitation of one another.[2] Its lead protagonist, Emilie, an alternative take on the 'other woman' through a nominative determinist sleight of hand, stands in for the film's director who briefly stands in for Emilie when Emilie stands in for her absent employer – a film director. Like *The Piano Teacher*, this temporary co-option centres on the voice. At the behest of a visiting film crew, Emilie voices Varda's script for *Documenteur*'s companion film *Mur Murs* (1980), a documentary that charts the murals of Los Angeles. The film crew plays back Emilie's recorded voice and where hers should be, Varda's instead sounds out. *We never recognise our own voice*, the film teasingly tells us – a tease that inadvertently scores a sliver of *Vital Resonance*'s corpus and their dubbed bodies. From the villagers of la Pointe Courte to a Francophone Vienna, the pragmatic, purposeful and playful dissolution of the phantasmatic body is an accidental by-product of this study.[3] In *Documenteur* the occasional bad French accent substitutes these dubbed bodies and accentuates Emilie, and Varda's, sense of displacement, whilst being a gentle intertextual and rasping reminder of Jean Seberg's Patricia in Godard's *Breathless* or Robert De Niro's phoneticised delivery alongside Catherine Deneuve in Varda's *A Hundred and One Nights* (1994). *Documenteur* thus concertinas Varda and Emilie and through these wrinkles, as we shall see below, the papery joins the pinnal and the epistolary enfolds subjectivity and a resonant materiality.

Indeed, following Hamid Naficy, exile and epistolarity are constitutively linked here too, and despite the ludic quality of the abovementioned scene, fundamentally *Documenteur*, and Sabine Mamou's performance, poignantly detail pain, recounting a woman's tentative recovery after the end of her marriage. This recovery is epistolary. Nine letters structure the film, seven scribed by Emilie and two written by an unknown male typist who lives in Emilie's neighbourhood. Yet what causes this pain is equally postal. The separation of bodies is, after all, the very foundation of the epistolary genre: 'Epistolarity is constitutionally a discourse of desire, for it mediates between distanced but desiring subjects.'[4] Indeed, the first epistle conjures the absent object of desire: Tom's body. Naked and prone on yellow and blue, these nude inserts recur throughout the film in flashbacks or fantasies of love-making – a tiny, private letter that we pen for our eyes only, a microcosmic erotic emissary from the subconscious. Emilie's gaze here is fundamental. In this first appearance her look first zooms in to frame Tom's genitals and then his chest as it gently rises and falls, and later inserts show their bodies intertwined – written from left to right with her eyes cast down towards their bodies. Tellingly too, Emilie and her son, Martin, discuss letter writing when thinking of things that make them sad: a pencil that is too small to write with, porridge left to go cold, a letter without a response. What is a letter without a recipient? Is it still a letter?

Documenteur's film letters do not necessarily receive a response, yet they dialogue with each other through the adoption of a similar logic. Emilie is frequently pictured seated at her desk in front of a large window overlooking the beach, sometimes typing, sometimes not, sometimes shot from the back, sometimes from the front. The sand and sea consistently form a littoral horizon – a terrestrial fold, its colour scheme anticipating Tom's first appearance. Significantly, the window doubles the screen, its diaphanous materiality at times capturing two spaces at once. Emilie at her desk and the beachscape which produces delicate, palimpsestic configurations: florid clusters which articulate the murmur of worldly sense. Moving from left to right, as if aping writing, the walkers, sunbathers, joggers, garbage pickers and sand combers further the epistolary character of these instances, whilst at times the film secretes smaller missives: a dumb T-shirt with a sarcastic message, names scrawled on walls and washer-dryers. In its most sustained epistolary endeavour, Emilie, the film's primary epistolarian, writes this postal separation over and over again. The typewriter carriage pinches the paper, the camera pinches the paper in the typewriter in close-up. The words *séparation de corps* dominate the page – repeated over and over again in a central column. Traces of mishits produce a spectral effect on the page, some letters cannibalised by others and sandwiched by briefer meditations on letters, death, words and the sea. Such separation of course murmurs beneath *Documenteur*, as does this missive's dearth of verbs. What kills, what breaks, what separates these bodies? This verbal absence also shapes the enumerations that rhythm its visual and soundtracks, helmed by Varda and voiced by Delphine Seyrig, which echo Nancy's iterative *corpus corporum*: faces, fish, murals, orphaned words. An exception to this verbal absence, however, is to do/*faire*.

To do/*Faire* is the most fundamental, all-encompassing verb of action and, if we recall, according to Nancy 'verbs [. . .] signify the work's *doing*, its manner of doing and making, what it does to sense or how it *makes sense*'.[5] Any discussion of the work's doing of course arabesques with the resonances of to film/*filmer* across Nancy's writing on cinema. To film/*Filmer* in the Nancean vernacular resonates. It is laminar. It carousels a panoply of meanings and doings. But if a verb-less separation murmurs beneath *Documenteur*, what does the film do to sense and how does it make sense? Its film letters do some of this work. Its lengthiest epistolary episode, during which Emilie receives a call from a friend who is unaware of her separation from Tom, is a devastating illustration of this doing and its inscription of pain (Figure 10). Emilie taps away and as she does so, she is not only surrounded by her usual office paraphernalia – wicker chair, telephones, typewriter – she is also framed by two large, light blue swatches. The beach's reflection pools on the window independently of the narrative frame. Sailing boats bob, the ocean glistens as the sun meets its surface, wispy clouds score the sky and through the window's diaphanous surface they enter Emilie's office. The outside world's intrusion here triplicates the screen and demonstrates how the image is but a placeholder for a *corpus corporum*, that is, for a *corpus imāginum*, or indeed for a cinematic corpus. The window becomes a second screen and the mosaicked beachscape accentuates how light supports and fluidifies the film's worldviews. The work's doing here, realised by the film letters, screens Emilie and Varda's concertinaed pain whereby to film/*filmer* secretes its lexical carousel, for here to film/*filmer* both shows and filters, even shields, the pain it undoubtedly inscribes. Cradled within this cinematic corpus, Emilie's anguish is obvious. Yet Varda's pain is obscured by the very work of to film/*filmer* as to show, and crucially the violence which separated the lovers' bodies is not simply reflected in Emilie's body, that is, in the tumble of her tears and the breaking of her voice, but in the material makeup of the film too. These film letters thus operate as resonant afterimages of violence. Their multiply material collages are the afterimage that violence seeks out and through its insistent inscription of pain, the film as a whole is an enduring afterimage of violence.

Like many Vardadian pictures, this pain is at once subjective – Varda's, Mathieu/Martin's, Emilie's – and objective: a remote observation of odd jobs, rough sleeping and relationship strife. In this way, *Documenteur* echoes and anticipates Varda's wider oeuvre: the lame, the old and the sick depicted in *L'Opéra-mouffe* (1958), the inscrutable, transient Mona

Figure 10 *Documenteur* (1981) a film by Agnès Varda © 1981 ciné-tamaris.

sketched out in *Vagabond* (1985) and the rejected potatoes in *The Gleaners & I*. Indeed, *Documenteur* attests to film as the ultimate resonance form, yet this is a form that even exceeds an understanding of such resonance as matter in movement, that is, how cinema's many component parts – cinematography, editing, mise-en-scène, colours, textures and sounds – resonate with and between each other in order to create meaning materially. For alongside its many parts, which also constitute the film's epistolary impulse, and make up its resonant afterimages of violence, its lead protagonist is the facsimile of the film's director; Emilie's anguish and quietness are Varda's as she confronts the breakdown of her own relationship with Jacques Demy, both heartbroken and displaced. The son of the film's lead protagonist is played by Varda's son, Mathieu Demy. Equally, the film houses images that are direct facsimiles of Varda's earlier filmography: buckets of squirming fish, nude inserts of lovers' bodies, skeleton hands, the murals of LA. Resonantly, this genealogy counterpoints the film's narrative of loneliness, as So Mayer describes:

> Perhaps one of Varda's answers [to whether a woman artist can do more than introduce herself through her oeuvre], then, is that she is not alone: there are other women

inventing and introducing themselves as well, observing and refracting each other. Her films with Jane Birkin (*Jane B. par Agnès V.* and *Kung Fu Master!*, both 1988) offer a similar sense of resonance as the friends dissect the complexity of celebrity, feminism, motherhood and female desire.[6]

Mayer calls this sense of resonance 'homocitation' and defines it as references to the existing 'feminist film community' to which, they argue, 'film critics traditionally pay too little attention' and by doing so 'miss the communities they build, introducing themselves as multiple, communal, complex and – above all – attentively discursive'.[7] Varda is, of course, a fundamental member of this community and Mayer's homocitation effectively casts such supersized resonance as cinema's doing, its way of making sense.

Documenteur is thus resonantly constituted and as an enduring afterimage of violence it resonates long after the film's conclusion, for Varda reincarnates this enduring reminder of her pain in the later career retrospective, *The Beaches of Agnès*, to pseudonymously elaborate on her separation from Demy where to film/*filmer* as to filter/*filtrer* clarifies somewhat but still 'creates a disjunctive combination of truth and fiction'.[8] Like Nancy, then, resonance is Varda's works doing and this doing echoes Nancy's observation that '[t]he only portrait of an artist [. . .] is his art (of a philosopher, his thought, of an engineer, his machines, of a politician, his politics).'[9] The portrait of the artist here is resonance, and Mayer's staking a claim for Vardadian perhaps does not go quite far enough, for as *Documenteur* shows, Varda is not an adjective, she is a verb.

Notes

1. So Mayer, 'The Varda Variations: (Re)introductions of the Auteure in *Documenteur* and Beyond', *cléo: a journal of film and feminism*, 6 (2018) <http://cleojournal.com/2018/04/11/varda-variations-documenteur/> (last accessed 13 June 2020).
2. See Bénézet (2014) and Conway (2015).
3. See Mary Ann Doane, 'The Voice in the Cinema: The Articulation of Body and Space', *Yale French Studies*, 60 (1980), 33–50.
4. Naficy (2001), p. 111.
5. Nancy (2005b), p. 74. Original emphasis.
6. Mayer (2018).
7. Ibid.
8. DeRoo (2017), p. 147.
9. Nancy (2011a), p. 79.

Bloody Resonance

I measure the distance from the mind to the body by means of the fluid that runs all through the body, like the ink in the calamus [. . .]. You must conceive this spiritual writing with blood, this hematography.[1]

In this book's introduction, Nancy's philosophy was described as the ultimate resonance chamber thanks to the lexical, thematic, conceptual and ontological whorls that arabesque across his work – this work's doing resonance itself. The stone, for instance, modest and hard, brute yet worldly, choreographs huge swathes of Nancy's thought. It is at the heart of his wasted heart. Like a wasted wish, he images his arrhythmia, his discourse, with the doubly rocky image of a pebble falling to the bottom of a well – a feeling which alerts him to his originary strangeness. The stone also manages our mineral technicity, distinguishing us from and drawing us towards all other bodies, whether made of stone, wood, plastic, or flesh, whilst the rocky cave wall irreducibly binds imagehood and subjecthood, and a fissure in a wall realises the spectators that we (later) are and indirectly apes the sonorous cave that we become.

Vital Resonances adds a further resonant chamber to Nancy's thinking on film, for each chapter features a rouge burst. The red flowers of Kiarostami's cinema, which disrupt the presiding timbre of his images, are here transplanted to the arboreal settings of *La Pointe Courte* and *Time of the Wolf* and through their ligneous, discreet touches their respective wooden matrices materialise. Eva's redness in *The Seventh Continent* swells her corporeality, transforming her into the filmic element whereby she ultimately takes over the textures of cinema itself. It is red, again, the blood of battlefields, that charges *Cleo from 5 to 7*'s local colour and its discussion of our compound mode of being, and seeing, and which works to restore the event in *Caché*. And finally, it is the understanding of the enduring afterimage of violence as resonant, and the seeping, gushing flow of blood that wounds (likely) entail, which realises another red pool in *The Piano Teacher* and less bloodily, but no less poignantly, in *Documenteur*. This red seam is especially curious because a frequent omission of Nancy's critical engagement with the body is blood. If we recall, he scathingly describes our insides as functionalist formalisms, and as Christina Howells summarises:

> For Nancy the truth of skin does not involve any kind of revelation, other than the fact that there is precisely *nothing* to reveal [...]. There are no hidden depths, no secret or sacred truths, nothing is concealed beneath the skin. And Nancy [...] plays with the etymology of the subject as *sub-jectum*, with nothing beneath it, simply its own fugitive being, here portrayed as [...] 'skin, the slenderness of skin, and its rosy [flesh-pink] tint'.[2]

Despite such consistency of thought, this rosiness hints at what lies beneath the skin – blood – and therefore begs the question: what lies on the inside of Nancy's thought and, moreover, what happens to his thought when it (actively) confronts our insides, not least because blood is a minor refrain amongst his writings on the image? Indeed, as Nancy contends in *The Ground of the Image*, a desire for spilt blood – 'the clots in which life suffers and dies' – stalks all images.[3] This bloodshed, he continues, 'does not seal any passage beyond death, but seals only the violent stupidity that believes it has produced death immediately before its eyes in a little puddle of matter'.[4] He continues: '*Every* image borders on such a puddle.'[5] Blood could thus be thought of as the anxious, internal silence of Nancy's thinking on the body – he even abstains from using the word in 'The Intruder', instead stating that 'I also know that I have to be grafted with a *type* O+ heart, thereby limiting the options'[6] – to echo the internal silence he experienced before his heart failed and his own body became a stranger, which in turn inspired his aesthetic turn. When blood is discussed, in *Corpus* for instance, it is in fact catalogued as *corpus corporum*:

> Tensions, squeezings, pressures, calluses, thromboses, aneurisms, anemias, hemolyses, hemorrhages, diarrheas, drugs, deliriums, capillary invasions, infiltrations, transfusions, soilings, cloacae, wells, sewers, froth, slums, megalopolises, sheet-roofs, dessications, deserts, crusts, trachomas, soil erosions, massacres, civil wars, deportations, wounds, rags, syringes, soilings, red crosses, red crescents, red bloods, black bloods, clotted bloods, bloods electrolyzed, perfused, infused, refused, spurted, imbibed, mired, plastified, cemented, vitrified, classified, enumerated, blood counts, blood banks, sense banks, cents banks, traffics, networks, flowings, flash-floods, splashes.[7]

The image is, of course, catalogued thus, that is, as *corpus imāginum*, and materially blood complements Nancy's particular understanding of to film/*filmer* and its fluidifying, jellifying, crystallising what is captures. Equally, blood's motility, its running, flowing, coagulating, sealing, suggests a vital, soulful writing, a hematography, which Nancy contends with in *Ego Sum* and his response to Descartes's twelfth rule '*Dum Scribo*': 'It is not what I write that I understand while I am writing, but I understand, or rather I gather that *I am writing*. I collect myself in writing. *Cogito, sum*, as it will be written later; here I am writing *scribo, intelligo*.'[8] This hematography, which is also a gathering, is reminiscent of resonance's percussive corporeality, a body beaten by its own sense of a body. In writing blood, in French, we find it collapsed into *sens*, which enjoys another peculiar Nancean resonance, because in *sens* (sãs) we hear *sang* (sã) – blood – as if auscultating our own body, its blood, its noise, its heart, we would hear this sense too, sense that is coterminous with the world and a coextensivity which pivots on a noisy hinge and quivers with our compound mode of being. Jacques Derrida listens in to Nancy's thinking thus and describes how Nancy 'tamper[s] with the relation between sense and blood, between a "stroke of sense" and a sanguineous "stroke" of blood'.[9] Indeed, in listening we might understand this coextensivity as a transposition of the altogether stranger, more intimate, orificial anatomy associated with Nancy's encounter with the image. After all, according to Nancy, '[o]penings for blood are identical to those of sense'[10] and our exposure to each other and to the world only ever admits access, that is, an opening up towards, but never ingress.[11] Sense, being, the world are thus holey by design, and resonance is of course attuned to these inherent hollows for in a corollary to skin's absence of hidden depths, sound has no hidden surface; and whilst an earlier Nancean whorl cites sound as the least incorporated of matter, a later one understands it as corporeally penetrating and propagating. Resonance thus attests to 'the ultimate human truth of blood, sinews and bones'.[12] The sense of the world blows through us. Howells's discussion of *Nus sommes* is again instructive here:

> Nancy clearly alludes to Freud's account [of the soul or psyche] in 'Trans', his study of Nan Goldin's portrait of *Joana's Back in the Doorway* of 2000, when he describes the meaning of the nude as inscribed 'on the skin of bodies and in the passage from one body to the next', and discusses psychoanalytic transference as 'the place where the psyche grasps itself as an extension and a spacing, which means that I have a body'. In this way transference is neither a process of identification nor of projection, but rather 'an experience of alterity' and 'an exposure to the extension which constitutes the psyche'. These complex phrases are attempts to account for the way in which subjectivity is not independent or self-identical but rather a part of mutual self-constitution, open to otherness with both its pains and its joys.[13]

These pains and joys, and their potential translations, are experienced by Nancy through an encounter with blood via cinema, specifically with Claire Denis's *Trouble Every Day*:

> Love – that by which we are bitten (as colloquial language would have it). Not an anatomical dissection but that which bursts and destroys the flesh leading not to death but to something that resembles it: to an irradiation causing a stabbing jolt to the heart, a contraction that at once freezes the blood and spills it out. This – this thing or this beast –, this chilling heartbreak, love, the transfixion or transfusion of that which (of he or she who) thought itself alone with itself, the breakdown of the specular and of the resembling image: the image bleeding, blinding.[14]

When compared with his response to Goldin's *Joana's Back in the Doorway*, Nancy here adopts a 'radically different' set of terms to consider our compound mode of being;[15] he draws on a bloody corpus – love, spills, transfixion, transfusion all lead to ichor – indicating that the abovementioned translation affects his thinking too. This hematography returns us to a vital, soulful writing:

> The truth of the soul is that of the pen. [. . .] For we see that spoken or written words excite all sorts of thoughts and emotions in our minds. With the same paper, pen and ink, if the tip of the pen is pushed across the paper in a certain way it will form letters which excite in the mind of the reader thoughts of battles, storms and violence, and emotions of indignation and sorrow; but if the movements of the pen are just slightly different they will produce quite different thoughts of tranquillity, peace and pleasure, and quite opposite emotions of love and joy.[16]

Blood moves Nancy's writing in this way and proves threatening to the very fabric of his thought – a frenzied bloodlust inaugurated by a 'mauve bite mark' – whereby his former anxious silence becomes fury.[17]

In the article produced in response to *Trouble Every Day*, Nancy mentions blood nearly fifty times – a veritable hematography – and, as Laura McMahon highlights, his encounter with the film questions the robustness of his ontology of touch and whether it is only 'able to engage [. . .] with the very extremes of touch',[18] 'where touching becomes searching, touching under the skin, tearing out what it covers up, what it protects and announces, what it signals as the layer and the stream that it encloses'.[19] The flow of blood, then, is almost too much for Nancy's philosophy to handle, exposing it to its own limits and transforming some of his principal tropes. It stymies the cataloguing of the body whereby the functionalist formalisms of our insides and *corpus corporum* of old collide: 'a living body', he writes, 'is a body of blood: blood is not simply one of its contents, it *is* its blood, it lives in its blood'.[20] Coterminous with the body, then, we might residually catalogue blood as *corpus* (as Nancy does above) but what in fact precipitates is a catalogue of the body as blood, blood, blood and nothing more. Is this the bloody end of Nancy's thinking, then? Exposed to the insides of his own thought, his body of work finds itself vulnerable to the agglutination it has so ardently fought against that centres essence through its exposure to cinema. For Nancy's thought to work, then, must blood remain extruding, exterior, ecstatic?[21]

Nancy's response to *Trouble Every Day*, however, bears many of his more typical rhetorical hallmarks. How we listen in to certain always key words, for example, is vital. The inaugural *baiser*, whence his reflections cascade, translates as both 'to kiss' and 'to fuck' and blood itself is parenthetically catalogued as both '*cruor*, blood erupting outside the skin, distinguished from *sanguis*, the blood circulating in the organs'.[22] A Nancean otology thus burgeons – a listening that picks at the scabs of a congealed understanding and like the wound is both inside and outside. The altogether stranger, more intimate, orificial anatomy at the heart of Nancy's encounter(s) with the image structures his thinking here too: the heart, mouth, ears, lungs, skin and eyes, and their effluvia, breath, saliva, blood, the soul litter his response to the film right down to the secret silence of blood. *Trouble Every Day*, according to Nancy, is 'almost a silent film – what dialogue there is is often in English, and nothing is said about the blood', as in Nancy.[23] According to a Nancean otology, however, in silence there is always blood. Indeed, the whole articulatory cinema of the mouth appears here – like the voice, face, lips, tongue, teeth are all seen in the bite and the mouth once more becomes an invitation for spectation – further suggesting that cinema might be Nancy's epic of the mouth. A kiss becomes a bite, a bite that tastes blood. A breathy kiss becomes a bloody bite. Blood subsumes saliva. Souls, the living body of flesh and blood, explode, rather than mingle. Arguably, then, our insides and the insides of Nancy's thought arabesque and they constitute not so much a bloody ending, but rather add a further resonance chamber to his oeuvre even when they appear alarmingly distinct. Once more, Nancy's work's doing is resonance, and blood – like bone, and Nancy's thought – arabesques; through these arabesques it demands that we (re)attune to its resonances. How we listen in to certain, always critical words again comes to the fore, further exposing how in blood we hear sense through Nancy's (residual) insistence that we listen hard(er) to his words whereby any encounter with his work operates as an exercise in our exposure to *sens* to which a Nancean otology is resolutely attuned. Indeed, the arabesque logic of Nancy's work listens to its own insides and discovers not destruction and agglutination, but resonance itself; and curiously, Varda's and Haneke's final cinematic outings, *Happy End* and *Varda by Agnès* (2019), respectively, involve the filmmakers listening to their own insides. Listening to the entirety of their cinematic universes, such listening adds further resonance chambers to their oeuvres, ones that do not develop a taste for blood but which do ask us to listen again.

Happy End: All Together Now

Michael Haneke's latest film, *Happy End*, is a resonance chamber. Indeed, his entire oeuvre is characterised by its steadfast commitment to bourgeois foibles, repeated names and an austere style. *Happy End*, however, perhaps inadvertently, pushes these narrative, stylistic and authorial tropes to a cannibalistic conclusion. Are we to believe, then, that Haneke is surreptitiously saying goodbye to audiences with this cinematic collage? Is its 'happy end' the final piece in the Haneke mind-game puzzle?[24] Likely not, although at the time of writing there are no known plans for a follow-up. Moreover, *Happy End* reads like an ending, or rather it feels like exhaustion, and not according to what we might consider typical Haneke means: unforgiving long takes, palpable violence on- or off-screen, coldness. Instead this sense of exhaustion precipitates from a sense of overfamiliarity, which begs a further question: have we spent too much time in this director's company? *Happy End*'s opening moments invite such reflection. Styled as if shot on a smartphone, that is, as a narrow, vertical oblong, it depicts the very pinnacle of domestic automatisms: the night-time bathroom routine. The peak of these automatisms, however, belongs to Haneke: the door ajar, accentuated by the imitative viewfinder, the everyday sounds, including water, the minor missives, that is, text messages, which narrate the on-screen action are all drawn from the warp and weft of his oeuvre. This is Haneke in microcosm. Some faces, moreover, are, of course, familiar – Isabelle Huppert and Jean-Louis Trintignant once again play father and daughter just as they did in *Amour* – whilst others' familiarity has been suppressed. Mathieu Kassovitz's face and hair, for instance, are unsettling smooth, shaving off elements of his recognisability. In effect, his face squirms even when it is still, or not being confronted with knowledge of extramarital affairs. It is not only this trio of French film stars which loans the film such cyclical contours, for *Happy End* rebaptises narrative and stylistic details from across Haneke's filmography, each of which telescopes key plot points. Teenage Eve cries Anne Schober's tears in the car. During a haircut Trintignant's paterfamilias dons the white ribbon, which elsewhere denotes patriarchal law, and here possesses further follicular resonances through memories of poor Peepsie's scissored crucifixion and Klara's sopping wet hair. Trintignant again maps this impulse when he confesses to having euthanised his wife a decade earlier and finally music(al performance), missives and sadomasochism are once more bound through Thomas's affair. We are also treated to lots of water. Indeed, in terms of the film's relationship to water, and the interrelationship between the mind and water that Haneke's work consistently demonstrates, and which is not accommodated elsewhere within his film style, *Happy End* is this project's logical conclusion.

Happy End is set in Calais, a long way from Haneke's usual city centres of European high culture and insidious, febrile conflict, such as Paris and Vienna; his hallmark bourgeois blindness is all the more acute here given the chronic humanitarian crisis unfolding there. Like the deaths of the 200 protestors on 17 October 1961, to which *Caché* obliquely testifies, there exists no official record of the number of would-be migrant deaths in the English Channel.[25] Remembrance relies on anecdote and the painstaking work of activists and volunteers, and despite its own attempts, *Happy End* does not offer a salve to this reality. Indeed, its diegetic clumsiness parrots this wilful myopia. Water, however, probes and exposes this silence. A beach visit nestles a seemingly banal choice of bottled water – there's no Evian, so will Badoit do? – alongside a discovery of bad faith, whilst the Laurent family mansion is limned by riparian paintings: white swans on an azure expanse in the dining room and a pastoral scene on the lounge wall. Flushed toilets also confect the film's soundtrack, whilst droplets of toilet water even secrete themselves into Thomas's sadomasochistic exchange. It is the film's closing sequence, at a beachside restaurant celebrating Anne's engagement to Lawrence Bradshaw (Toby Jones), however, which lionises the hydrous and psychical seam of Haneke's oeuvre through the horizon's perfect blue line which unerringly bisects the frame. The tableau-like shots that capture the Laurent family against this blue backdrop, who are pictured in all white and insouciance, concerned only with the banalities of babysitting and main courses, and in a manner whereby they would be perfectly at home on the walls of their own home, crystallise the sense of refused responsibility. Indeed, its pictorial insistence, which echoes that of the river painting in *Caché*'s Laurent family apartment, stalks and silently scores the family's failings even as the film attempts to pronounce them when Pierre, Anne's son (Franz Rogowski), arrives at the party with five refugees in tow, wishing to disclose details of their journeys to Europe. Once again, Haneke attempts to defy water's logic here, for its horizon is discomfitingly static until Georges punctures its steady blue line, exposing what lies beneath, laying bare the invisible like the bite. Immersing himself in the now far murkier-looking depths of *la Manche*, renaissance-perspective-defying grey-blue as far as the eye can see comes to fill the frame and for the first time in Haneke's filmography, we are in water that has not been piped, treated, chlorinated: a watery expanse that opens onto the world (Figure 11).

We are in the commons and we are also unusually close to one of Haneke's protagonists here – a nape, or over-shoulder shot, is generally as far or near as we get. We are, then, in the commons with Georges, spatially and experientially close, and like Georges we are fixed to our seats. Arguably, Haneke here turns the textures of the bleakly aestheticised sentimentality he demonstrates during the first frames of his first feature film inside out. In *Happy End* the stasis of the driver/passenger remains, yet the viscous bowels of the carwash inundate Georges and the screen. Despite the overwhelmingly derivative nature of *Happy End*, then, Georges's submersion disrupts the Hanekian timbre. Contrary to the critical reception of Haneke's most recent film, which perceives a satirical lightness of touch amongst its textures, this shift risks making *Happy End* Haneke's most pessimistic film to date because any esteemed lightness in fact accentuates the bourgeois insularity that his films outwardly pursue, whilst its closing frames are downright condemnatory of the inaction of spectatorship. Anne's scathing look towards Eve indicates as much. Nothing changes if we all just sit there watching like spectator-fish in a tank.

On the surface, Haneke's films seem violent, sadistic, uncaring and cruel, even unconcerned with the spectator. Indeed, they might appear to show concern only for their own deafening intrusion into our lives, reminding us of our complicity in the worldviews that they present.

Figure 11 *Happy End* (Michael Haneke, 2017). Reproduced with kind permission of the director.

Attuning to Haneke's film worlds is not, however, a case of falling into line with what we see and hear. There is an asymmetry between their narrative and material frames. We might see inhumanity, hear hostility, understand hopelessness, but in resonance what we encounter is altogether different. It is only in resonance that the(se) film(s) makes sense; a sense that remains open-ended and uncertain. Despite appearances, then, Haneke's door, another material-ethico frame of his oeuvre, is, however slightly, always ajar. In resonance, however, some voices might prove louder than others and thus we might need to listen harder. We might even need to speak up, to join a chorus of other voices to strengthen the coordination of our co-articulation of a world we want to live in. Akin to how Haneke's door ajar invites us to listen in despite its apparent restraint, we must seek fundamentally to leave ourselves open to resonance, to eschew the cacophonous understanding of political discourse. Where others will not, then, we must leave our doors ajar because even a slightly open door leads somewhere, after all . . . to hope, to hospitality, to humanity. What the commons reveal to us, then, is our responsibility – a responsibility that resonance seals thanks to our earlier contact with Haneke's hydrous film worlds.

Varda by Agnès: All Together Now for One Last Time

Hospitality is at the heart of Varda's final film, *Varda by Agnès*, which she stages as a causerie. In an unusual intermedial inclusion, *Varda by Agnès* also makes mention of the current refugee crisis through news footage and the widely circulated photograph of three-year-old Syrian refugee Alan Kurdi, a series of enduring afterimages of violence, and its mere mention here powerfully disrupts one of Varda's primary automatisms: the beach. Varda is a filmmaker for whom the beach is a primal scene – 'if you were to open me up you'd find beaches', she says in *The Beaches of Agnès* – and it is an environment that spans not only her entire career from *La Pointe Courte* to *Varda by Agnès*, but likewise her three lives: photographer, filmmaker, and visual artist.[26] It would be impossible for me to rehearse the wealth of work on Varda's cinema at the shoreline but what is remarkable about its inclusion here is how it pivots the beach away from the usual personal fabric of the beachscape within her filmography.[27] In essence, we might say that the beach changes timbre. Not that the beach, up until this point in Varda's oeuvre, has been treated as an exclusively jovial place of sandcastles, candy floss and cliché, although it has certainly been approached thus through the playfulness of works such as *Du côté de la côte* (1958) and *L'Île et Elle* (2006). In fact, in Varda's work the beach is no stranger to death and mourning, including her own grief, for instance in *Jacquot de Nantes* (1991) and *The Widows of Noirmoutier* (2006). Such a shift in her littoral timbre, however, is curious in light of the broader contours of the film: a career-spanning retrospective. Why change the habit of a lifetime?

Lifetime is a telling time and the titular informality of the film belies the significant labour involved in over six decades of filmmaking and image-making, an understatement perhaps best epitomised by Varda's comments upon receiving an honorary Palme d'Or: 'I have an entire bestiary of prizes with bears, dogs, etc. but people still don't give me funding. As fishermen say, "A little less thanks, and a little more money!"'[28] This labour, moreover, requires an 'active involvement with the afterlife of her projects' – an afterlife which is emphatically verbal: 'supplementing her projects, reframing them and adding new variations, exploring their existence in time and in interaction with her viewers'.[29] *Varda by Agnès* is the ultimate embodiment of this project, and the film acknowledges this work, and, moreover, its own, which are one and the same, from its first frames, for the opening credits consist of a series of overexposed, haptic stills taken from across Varda's filmography that have been further manipulated so that particular details are blown up, resulting in a slightly askew re-presentation of her film worlds. Their fuzziness effectively stymies any (threatened) sense of overfamiliarity and pictorialises the poring over the details of the past that *Varda by Agnès* enacts. Varda's filmmaking thus adopts something of an arabesque logic. Technical and sensible, her oeuvre becomes a florid line that whorls and flows, splaying and stringing out its materiality and vitality and reimagining them in manifold ways to establish new configurations.

If, however, the film's calls to labour appear underdeveloped, causerie does warmly imply hospitality. Across the film's near two-hour runtime Varda plays host to a series of different audiences, including the contemporary cinematic one, and from the various stages she occupies, some seen, some supposed – theatres, her archive at her rue Daguerre home, the editing table where she patchworks together material from her three lives, the Fondation Cartier in Paris, a series of lecture theatres – Varda introduces her work. Briefly transformed into a debutante, as *Uncle Yanco* (1967) presents her to film society, *Varda by Agnès* temporarily abandons Paris for California just as Varda did fifty years earlier, yet a sense of continuity remains through the colour purple that Varda dons in the late sixties and in 2018. Next, Varda discusses *Cleo from 5 to 7*, initially from the original auditorium, then by means of a televised interview. In this interview extract, Varda meditates on the film's peculiar relationship to time and her attempts to record both subjective time, that is, time lived according to the banalities and urgencies of everyday life, and mechanical time measured by clocks. Thanks to Varda's jumps in time and space, this theme becomes all the more resonant and it is from this time travel that the work of *Varda by Agnès* becomes manifest. Indeed, Varda's ability to draw from a rich archive of interviews, that span as many decades as her creative output, discreetly signals labour.

Her later discussion of *Documenteur* reflects this pattern. In another interview, from another time, Varda talks about this deeply personal film which, as already explored, substitutes Sabine Mamou for Varda, whilst the *douleur douce*, and Mamou's co-star, that Varda mentions in relation to the film, is all hers. Subtly reinforcing the doubling at work in *Documenteur*, during these reflections we return to one of *Varda by Agnès*'s principal costumes and settings where Varda recalls, in great detail, a sequence towards the end of *Documenteur*. Overlaid with Varda's thoughts in voice-over/voice-off, the sequence in question is then screened: a woman playing with her slightly greasy hair in a laundromat shot through a window and thereby doubly screened – shown by and filtered through cinema and the glass pane. Varda describes how the scene, the gestures, narrate 'an extraordinary sensual solitude' and the resonance of small gestures soon precipitates with a fade out to black, followed by a fade in from black to *L'Opéra-mouffe*. Producing an unusual gap in *Varda by Agnès*'s audio-visual material, these fades do not observe the original editing of either *Documenteur* or *L'Opéra-mouffe*. Their use is therefore telling for they create an absence, a moment of stillness and quiet that has been retroactively imposed on both films. These fades thus resonate. Why pause things here, even momentarily?

The answer may lie in the *douleur douce* that the former recounts and the anxiety that the latter stages. Resonance articulates this anxiety. Indeed, resonance is the only way to make sense of *L'Opéra-mouffe*. The film opens with the image of a nude, pregnant woman and the opening credits cast it as a diary of a pregnant woman. Yet pregnancy is not simply a thematic concern, but a formal, material one too for its fullness, suggestiveness, expressiveness, roundness, vitality and fragility, as well as the woman's nudity, resonate across the film's visual, tactile and visceral registers. The curvature of her swollen belly is reiterated by the contours of a woman's hips, by the looped nodes of exposed wood grain, by bulbous flora whence life squirms, grows or is ripped, by unblinking fish eyes, by the quivering body of a new-born chick and by the exposed flesh of meat. In effect, *L'Opéra-mouffe* deals with matter in movement. This preoccupation with pregnancy, however, is not overtly uttered by these images, and ostensibly pregnancy, like resonance, is bracketed off in its own chapter. We nonetheless grasp a keen sense of pregnancy across the film: it becomes our very touch with the world and 'La Mouffe'. Pregnancy dovetails with community as the film increasingly takes in visions of the many people and things that make Paris's rue Mouffetard their home: root vegetables, summer fruits, flowers, lovers, the elderly, the lame, the fluey. These people and things are not brought together by the flow of narrative but through resonance, by material bursts that resonate. Roundness and fullness, for instance, reverberate between swollen bellies, pumpkins and faces; vitality vibrates between eggs, onions and children and lovers. 'La Mouffe', the film suggests, like a swollen, pregnant belly, is bursting with life, life tinged with desire, daily walks and desperation. In essence, the resonance of pregnancy is the film's common movement, transforming the slightest curve and filling up all the film.

Pregnancy, however, does not congeal into a phoney third term as typified by Richard Neupert's appraisal: 'Varda's earliest films were vital to revising French film language, and her inspiring pregnancy with her daughter Rosalie became symbolic of France giving birth to a new cinema.'[30] Apparently encompassing wonder, renewal and flux, Neupert here attunes to an essentialist key, much like Nancy's correlation between femininity and materiality and his corresponding claims for life bursting forth from the enwombed cries of the foetus, and risks transforming Varda's filmography into a mucous, mythic space. Instead *L'Opéra-mouffe* testifies to the many textures of Varda's cinema: the personal and its graffitied *colocataire*, the political, the marginal, the mundane and the surreal. And, of course, women: their bodies, their voices, their experiences, their (in)visibility. Its textures, moreover, are matricial with this study in particular. Wood's internal textured ornament returns here, whilst the intertwined bodies of lovers – a corporeal choreography that Varda repeats in *Le Bonheur* – features for the first time, as do Dorothée Blanck, one of the lovers, and Antoine Bourseiller, who later appear in *Cleo from 5 to 7*; *Varda by Agnès*, of course, generates the link between the two films. *L'Opéra-mouffe* is thus an arabesque in microcosm, and these fades sprout a new whorl within the very fabric of Varda's filmography that, like blood in Nancy, reattunes us to her filmmaking. Varda, after all, is verbal.

Despite this fullness, and the enduring fullness of Varda's career, it is somewhat alarming, and perhaps troublingly pessimistic, that the final image of her entire oeuvre is murky (Figure 12). Renaissance-perspective-defying grey as far as the eye can see. Taken from footage shot for her collaborative documentary with muralist JR, *Faces Places* (2017), in the moments before this murk takes hold, the duo is seated on the beach at Saint-Aubin-sur-Mer and in voiceover (from the later film), Varda explains how they had originally intended on finishing *Faces Places* with this sequence that gradually fills with sand, rather than her thwarted

Figure 12 *Varda by Agnès* (2019), a film by Agnès Varda © 2019 ciné-tamaris.

meeting with the 'rat' Jean-Luc Godard. Although risking pessimism, once more here Varda declines the 'blank screen' so often used to articulate 'an ending that is purely cinematic',[31] and one that often collapses 'the story's end with a human end',[32] again choosing an image of the seashore instead – perhaps most poignantly used to close *Jacquot de Nantes* – which cinematically refutes cruelty's stupidity.[33] Both endings, then, suggest 'an *ongoing* imprint', rather than a deathly index, and as sea, sand and wind swirl we find ourselves back in the commons.[34] The closing moments of both Varda's and Haneke's final films, then, suggest that cinema is another commons, like blood and bones and resonance: it is another measure of our common experience, something that we all share, yet like resonance, it is simultaneously only available to me, whoever this I might be. Varda's final frames, then, represent a sedimentation of resonance. Murky, wavy, ambiguous, corporeal, brushing up against and blowing through us, it is matter in movement without hierarchy. These final frames are thus a placeholder for the image, a *corpus imāginum*, through which we become a *corpus corporum*, for they call upon the altogether stranger, more intimate anatomy associated with Nancy's work on cinema: the heart, mouth, lungs, ears and skin. We resonate. Likewise, these final frames are a placeholder for an ending. After all, the afterlives of Varda's (and Haneke's) cinema will outlive us all. But in resonance we briefly partake in their film worlds. I have to end here, though; and like Varda, and possibly Haneke, *je vous quitte . . .*

Notes

1. Nancy (2016a), pp. 34–5.
2. Howells (2018), pp. 167–8.
3. Nancy (2005b), p. 25.
4. Ibid.
5. Ibid.
6. Nancy (2008a), p. 164.
7. Ibid. pp. 105–7.
8. Nancy (2016a), p. 23.
9. Derrida (2005), p. 55.
10. Nancy (2008a), p. 105.
11. Nancy (2000c), p. 14.
12. Howells (2018), p. 171.
13. Ibid. pp. 168–9.
14. Nancy (2008b), p. 9.
15. McMahon (2012), p. 131.
16. Nancy (2016a), p. 38.
17. Nancy (2008b), p. 1.
18. McMahon (2012), p. 132.
19. Nancy (2008b), p. 3.
20. Ibid. p. 2.
21. McMahon's (2012) account of Nancy's remarkable departure from his usual handling of touch here suggests that it may residually remain for its 'destructive urge [. . .] is destroyed by its own desire' (p. 132).
22. Nancy (2008b), p. 4.
23. Ibid. p. 6.
24. See Elsaesser (2010).
25. See Calais Migrant Solidarity <https://calaismigrantsolidarity.wordpress.com/deaths-at-the-calais-border/> and UNITED for Intercultural Action <http://www.unitedagainstracism.org/campaigns/refugee-campaign/fortress-europe/> (both last accessed 15 June 2020).
26. DeRoo (2017), p. 9.
27. See Handyside (2014), Cybelle H. McFadden, *Gendered Frames, Embodied Cameras: Varda, Akerman, Cabrera, Calle, and Maïwenn* (Madison: Fairleigh Dickinson University Press, 2014) and Emma Wilson, *Love, Mortality and the Moving Image* (Basingstoke: Palgrave Macmillan, 2012).
28. Agnès Varda quoted in Elsa Keslassy, 'Cannes' Honoree Agnès Varda Touts *Girls*, Says Money is the Biggest Problem', *Variety*, 24 May 2015 <https://variety.com/2015/film/festivals/cannes-honoree-agnes-varda-talks-women-film-1201504425/> (last accessed 15 June 2020).
29. Wilson (2012), p. 22.
30. Neupert (2007), p. 333.

31. Laura Mulvey, *Death 24x a Second: Stillness and the Moving Image* (London: Reaktion Books, 2006), p. 78.
32. Ibid. p. 76.
33. Ibid. p. 78.
34. Wilson (2012), p. 8.

Bibliography

Acker, Ally, *Reel Women: Pioneers of the Cinema 1896 to the Present* (London: B. T. Batsford, 1991).
Adamek, Philip M., 'The Intimacy of Jean-Luc Nancy's *L'Intrus*', *CR: The New Centennial Review*, 2 (2002), 189–201.
Ahmed, Sara, *The Promise of Happiness* (Durham, NC: Duke University Press, 2010).
Allan, Tony, *Virtual Water: Tackling the Threat to Our Planet's Most Precious Resource* (London: I. B. Tauris, 2011).
Anonymous, 'Agnès Varda, la grande Dame de la Nouvelle Vague est morte', *Paris Match*, 29 March 2019 <https://www.parismatch.com/Culture/Cinema/Agnes-Varda-figure-de-la-Nouvelle-Vague-est-morte-1615647> (last accessed 16 May 2020).
Anonymous, 'La Pointe Courte', *Le Monde*, 9 June 1955.
Anonymous, '*La Pointe Courte* et le spectacle du Studio Parnasse', *Le Monde*, 12 January 1956.
Antunes, Luis R., *The Multisensory Film Experience: A Cognitive Model of Experiential Film Aesthetics* (Bristol: Intellect, 2016).
Armstrong, Philip, 'From Appearance to Exposure', *Journal of Visual Culture* (2010), 11–27.
———. *Reticulations: Jean-Luc Nancy and the Networks of the Political* (Minneapolis: University of Minnesota Press, 2009).
Bachelard, Gaston, *Water and Dreams: An Essay on the Imagination of Matter*, trans. by Edith R. Farrell (Dallas: Dallas Institute of Humanities and Culture, 1983).
Backman Rogers, Anna, 'Lena Dunham's *Girls*: Can-Do Girls, Feminist Killjoys, and Women Who Make Bad Choices', in *Feminisms: Diversity, Difference and Multiplicity in Contemporary Film Cultures*, ed. by Laura Mulvey and Anna Backman Rogers (Amsterdam: Amsterdam University Press, 2015), pp. 44–53.
Bakker, Karen J., *Privatizing Water: Governance Failure and the World's Urban Water Crisis* (Ithaca: Cornell University Press, 2010).
Balfour, Ian, 'Nancy on Film: Regarding Kiarostami, Re-thinking Representation (with a Coda on Claire Denis)', *Journal of Visual Culture* (2010), 29–43.

Barker, Jennifer M., *The Tactile Eye: Touch and the Cinematic Experience* (Berkeley: University of California Press, 2009).

Barker, Stephen, 'De-monstration and the *Sens* of Art', in *Jean-Luc Nancy and Plural Thinking: Expositions of World, Ontology, Politics, and Sense*, ed. by Peter Gratton and Marie-Eve Morin (New York: State University of New York Press, 2012), pp. 175–90.

Barnfield, Jessica, 'Being Is an Octopus: Exploring Octopuses, Organs and Outsides in Jean Painlevé's *Les amours de la pieuvre* and Philip Warnell's *Outlandish*', *HARTS & Minds: The Journal of the Humanities and Arts*, 7 (2016) <https://www.harts-minds.co.uk/haptics-the-senses> (last accessed 27 June 2020).

Baross, Zsuzsa, *Encounters: Gérard Titus-Carmel, Jean-Luc Nancy, Claire Denis* (Eastbourne: Sussex University Press, 2015).

Barthes, Roland, *The Grain of the Voice: Interviews, 1962–1980*, trans. by Linda Coverdale (Evanston: Northwestern University Press, 2009).

———. *Camera Lucida: Reflections on Photography* (London: Vintage, 2000).

———. 'Leaving the Movie Theater', in *The Rustle of Language*, trans. by Richard Howard (Berkeley: University of California Press, 1989).

Bastide, Bernard, '*La Pointe Courte* ou comment réaliser un film à Sète (Hérault) en 1954', *Cahiers de la cinémathèque* (1994), 30–5.

Bellour, Raymond and Jean Michaud, 'Agnès Varda de A à Z', *Cinéma 61* (1961), 3–20.

Bénézet, Delphine, *The Cinema of Agnès Varda: Resistance and Eclecticism* (London: Wallflower Press, 2014).

Benjamin, Walter, 'The Work of Art in the Age of Mechanical Reproduction', in *Illuminations*, ed. by Hannah Arendt, trans. by Harry Zohn (New York: Schocken Books, 1985), pp. 217–51.

Bennett, Jane, *Vibrant Matter: A Political Ecology of Things* (Durham, NC: Duke University Press, 2010).

Betz, Mark, *Beyond the Subtitle: Remapping European Art Cinema* (Minneapolis: University of Minnesota Press, 2009).

Beugnet, Martine, 'The Practice of Strangeness: *L'Intrus* – Claire Denis (2004) and Jean-Luc Nancy (2000)', *Film-Philosophy*, 12 (2008), 31–48.

———. *Cinema and Sensation: French Film and the Art of Transgression* (Edinburgh: Edinburgh University Press, 2007).

Beylie, Claude, 'La Pointe Courte', *Télérama*, 6 March 1962, pp. 29–30.

Bingham, Adam, 'Life, or Something Like It: Michael Haneke's *Der siebente Kontinent*', *Kinoeye*, 1 (2004) <https://www.kinoeye.org/04/01/bingham01_no2.php> (last accessed 12 May 2020).

Brakhage, Stan, 'From *Metaphors on Vision*', in *The Avant-Garde Film: A Reader of Theory and Criticism*, ed. by P. Adams Sitney (New York: Anthology Film Archives, 1987), pp. 120–8.

Brinkema, Eugenie, *The Forms of the Affects* (Durham, NC: Duke University Press, 2014).

——. 'How to Do Things with Violences', in *A Companion to Michael Haneke*, ed. by Roy Grundmann (Oxford: Wiley-Blackwell, 2010), pp. 354–70.

Brown, Christopher and Pam Hirsch, 'Introduction: The Cinema of the Swimming Pool', in *The Cinema of the Swimming Pool*, ed. by Christopher Brown and Pam Hirsch (Oxford: Peter Lang, 2014), pp. 1–20.

Brunette, Peter, *Michael Haneke* (Chicago: University of Illinois Press, 2010).

Bui, Hoai-Tran, 'Agnès Varda, Filmmaker and "Godmother of the French New Wave", Dies at 90', *Washington Post*, 29 March 2019 <https://www.washingtonpost.com/local/obituaries/agnes-varda-godmother-of-the-french-new-wave-dies-at-90/2019/03/29/1bcf32d0-5225-11e9-88a1-ed346f0ec94f_story.html> (last accessed 16 May 2020).

Chamarette, Jenny, *Phenomenology and the Future of Film: Rethinking Subjectivity beyond French Cinema* (Basingstoke: Palgrave Macmillan, 2012).

Champagne, John, 'Undoing Oedipus: Feminism and Michael Haneke's *The Piano Teacher*', *Bright Lights Film Journal* (2002) <https://brightlightsfilm.com/undoing-oedipus-feminism-michael-hanekes-piano-teacher/#.XvkBWZNKi9Y> (last accessed 28 June 2020).

Chapman, Mark, '*La Pianiste*: Michael Haneke's Aesthetic of Disavowal', *Bright Lights Film Journal* (2011) <https://brightlightsfilm.com/la-pianiste-michael-hanekes-aesthetic-of-disavowal/#.XvCdQpNKhmA> (last accessed 22 June 2020).

Chauvet, Louis, 'La Pointe Courte', *Le Figaro*, 10 January 1956.

Connolly, Maeve, 'Outlandish: Introduction by Maeve Connolly', *Vdrome* (n.d.) <http://www.vdrome.org/phillip-warnell-outlandish/> (last accessed 16 April 2019).

Conrad, Peter, 'Michael Haneke: There's No Easy Way to Say This...', *The Observer*, 4 November 2012 <http://www.guardian.co.uk/film/2012/nov/04/michael-haneke-amour-director-interview> (last accessed 29 June 2020).

Conway, Kelley, *Agnès Varda* (Urbana: University of Illinois Press, 2015).

Cooper, Sarah, *The Soul of Film Theory* (Basingstoke: Palgrave Macmillan, 2013).

——. 'Film Theory in France', *French Studies*, 66 (2012), 376–82.

Coulthard, Lisa, 'Haptic Aurality: Listening to the Films of Michael Haneke', *Film-Philosophy*, 16 (2012), 16–29.

——. 'Ethical Violence: Suicide as Authentic Act in the Films of Michael Haneke', in *The Cinema of Michael Haneke: Europe Utopia*, ed. by Ben McCann and David Sorfa (London: Wallflower Press, 2011a), pp. 38–48.

——. 'Interrogating the Obscene: Extremism and Michael Haneke', in *The New Extremism in Cinema: From France to Europe*, ed. by Tanya Horeck and Tina Kendall (Edinburgh: Edinburgh University Press, 2011b), pp. 180–91.

——. 'Listening to Silence in the Films of Michael Haneke', *Cinephile*, 6 (2010), 18–24.

Crowley, Patrick, 'When Forgetting Is Remembering: Haneke's *Caché* and the Events of October 17, 1961', in *On Michael Haneke*, ed. by Brian Price and John David Rhodes (Detroit: Wayne State University Press, 2010), pp. 267–79.

Curot, Frank, 'L'Écriture de *La Pointe Courte*', in *Agnès Varda: Études cinématographiques*, ed. by Michel Estève (Paris: Lettres modernes Minard, 1991), pp. 85–99.

de Luca, Tiago, *Realism of the Senses in World Cinema: The Experience of Physical Reality* (London: I. B. Tauris, 2013).

del Río, Elena, *The Grace of Destruction: A Vital Ethology of Extreme Cinemas* (New York: Bloomsbury, 2016).

Deleuze, Gilles, *Cinema 2: The Time-Image*, trans. by Hugh Tomlinson and Robert Galeta (London: The Athlone Press, 1989).

——. *Cinema 1: The Movement-Image*, trans. by Hugh Tomlinson and Barbara Habberjam (London: Continuum, 2005).

DeRoo, Rebecca J., *Agnès Varda between Film, Photography, and Art* (Oakland: University of California Press, 2017).

Derrida, Jacques, *On Touching – Jean-Luc Nancy*, trans. by Christine Irizarry (Stanford: Stanford University Press, 2005).

Dixon, Wheeler Winston, *Visions of the Apocalypse: Spectacles of Destruction in American Cinema* (London: Wallflower Press, 2003).

Doane, Mary Ann, *The Emergence of Cinematic Time: Modernity, Contingency, the Archive* (Cambridge, MA: Harvard University Press, 2002).

——. 'The Voice in the Cinema: The Articulation of Body and Space', *Yale French Studies*, 60 (1980), 33–50.

Donaldson, Lucy Fife, *Texture in Film* (Basingstoke: Palgrave Macmillan, 2014).

Dousteyssier-Khoze, Catherine, 'Mise-en-abyme, Irony and Visual Cliché in Agnès Varda's *Le Bonheur* (1964)', in *Agnès Varda Unlimited: Image, Music, Media*, ed. by Marie-Claire Barnet (Cambridge: Legenda, 2016), pp. 97–107.

Elkin, Lauren, *Flâneuse: Women Walk the City in Paris, New York, Tokyo, Venice* (London: Chatto & Windus, 2016).

Elsaesser, Thomas, 'Performative Self-Contradictions: Michael Haneke's Mind Games', in *A Companion to Michael Haneke*, ed. by Roy Grundmann (Oxford: Wiley-Blackwell, 2010), pp. 53–74.

Ezra, Elizabeth 'Cléo's Masks: Regimes of Objectification in the French New Wave', *Yale French Studies*, 118/119 (2010), 177–90.

Ezra, Elizabeth and Jane Sillars, '*Hidden* in Plain Sight: Bringing Terror Home', *Screen* (2007), 215–21.

Fairfax, Daniel, 'Montage as Resonance: Chris Marker and the Dialectical Image', *Senses of Cinema* (2012) <http://sensesofcinema.com/2012/feature-articles/montage-as-resonance-chris-marker-and-the-dialectical-image/> (last accessed 15 July 2019).

Flitterman-Lewis, Sandy, *To Desire Differently: Feminism and the French Cinema* (New York: Columbia University Press, 1996).

Foundas, Scott, 'Michael Haneke on Amour: "When I Watched It with the Audience, They Gasped!"', *The Village Voice* (2012) <https://www.village

voice.com/2012/12/20/michael-haneke-on-amour-when-i-watched-it-with-the-audience-they-gasped/> (last accessed 12 May 2020).

——. 'Michael Haneke: The Bearded Prophet of *Code Inconnu* and *The Piano Teacher*', *IndieWire* (2001) <https://www.indiewire.com/2001/12/interview-michael-haneke-the-bearded-prophet-of-code-inconnu-and-the-piano-teacher-2-80636/> (last accessed 22 May 2020).

Frey, Mattias, 'A Cinema of Disturbance: The Films of Michael Haneke in Context', *Senses of Cinema* (2010) <http://sensesofcinema.com/2010/great-directors/michael-haneke/> (last accessed 9 May 2013).

Galt, Rosalind, *Pretty: Film and the Decorative Image* (New York: Columbia University Press, 2011).

——. 'The Functionary of Mankind: Haneke and Europe', in *On Michael Haneke*, ed. by Brian Price and John David Rhodes (Detroit: Wayne State University Press, 2010), pp. 221–42.

——. 'Pretty: Film, Theory, Aesthetics, and the History of the Troublesome Image', *Camera Obscura*, 24 (2009), 1–41.

——. 'The Obviousness of Cinema', *World Picture Journal* (2008) <http://www.worldpicturejournal.com/WP_2/Galt.html> (last accessed 9 May 2013).

Gibbs, John, *Mise-en-scène: Film Style and Interpretation* (London: Wallflower, 2002).

Gorbman, Claudia, 'Varda's Music', *Music and the Moving Image*, 1 (2008), 27–34.

——. '*Cléo from 5 to 7*: Music as Mirror', *Wide Angle*, 4 (1981), 38–49.

Grønstad, Asbjørn, *Screening the Unwatchable: Spaces of Negation in Post-Millennial Art Cinema* (Basingstoke: Palgrave Macmillan, 2012).

Guyer, Sara, 'Buccality', in *Derrida, Deleuze, Psychoanalysis*, ed. by Gabriele Schwab and Erin Ferris (New York: Columbia University Press, 2007), pp. 77–104.

Halpern Martineau, Barbara, 'Subjecting Her Objectification, or Communism Is Not Enough', in *Notes on Women's Cinema*, ed. by Claire Johnston (London: Society for Education in Film and Television, 1973), pp. 32–40.

Handyside, Fiona, *Cinema at the Shore: The Beach in French Film* (Oxford: Peter Lang, 2014).

Haneke, Michael, 'Terror and Utopia of Form: Robert Bresson's *Au hasard Balthazar*', in *A Companion to Michael Haneke*, ed. by Roy Grundmann (Oxford: Wiley-Blackwell, 2010), pp. 565–74.

Hickmott, Sarah, '(En)Corps Sonore: Jean-Luc Nancy's "Sonotropism"', *French Studies*, 69 (2015), 479–93.

Hole, Kristin Lené, *Towards a Feminist Cinematic Ethics: Claire Denis, Emmanuel Levinas and Jean-Luc Nancy* (Edinburgh: Edinburgh University Press, 2016).

Horton, Andrew J., 'De-icing the Emotions', *Central Europe Review* (1998) <http://www.ce-review.org/kinoeye/kinoeye5old.html> (last accessed 6 March 2013).

Howells, Christina, 'Jean-Luc Nancy and *La Peau des images*: Truth Is Skin-Deep', *Body and Society*, 24 (2018), 166–74.

Hutchens, B. C., *Jean-Luc Nancy and the Future of Philosophy* (Chesham: Acumen, 2005).
Irigaray, Luce, *The Forgetting of Air in Martin Heidegger*, trans. by Mary Beth Mader (London: Athlone Press, 1999).
Jacobus, Mary, *Romantic Things: A Tree, a Rock, a Cloud* (Chicago: University of Chicago Press, 2012).
James, Ian, 'Immanence and Technicity', *Sense & Society*, 8 (2013), 14–25.
——. *The New French Philosophy* (Cambridge: Polity Press, 2012).
——. 'The Evidence of the Image', *L'Esprit Créateur*, 47 (2007), 68–79.
——. *The Fragmentary Demand: An Introduction to the Philosophy of Jean-Luc Nancy* (Stanford: Stanford University Press, 2006).
——. 'Art – Technics', *Oxford Literary Review*, 27 (2005), 83–102.
James, Nick, 'Darkness Falls', *Sight & Sound*, 13 (2003), 16–18.
Jameson, Fredric, *Postmodernism, or, the Cultural Logic of Late Capitalism* (London: Verso, 1991).
Janus, Adrienne, 'Introduction: Jean-Luc Nancy and the Image of Visual Culture', in *Jean-Luc Nancy and Visual Culture*, ed. by Carrie Giunta and Adrienne Janus (Edinburgh: Edinburgh University Press, 2016), pp. 1–20.
——. 'Soundings: The Secret of Water and the Resonance of the Image', *Sense & Society*, 8 (2013), 72–84.
——. 'Listening: Jean-Luc Nancy and the "Anti-Ocular" Turn in Continental Philosophy and Critical Theory', *Comparative Literature*, 63 (2011), 182–202.
Jefferson Kline, T. (ed.), *Agnès Varda: Interviews* (Jackson: University Press of Mississippi, 2014).
Johnston, Claire, 'Women's Cinema as Counter-Cinema', in *Notes on Women's Cinema*, ed. by Claire Johnston (London: Society for Education in Film and Television, 1973), pp. 24–31.
Kamuf, Peggy, 'Béance', *CR: The New Centennial Review*, 2 (2002), 37–56.
Kane, Brian, 'Resonance', in *The Nancy Dictionary*, ed. by Peter Gratton and Marie-Eve Morin (Edinburgh: Edinburgh University Press, 2015), pp. 143–4.
——. 'Jean-Luc Nancy and the Listening Subject', *Contemporary Music Review*, 31 (2012), 439–47.
Kenaan, Hagi, 'What Makes an Image Singular Plural? Questions to Jean-Luc Nancy', *Journal of Visual Culture*, 9 (2010), 63–76.
Keslassy, Elsa, 'Cannes' Honoree Agnès Varda Touts *Girls*, Says Money is the Biggest Problem', *Variety*, 24 May 2015 <https://variety.com/2015/film/festivals/cannes-honoree-agnes-varda-talks-women-film-1201504425/> (last accessed 15 June 2020).
Kristeva, Julia, *Powers of Horror: An Essay on Abjection*, trans. by Léon S. Roudiez (New York: Columbia University Press, 1982).
Lawrence, Matthew, 'Haneke's Stable: The Death of an Animal and the Figuration of the Human', in *On Michael Haneke*, ed. by Brian Price and John David Rhodes (Detroit: Wayne State University Press, 2010), pp. 63–84.

Le Cain, Maximilian, 'Do the Right Thing: The Films of Michael Haneke', *Senses of Cinema* (2003) <http://sensesofcinema.com/2003/26/michael-haneke/haneke/> (last accessed 10 February 2021).

Lee, Mark, 'Re-viewing Varda's *Le Bonheur* (1964): Accident? Suicide? Or the Natural Order? That Is the Question', in *Agnès Varda Unlimited: Image, Music, Media*, ed. by Marie-Claire Barnet (Cambridge: Legenda, 2016), pp. 87–95.

Loren, Scott and Jörg Metelmann, *Irritation of Life: The Subversive Melodrama of Michael Haneke, David Lynch and Lars Von Trier* (Marburg: Schüren, 2013).

Lübecker, Nikolaj, *The Feel-Bad Film* (Edinburgh: Edinburgh University Press, 2015).

Ma, Jean, 'Discordant Desires, Violent Refrains: *La Pianiste* (*The Piano Teacher*)', in *A Companion to Michael Haneke*, ed. by Roy Grundmann (Oxford: Wiley-Blackwell, 2010), pp. 511–31.

McFadden, Cybelle H., *Gendered Frames, Embodied Cameras: Varda, Akerman, Cabrera, Calle, and Maïwenn* (Madison: Fairleigh Dickinson University Press, 2014).

McMahon, Laura, 'Dislocation of the Senses: Nancy on Klotz's *La Blessure*', *Senses & Society*, 8 (2013), 62–71.

——. *Cinema and Contact: The Withdrawal of Touch in Nancy, Bresson, Duras and Denis* (Oxford: Legenda, 2012).

——. 'Deconstructing Community and Christianity: "A-religion" in Nancy's Reading of *Beau Travail*', *Film-Philosophy*, 12 (2008), 63–78.

McMahon, Orlene Denice, *Listening to the French New Wave: The Film Music and Composers of Postwar French Art Cinema* (Berlin: Peter Lang, 2014).

Mandell, Charlotte, 'Translator's Note to *Listening*', in Jean-Luc Nancy, *Listening*, trans. by Charlotte Mandell (New York: Fordham University Press, 2007), pp. xi–xii.

Marks, Laura U., *Enfoldment and Infinity: An Islamic Genealogy of New Media Art* (Cambridge, MA: The MIT Press, 2010).

——. 'Haptic Visuality: Touching with the Eyes', *Framework: The Finnish Art Review*, 2 (2004), 78–82.

——. *Touch: Sensuous Theory and Multisensory Media* (Minneapolis and London: University of Minnesota Press, 2002), pp. 91–110.

——. *The Skin of the Film: Intercultural Cinema, Embodiment, and the Senses* (Durham, NC: Duke University Press, 2000).

Massumi, Brian, *Parables for the Virtual: Movement, Affect, Sensation* (Durham, NC: Duke University Press, 2002).

Mauriac, Claude, 'La Pointe Courte', *Le Figaro littéraire*, 14 January 1956.

Mayer, So, 'The Varda Variations: (Re)introductions of the Auteure in *Documenteur* and Beyond', *cléo: a journal of film and feminism*, 6 (2018) <http://cleojournal.com/2018/04/11/varda-variations-documenteur/> (last accessed 13 June 2020).

Mayne, Judith, *The Woman at the Keyhole: Feminism and Women's Cinema* (Bloomington: Indiana University Press, 1990).

Metz, Christian, *The Imaginary Signifier: Psychoanalysis and the Cinema*, trans. by Celia Britton, Annwyl Williams, Ben Brewster and Alfred Guzzetti (Basingstoke: Macmillan Press, 1982).

Minkowski, Eugène, *Vers une cosmologie: Fragments philosophiques* (Paris: Fernand Aubier, 1936).

Monod, Martine, 'La Pointe Courte', *Les Lettres françaises*, 12 January 1956.

Morin, Marie-Eve, '*Corps propre* or *corpus corporum*: Unity and Dislocation in the Theories of Embodiment of Merleau-Ponty and Jean-Luc Nancy', *Chiasmi International*, 18 (2016), 333–51.

——. 'Matter/Materiality', in *The Nancy Dictionary*, ed. by Peter Gratton and Marie-Eve Morin (Edinburgh: Edinburgh University Press, 2015), pp. 156–8.

——. *Jean-Luc Nancy* (Cambridge: Polity Press, 2012).

Morrey, Douglas, 'Listening and Touching, Looking and Thinking: The Dialogue in Philosophy and Film between Jean-Luc Nancy and Claire Denis', in *European Film Theory*, ed. by Temenuga Trifonova (London: Routledge, 2009), pp. 122–33.

Mouton, Janice, 'From Feminine Masquerade to Flâneuse: Agnès Varda's Cléo in the City', *Cinema Journal*, 40 (2001), 3–16.

Mroz, Matilda, *Temporality and Film Analysis* (Edinburgh: Edinburgh University Press, 2012).

Mulvey, Laura, *Death 24x a Second: Stillness and the Moving Image* (London: Reaktion Books, 2006).

——. 'Visual Pleasure and Narrative Cinema', *Screen*, 16 (1975), 6–18.

Naficy, Hamid, *An Accented Cinema: Exilic and Diasporic Filmmaking* (Princeton: Princeton University Press, 2001).

Nancy, Jean-Luc, *Ego Sum: Corpus, Anima, Fabula*, trans. by Marie-Eve Morin (New York: Fordham University Press, 2016a).

——. 'Rien sur le cinéma', *Trafic*, 100 (2016b), 194–9.

——. 'En Tournage Avec R.A.-Z.', *Trafic* (2011a), 79–86.

——. 'Making Sense', trans. by Emma Wilson, in *Making Sense: For an Effective Aesthetics*, ed. by Lorna Collins and Elizabeth Rush (Oxford: Peter Lang, 2011b), pp. 215–20.

——. *Corpus*, trans. by Richard A. Rand (New York: Fordham University Press, 2008a).

——. 'Icon of Fury: Claire Denis's *Trouble Every Day*', trans. by Douglas Morrey, *Film-Philosophy*, 12 (2008b), 1–9.

——. *Noli me Tangere: On the Raising of the Body*, trans. by Sarah Clift, Pascale-Anne Brault and Michael Naas (New York: Fordham University Press, 2008c).

——. *Listening*, trans. by Charlotte Mandell (New York: Fordham University Press, 2007).

——. 'La blessure, la cicatrice', *Remue* (2005a) <http://remue.net/spip.php?article742> (last accessed 5 September 2014).

——. *The Ground of the Image*, trans. by Jeff Fort (New York: Fordham University Press, 2005b).

——. 'L'Intrus selon Claire Denis', *Remue* (2005c) <http://remue.net/spip.php?article679> (last accessed 5 September 2014).
——. 'Cinéfile et cinémonde', *Trafic*, 50 (2004), 183–90.
——. 'L'Areligion', *Vacarme* (2001a) <http://www.vacarme.org/article81.html> (last accessed 2 January 2020).
——. 'Icône de l'acharnement', *Trafic*, 39 (2001b), 58–64.
——. *The Evidence of Film* (Brussels: Yves Gevaert, 2001c).
——. *L'Intrus* (Paris: Galilée, 2000a).
——. 'The Technique of the Present', *Tympanum* (2000b) <http://www.usc.edu/dept/comp-lit/tympanum/4/nancy.html> (last accessed 24 June 2012).
——. *Being Singular Plural*, trans. by Robert D. Richardson and Anne E. O'Byrne (Stanford: Stanford University Press, 2000c).
——. *The Muses*, trans. by Peggy Kamuf (Stanford: Stanford University Press, 1997a).
——. *The Sense of the World*, trans. by Jeffrey S. Librett (Minneapolis: University of Minnesota Press, 1997b).
——. *The Inoperative Community*, trans. by Peter Connor, Lisa Garbus, Michael Holland and Simona Sawhney (Minneapolis: University of Minnesota Press, 1991).
Nancy, Jean-Luc and Federico Ferrari, *Nus sommes: La peau des images* (Brussels: Yves Gevaert, 2006).
Naqvi, Fatima and Christophe Koné, 'The Key to Voyeurism: Haneke's Adaptation of Jelinek's *The Piano Teacher*', in *On Michael Haneke*, ed. by Brian Price and John David Rhodes (Detroit: Wayne State University Press, 2010), pp. 127–50.
Nelson, Roy Jay, 'Reflections in a Broken Mirror: Varda's *Cléo de 5 à 7*', *The French Review*, 56 (1983), 735–43.
Neupert, Richard, *A History of the French New Wave* (Madison: University of Wisconsin Press, 2007).
Noys, Benjamin, 'Attenuating Austria: The Construction of Bourgeois Space in *The Seventh Continent*', in *The Cinema of Michael Haneke: Europe Utopia*, ed. by Ben McCann and David Sorfa (London: Wallflower Press, 2011), pp. 141–50.
O'Byrne, Anne, 'Nancy's Materialist Ontology', in *Jean-Luc Nancy and Plural Thinking: Expositions of World, Ontology, Politics, and Sense*, ed. by Peter Gratton and Marie-Eve Morin (New York: State University of New York Press, 2012), pp. 79–93.
——. *Natality and Finitude* (Bloomington: Indiana University Press, 2010).
Orpen, Valerie, *Cléo de 5 à 7* (London and New York: I. B. Tauris, 2007).
Osterweil, Ara, *Flesh Cinema: The Corporeal Turn in American Avant-Garde Film* (Manchester: Manchester University Press, 2014).
Penz, François, 'From Topographical Coherence to Creative Geography: Rohmer's *The Aviator's Wife* and Rivette's *Pont du Nord*', in *Cities in Transition: The Moving Image and the Modern Metropolis*, ed. by Emma Wilson and Andrew Webber (London: Wallflower Press, 2008), pp. 123–40.

Pethő, Ágnes, 'Intermediality as Metalepsis in the "Cinécriture" of Agnès Varda', *Acta Universitatis Sapientiae Film and Media Studies*, 3 (2010), 69–94.

Peucker, Brigitte, 'Games Haneke Plays: Reality and Performance', in *On Michael Haneke*, ed. by Brian Price and John David Rhodes (Detroit: Wayne State University Press, 2010), pp. 15–33.

——. *The Material Image: Art and the Real in Film* (Stanford: Stanford University Press, 2006).

Pingaud, Bernard, 'Agnès Varda et la réalité', *Artsept* (1963), 124–41.

Prédal, René, 'Genèse d'une oeuvre: Agnès Varda et *La Pointe Courte*', in *Agnès Varda: Le cinéma et au-delà*, ed. by Antony Fiant, Roxane Hamery and Éric Thouvenel (Rennes: Presses Universitaires de Rennes, 2009), pp. 101–12.

Quart, Barbara Koenig, *Women Directors: The Emergence of a New Cinema* (New York: Praeger, 1988).

Quinlivan, Davina, *The Place of Breath in Cinema* (Edinburgh: Edinburgh University Press, 2012).

Rhodes, John David, 'The Spectacle of Skepticism', in *On Michael Haneke*, ed. by Brian Price and John David Rhodes (Detroit: Wayne State University Press, 2010), pp. 87–102.

Ricco, John Paul, 'Drool: Liquid Fore-speech of the Fore-scene', *World Picture*, 10 (2015) <http://www.worldpicturejournal.com/WP_10/Ricco_10.html> (last accessed 3 July 2020).

Rodowick, D. N., *Gilles Deleuze's Time Machine* (Durham, NC: Duke University Press, 1997).

Rosello, Mireille, *The Reparative in Narratives: Works of Mourning in Progress* (Liverpool: Liverpool University Press, 2010).

Ross, Kristin, *Fast Cars, Clean Bodies: Decolonization and the Reordering of French Culture* (Cambridge, MA: The MIT Press, 1995).

Rowe, Christopher, *Michael Haneke: The Intermedial Void* (Evanston: Northwestern University Press, 2017).

Royer, Michelle, *The Cinema of Marguerite Duras: Multisensoriality and Female Subjectivity* (Edinburgh: Edinburgh University Press, 2019).

Rushton, Richard, 'Absorption and Theatricality in the Cinema: Some Thoughts on Narrative and Spectacle', *Screen*, 48 (2007), 109–12.

——. 'Early, Classical and Modern Cinema: Absorption and Theatricality', *Screen* (2004), 226–44.

Russell, Dennis Eugene, *The Portrayal of Social Catastrophe in the German-Language Films of Austrian Filmmaker Michael Haneke (1942–): An Examination of The Seventh Continent (1989), Benny's Video (1992), 71 Fragments of a Chronology of Chance (1994), and Funny Games (1997)* (Lewiston: The Edwin Mellen Press, 2010).

Rutherford, Anne, *What Makes a Film Tick? Cinematic Affect, Materiality and Mimetic Innervation* (Berlin: Peter Lang, 2011).

Saxton, Libby, 'Close Encounters with Distant Suffering: Michael Haneke's Disarming Visions', in *Five Directors: Auteurism from Assayas to Ozon*, ed. by Kate Ince (Manchester: Manchester University Press, 2008), pp. 84–111.

Schoonover, Karl, 'Wastrels of Time: Slow Cinema's Labouring Body, the Political Spectator and the Queer', in *Slow Cinema*, ed. by Tiago de Luca and Nuno Barradas Jorge (Edinburgh: Edinburgh University Press, 2016), pp. 153–68.

Seeßlen, Georg, 'Structures of Glaciation: Gaze, Perspective, and Gestus in the Films of Michael Haneke', in *A Companion to Michael Haneke*, ed. by Roy Grundmann (Oxford: Wiley-Blackwell, 2010), pp. 323–36.

Sellier, Geneviève, *Masculine Singular: French New Wave Cinema*, trans. by Kristin Ross (Durham, NC: Duke University Press, 2008).

Sharrett, Christopher, 'Haneke and the Discontents of European Culture', in *On Michael Haneke*, ed. by Brian Price and John David Rhodes (Detroit: Wayne State University Press, 2010), pp. 207–19.

——. 'The World That Is Known', *Kinoeye*, 4 (2004) <http://www.kinoeye.org/04/01/interview01.php> (last accessed 22 May 2020).

Shaviro, Steven, *The Cinematic Body* (Minneapolis: University of Minnesota Press, 1993).

Sherlock, Amy, 'Multiple Expeausures: Identity and Alterity in the "Self-Portraits" of Francesca Woodman', *Paragraph*, 36 (2013), 376–91.

Shiva, Vandana, *Water Wars: Privatization, Pollution, and Profit* (London: Pluto Press, 2002).

Smith, Alison, *Agnès Varda* (Manchester: Manchester University Press, 1998).

Sobchack, Vivian, *Carnal Thoughts: Embodiment and Moving Image Culture* (Berkeley: University of California Press, 2004).

——. *The Address of the Eye: A Phenomenology of Film Experience* (Princeton: Princeton University Press, 1992).

Sorfa, David, 'Uneasy Domesticity in the Films of Michael Haneke', *Studies in European Cinema*, 3 (2006), 93–104.

Speck, Oliver C., *Funny Frames: The Filmic Concepts of Michael Haneke* (London: Continuum, 2010).

Stewart, Garrett, 'Pre-war Trauma: Haneke's *The White Ribbon*', *Film Quarterly* (2010), 40–7.

Stewart, Susan, *On Longing: Narratives of the Miniature, the Gigantic, the Souvenir, the Collection* (Durham, NC: Duke University Press, 1993).

Syrotinski, Michael, 'Introduction', *Sense & Society*, 8 (2013), 5–49.

Szendy, Peter, 'The Archi-Road Movie', *Senses & Society*, 8 (2013), 50–61.

Tardy, Michel, 'Notes sur deux films d'Agnès Varda', *Image et Son* (1960), 10–11.

Tassone, Aldo (ed.), *Que reste-t-il de la Nouvelle Vague?* (Paris: Stock, 2003).

Thomas, Jonathan, 'Michael Haneke's New(s) Image', *Art Journal* (2008), 80–5.

Thompson, Kirsten Moana, *Apocalyptic Dread: American Film at the Turn of the Millennium* (Albany: State University of New York Press, 2007).

Torner, Evan, 'Civilization's Endless Shadow: Haneke's *Time of the Wolf*', in *A Companion to Michael Haneke*, ed. by Roy Grundmann (Oxford: Wiley-Blackwell, 2010), pp. 532–50.
Trémois, Claude-Marie, 'La Pointe Courte', *Le Cinéma Chez Soi* (1956), 28–31.
Truffaut, François, '*La Pointe Courte* d'Agnès Varda', in *Les Films de ma vie* (Paris: Flammarion, 1975), pp. 325–7.
Tucker, Thomas Deane, *The Peripatetic Frame: Images of Walking in Film* (Edinburgh: Edinburgh University Press, 2020).
Tweraser, Felix W., 'Images of Confinement and Transcendence: Michael Haneke's Reception of Romanticism in *The Piano Teacher*', in *The Cinema of Michael Haneke: Europe Utopia*, ed. by Ben McCann and David Sorfa (London: Wallflower Press, 2011), pp. 195–205.
Ungar, Steven, *Cléo de 5 à 7* (Basingstoke: Palgrave Macmillan, 2008).
Uytterhoeven, Pierre, 'Agnès Varda de 5 à 7', *Positif* (1962), 1–14.
Varda, Agnès, 'Comment j'ai fait *La Pointe Courte*', *Positif* (2009), 58–9.
——. *Varda par Agnès* (Paris: Cahiers du cinéma, 1994).
Vincendeau, Ginette, '*La Pointe Courte*: How Agnès Varda "Invented" the New Wave', *Current: The Criterion Collection* (2008) <http://www.criterion.com/current/posts/497-la-pointe-courte-how-agnes-varda-invented-the-new-wave> (last accessed 6 July 2013).
Virtue, Nancy E., 'Memory, Trauma, and the French-Algerian War: Michael Haneke's *Caché* (2005)', *Modern & Contemporary France* (2011), 281–96.
Vogel, Amos, 'Of Nonexisting Continents: The Cinema of Michael Haneke', *Film Comment*, 32 (1996), 73–5.
Walker, Elsie, *Hearing Haneke: The Sound Tracks of a Radical Auteur* (Oxford: Oxford University Press, 2018).
Warren, Charles, 'The Unknown Piano Teacher', in *A Companion to Michael Haneke*, ed. by Roy Grundmann (Oxford: Wiley-Blackwell, 2010), pp. 494–510.
Watkin, Christopher, *Phenomenology or Deconstruction? The Question of Ontology in Maurice Merleau-Ponty, Paul Ricoeur, and Jean-Luc Nancy* (Edinburgh: Edinburgh University Press, 2009).
——. 'A Different Alterity: Jean-Luc Nancy's "Singular Plural"', *Paragraph*, 30 (2007), 50–64.
Wheatley, Catherine, *Caché (Hidden)* (London: Palgrave Macmillan, 2011).
——. *Michael Haneke's Cinema: The Ethic of the Image* (Oxford: Berghahn Books, 2009).
——. 'The Masochistic Fantasy Made Flesh: Michael Haneke's *La Pianiste* as Melodrama', *Studies in French Cinema*, 6 (2006), 117–27.
Williams, Linda, 'Film Bodies: Gender, Genre, and Excess', *Film Quarterly*, 44 (1991), 2–13.
Wilson, Emma, *Love, Mortality and the Moving Image* (Basingstoke: Palgrave Macmillan, 2012).
Wood, Robin, '"Do I Disgust You?" or, tirez pas sur *La Pianiste*', *CineAction*, 59 (2002), 54–60.

Wortham, Simon Morgan, *The Poetics of Sleep: From Aristotle to Nancy* (New York: Bloomsbury, 2013).

Wray, John, 'Minister of Fear', *New York Times Magazine*, 23 September 2007, <http://www.nytimes.com/2007/09/23/magazine/23haneke-t.html?pagewanted=all&_r=3&> (last accessed 18 May 2020).

Wrye, Harriet, 'Perversion Annihilates Creativity and Love: A Passion for Destruction in *The Piano Teacher* (2001)', *International Journal of Psycho-Analysis*, 86 (2005), 1205–12.

Wyatt, Jean, 'Jouissance and Desire in Michael Haneke's *The Piano Teacher*', *American Imago*, 62 (2005), 453–82.

Žižek, Slavoj, *Welcome to the Desert of the Real! Five Essays on September 11 and Related Dates* (London: Verso, 2002).

Index

absorption, 143–4
Acker, Ally, 58
Adamek, Philip, 28, 31
Ahmed, Sara, 112, 114, 116
Allan, Tony, 95
   virtual water, 95
Ameur-Zaïmeche, Rabah, 20, 49
   Les Chants de Mandrin, 20
Angelopoulos, Theo, 4–5
   Ulysses' Gaze, 5
Arcimboldo, Giuseppe, 74
Armstrong, Philip, 136

Bachelard, Gaston, 105
Balfour, Ian, 26
Barbaud, Pierre, 61, 63, 75
Barison, David, 20
   The Ister, 20
Barker, Jennifer M., 8, 11–12
   musculature, 11–12
Barker, Stephen, 34, 123
Barnfield, Jessica, 29
Baross, Zsuzsa, 38
Barthes, Roland, 2–4, 11, 21
Bazin, André, 60, 62
Bénézet, Delphine, 116
Benjamin, Walter, 126
Bennett, Jane, 6–8, 35, 41
Berg, Alban, 101
Bergman, Ingmar, 74
   Persona, 74
Beugnet, Martine, 8
Bingham, Adam, 101
Birkin, Jane, 176
Blade Runner, 2
Blanck, Dorothée, 188
Bourseiller, Antoine, 188
Brakhage, Stan, 4, 7, 65
Brechtian, 60–2
Brinkema, Eugenie, 137
Brown, Christopher, 95

Chamarette, Jenny, 8
Chion, Michel, 5
Conway, Kelley, 59, 62
Cooper, Sarah, 20
Coulthard, Lisa, 96, 98, 151, 154, 157

de Luca, Tiago, 6, 8
De Niro, Robert, 172
del Río, Elena, 5, 8
Deleuze, Gilles, 7, 23
   heautonomy, 165–7
   sensory motor schema, 83
Demy, Jacques, 175–6
Demy, Mathieu, 175
Deneuve, Catherine, 172
Denis, Claire, 6, 20, 24, 30, 47, 180
   Beau Travail, 30, 32–3, 41
   L'Intrus, 6, 20
   Trouble Every Day, 47, 180–1
   Vers Nancy, 20, 24
DeRoo, Rebecca, 62–3, 113
Derrida, Jacques, 26, 29, 179
Descartes, René, 179
Donaldson, Lucy Fife, 58
Duras, Marguerite, 165–6
   India Song, 165–6

epistolarity, 82–4, 151, 153–67, 172–5
Ezra, Elizabeth, 126–7, 144

Fairfax, Daniel, 132
Fanon, Frantz, 127
Ferrari, Federico, 121, 123–4
Flitterman-Lewis, Sandy, 127, 131
Foundas, Scott, 88
Freud, Sigmund, 179
Frey, Mattias, 82
Friedan, Betty, 114

Galt, Rosalind, 6, 37

Godard, Jean-Luc, 62, 119, 121, 126, 172, 189
  Breathless, 172
Goldin, Nan, 179–80
  Joana's Back in the Doorway, 179–80
Grün, Mark, 20, 27, 120
  Le Corps du philosophe, 20, 27, 120
Guattari, Félix, 7
Guyer, Sara, 32

Haneke, Michael, 13, 24, 80–3, 85, 88–90, 92, 94–102, 106, 113, 142–9, 151, 153–8, 160–3, 167–8, 181–5, 189
  Amour, 13, 102, 146, 153, 155–6, 182
  Benny's Video, 88, 97, 147
  Caché, 24, 97, 99, 102, 142–9, 151, 153, 155, 177, 183
  Code Unknown, 96, 146, 153, 155
  Funny Games, 82, 147, 167
  Happy End, 13, 97, 146, 181–5
  The Piano Teacher, 24, 146, 151–68, 172, 178, 183
  The Seventh Continent, 24, 82, 88–107, 112–14, 119, 123, 146, 153, 155, 157, 162, 177, 182, 184
  71 Fragments of a Chronology of Chance, 88
  The White Ribbon, 14–15, 96–7, 146–7, 153, 155, 157, 182
  Time of the Wolf, 24, 76, 80–6, 88, 95–6, 153, 155–6, 162, 177
Hegel, Georg Wilhelm Friedrich, 20
Heidegger, Martin, 24–5, 76
Hickmott, Sarah, 38, 40
Hirsch, Pam, 95
Hitchcock, Alfred, 137
  Psycho, 137
Hole, Kristen Lené, 23, 165
Howells, Christina, 124, 178–9

James, Ian, 67
Janus, Adrienne, 38, 46, 91–3
Jelinek, Elfriede, 152
Johnston, Claire, 113

Kamuf, Peggy, 31
Kane, Brian, 35
Kant, Immanuel, 20, 45
Kassovitz, Mathieu, 182
Kawara, On, 122–4, 132–3, 145
  Today series, 122, 132–3, 142, 145
  Viet-Nam triptych, 123
Kiarostami, Abbas, 20, 45, 49, 69, 90, 101, 177

Life, and Nothing More, 44–5, 69
Kingsolver, Barbara, 86
Klotz, Nicolas, 20, 30, 47
  La Blessure, 20, 30, 47–9

Londe, Albert, 134
Lübecker, Nikolaj, 168

Ma, Jean, 151
McMahon, Denice Orlene, 61
McMahon, Laura, 22, 165–6, 180
Mandell, Charlotte, 155
Marks, Laura U., 8, 10–11, 70
  haptic visuality, 8–11, 129–30
Massumi, Brian, 7
Mayer, So, 175–6
Mayne, Judith, 126–7
Metz, Christian, 1–2, 8
Minkowski, Eugène, 12
modernity, 72, 88, 101–2
Monfort, Silvia, 60–1
Morin, Marie-Eve, 25–6
Mroz, Matilda, 4, 11

Naficy, Hamid, 154, 172
  accented cinema, 154, 165
Nancy, Jean-Luc, 15, 20–50, 58–9, 63–74, 76, 81, 90–3, 100–1, 104, 120–6, 129, 131–7, 142, 145, 151–5, 157–8, 161, 164–8, 174, 176–81, 188
  Being Nude: The Skin of Images, 26, 121, 179
  being singular-plural, 36–9, 41–3, 65–6, 69, 71, 93, 101, 104, 120–2, 129, 132–8, 143, 149, 165, 177, 179–80
  blood, 26, 123, 158, 177–82, 188–9
  body, 23–30, 32–6, 38, 39–43, 46, 65–6, 69, 93, 104, 107, 120–4, 129–30, 133–5, 137, 155, 161, 168, 177–81
  car, 90–2, 94, 106–7
  carnation see local colour
  'Cinéfile et cinémonde', 21
  cinémonde, 45, 47
  compearance, 22–3, 25, 32, 34
  corporeality *see* body
  Corpus, 28–30, 47, 178
  corpus corporum, 28, 44, 46–7, 66, 68, 72, 89, 123, 136, 160, 168, 174, 178, 180, 189
  Ego Sum, 28, 30, 179
  evidence, 21, 27, 29, 46, 67–9, 91, 120, 130, 158–9, 164, 167
  expeausition, 29–30, 47, 58

exposure, 22, 24, 35, 41, 65, 107, 152, 179, 181
exscription, 26, 28–9, 32, 68
gaping, 28–32, 34–5, 38, 42, 120, 154
image, 22, 26–9, 31, 33–4, 36–7, 42–8, 59, 66–72, 89–93, 100–1, 105, 121, 123, 125, 130, 135–7, 145, 158–60, 163–4, 166–8, 174–81, 185, 189
listening, 20, 23, 34–5, 37–42, 46, 48, 62–3, 70, 72, 86, 90, 92, 96, 104, 107, 127, 143, 149, 151–2, 155, 158, 168, 179, 181–2
Listening, 35, 38–9, 155
literature, 22–4, 122, 166
local colour, 122–5, 136, 138, 145, 177
matter, 23, 33, 39, 42–4, 63, 178–9
minerality, 24–5, 27, 36, 41, 43, 45, 76, 93, 97, 133, 177, 179, 181, 189
mouth, 26, 28, 30–3, 35, 40–4, 48, 63, 65, 68, 93, 104, 120, 124, 133, 153, 161, 181, 189
regard, 34, 44–5, 60, 67
renvoi, 154–5, 166
sens, 23, 25, 30, 32, 34–5, 37, 39–41, 47, 49, 65, 68–70, 85, 91–3, 101, 104–5, 119–20, 155–6, 168, 174, 176, 178–9, 181, 185, 187
sense *see* sens
sense of the world, 25, 37–42, 46, 48–50, 63–6, 68, 70–1, 74, 76, 85, 93, 104, 120, 122, 124, 133, 136, 143, 155, 168, 173, 177, 179
sonority, 23–4, 29–33, 37–43, 49, 58, 63, 65–6, 93, 96, 101, 104, 106, 121, 133, 142, 152, 155, 168, 179
The Evidence of Film, 20–1, 26–7, 44–5, 67, 92
The Ground of the Image, 26, 31, 36, 157, 178
The Inoperative Community, 28, 30
'The Intruder', 26–8, 30–1, 35, 178
The Muses, 26–7
The Sense of the World, 23, 37
timbre, 39–40, 48, 69, 71, 100, 177, 184–6
violence, 153–4, 157–60, 162–4, 166–8, 174–8, 180, 185
Nelson, Roy Jay, 137
Neupert, Richard, 188
Noiret, Philippe, 60–1

O'Byrne, Anne, 29
Ono, Yoko, 1

Orpen, Valerie, 125, 128, 131
Osterweil, Ara, 1, 3, 8

Peucker, Brigitte, 99–100, 151, 154, 156
Plato, 20

Quinlivan, Davina, 3, 8
breathing visuality, 3, 113

Rembrandt, 123
Bathsheba at Her Bath, 123
resonance, 1–2, 4–12, 15, 23–6, 32, 35, 37–50, 63, 65–71, 74, 76, 82, 84–6, 90–4, 96, 100–7, 115–16, 120, 122–4, 129, 132–3, 135, 137–8, 149, 152–5, 157, 159–63, 167–8, 172, 174–7, 179, 181, 185, 187–9
Reygadas, Carlos, 5
Battle of Heaven, 5
Ricco, John Paul, 120
Ross, Daniel, 20
The Ister, 20
Rowe, Christopher, 102, 145–6
Rushton, Richard, 143–4
Rutherford, Anne, 4, 8

Saxton, Libby, 99
Seyrig, Delphine, 174
Sharrett, Christopher, 101–2
Shaviro, Steven, 10
Sherlock, Amy, 22
Sillars, Jane, 144
Smith, Alison, 61–2
Sobchack, Vivian, 1–2, 5–6, 8–9, 11, 13, 70
Sorfa, David, 82, 96, 151–2
Speed, 5
Spinoza, Baruch, 7
Stewart, Garrett, 147
Szendy, Peter, 91

theatricality, 143–5
The Piano, 5–6
Thomas, Jonathan, 145
Torner, Evan, 82
Toy Story, 5
Truffaut, François, 59–60, 62
The 400 Blows, 59–60

Varda, Agnès, 13, 24, 58–62, 64, 70–1, 76, 101, 112–14, 116, 119, 125–6, 137, 142, 172, 174–6, 181, 185–9
A Hundred and One Nights, 172

Varda (*cont.*)
  Cleo from 5 to 7, 24, 119–38, 142–3, 152, 177, 186, 188
  Documenteur, 24, 172–6, 178, 187
  Du côté de la côte, 185
  Faces Places, 188–9
  Jacquot de Nantes, 185, 189
  Jane B. par Agnès V., 176
  Kung Fu Master!, 176
  L'Île et Elle, 185
  L'Opéra-mouffe, 174, 187–8
  La Pointe Courte, 24, 58–76, 94, 172, 177, 185
  Le Bonheur, 24, 112–16, 119, 134, 188
  Mur Murs, 172
  The Beaches of Agnès, 76, 176, 185
  The Gleaners & I, 13–15, 175
  The Widows of Noirmoutier, 186
  Uncle Yanco, 186
  Vagabond, 174–5
  Varda by Agnès, 181, 185–9

Walker, Elsie, 155
Warnell, Phillip, 20, 92
  Ming of Harlem, 20
  Outlandish: Strange Foreign Bodies, 20, 92
Watkin, Christopher, 36
Wheatley, Catherine, 80, 82, 99, 145, 155, 163
Williams, Linda, 80
  body genres, 80
Woodman, Francesca, 22

EU representative:
Easy Access System Europe
Mustamäe tee 50, 10621 Tallinn, Estonia
Gpsr.requests@easproject.com

www.ingramcontent.com/pod-product-compliance
Lightning Source LLC
Chambersburg PA
CBHW070824250426
43671CB00036B/2043